# THE IMPOSING PREACHER

# THE IMPOSING PREACHER

## SAMUEL DEWITT PROCTOR AND BLACK PUBLIC FAITH

ADAM L. BOND

Fortress Press
Minneapolis

THE IMPOSING PREACHER

Samuel DeWitt Proctor and Black Public Faith



Cover image: Abyssinian Baptist Church Archives

Cover design: Laurie Ingram

*Library of Congress Cataloging-in-Publication Data is available*

Print ISBN: 978-0-8006-9972-7

eBook ISBN: 978-1-4514-5224-2

The paper used in this publication meets the minimum requirements of American National Standard for Information Sciences — Permanence of Paper for Printed Library Materials, ANSI Z329.48-1984.

Manufactured in the U.S.A.

This book was produced using PressBooks.com, and PDF rendering was done by PrinceXML.

# CONTENTS

# Acknowledgments

Books are the products of teamwork. Though the ideas and words belong to the authors, someone (or several people) created an environment in which the authors could flourish. Such has been the case in my life. Several people worked with me and on my behalf to make this book possible.

A special note of thanks goes to Fortress Press and its Innovations series editors, Dr. Anthony B. Pinn and Dr. Katie G. Cannon. I appreciate their support for this work and the time they invested in it. Countless conversations with them helped this project become better. Those conversations also made me much more aware of why the academy holds them in such high esteem. I count it an honor to have a book in the Innovations series. The staff members at Fortress Press are some of the kindest people one will ever meet. Will Bergkamp "rolled out the red carpet" for this book. Lisa Gruenisen, Marissa Wold, and Karen Schenkenfelder's keen editorial eyes improved this manuscript a great deal. I offer my gratitude to Lisa, Marissa, and Karen.

I began this project as a dissertation at Marquette University. Countless conversations with professors and classmates helped me clarify some of the larger concerns that find their way into this text. The Marquette experience might not have been possible, however, without the encouragement and support of Dr. M. Shawn Copeland. God endows some people with wisdom "from on high." Dr. Copeland is one of those people. Her counsel led me to Dr. Patrick W. Carey and Dr. David D. Daniels III (McCormick Theological Seminary). I can never repay the debt I owe to her for her investment in my vocation. The fact that this book will appear in a series that includes one of her works is both exciting and humbling.

Pat Carey became my academic adviser when Dr. Copeland returned to Boston College. He guided me through the Ph.D. program and was my adviser for the dissertation process. I spent many hours in class admiring the ways in which he interpreted historical periods. Additional hours in his office helped me remain focused on writing.

David Daniels has remained a part of my formation as an academic. He unintentionally talked me into writing my dissertation on Samuel DeWitt Proctor. I went to him for advice about research materials on Bishop Charles Harrison Mason, founder of the Church of God in Christ. I walked out of his office convinced that I needed to write about Proctor. That was a good thing!

Dr. Daniels challenged me at several stages to ground Proctor within the larger black Christian experience. Dr. Daniels's mentoring spirit and scholarly insights inspire my own sense of vocation in the church and academy.

I must acknowledge the larger family of which I am a member. My father, Leon Bond Sr., is a masterful storyteller. I learned to appreciate history by sitting at his feet. My mother, Loretta Bond, a master of pedagogical devices and instructional methods, has been a model teacher and researcher. (She earned her Ph.D. in 2012!) They are models of faith and practitioners of love. The Bond, Smith, and Rogers families believed in me throughout the long years of seminary and graduate school. That vote of confidence means a great deal to me. These families and my families of faith have cheered me on every step of the way.

The world would not function well without librarians, archivists, and historians who have planted timely clues and hints in accessible places. The Marquette Raynor Library Research and Outreach staff, Interlibrary Loan Department, Circulation staff, and Library Systems technicians consist of some of the greatest people you will ever meet. Thank you. Other research librarians provided assistance in various locations. Dr. Tommy Bogger and the City of Norfolk forwarded me a copy of the transcript for Dr. Proctor's interview on Norfolk history. Bela Teixeira from the Rhode Island Black Heritage Society helped me identify sources from Dr. Proctor's early career. Dr. Virgil Wood, former pastor of the Pond Street Baptist Church, gave me a history of the Providence congregation—thank you. The Providence College library staff gave me a seemingly unlimited budget for photocopies. The Boston University School of Theology library staff located Dr. Proctor's dissertation and made it available to me. And Selicia Allen at the L. Douglas Wilder Library at Virginia Union University helped me sift through the resources in the presidential archives of the university. The Morton Library at Union Presbyterian Seminary in Richmond, Virginia, made audiocassettes available. The sharing of information is a marvelous activity.

I owe a great deal to the Reverend Dr. Calvin O. Butts III and the Abyssinian Baptist Church family for making several Proctor resources available to me. The church archivist, Dr. Kevin McGruder, tutored me on Harlem, Abyssinian, and the resources at the church almost simultaneously. I am grateful for their acts of kindness on my behalf.

Mrs. Bessie Proctor, Dr. Proctor's widow, encouraged me to complete this project from the first time I spoke to her. It was moving to hear her recount some of the details of Dr. Proctor's life. She also referred me to her son, Samuel T. Proctor, who shared his enthusiasm for my project.

The Samuel DeWitt Proctor School of Theology at Virginia Union University is a special place. I am a graduate of this seminary and now work there. This has been a blessing to me. My office is in the same building that was Dr. Proctor's dorm during his college years. Dr. John William Kinney, Dean of the Samuel DeWitt Proctor School of Theology, gave me time away from teaching and meetings to write this book. The faculty, staff, and students at the school all contributed in meaningful ways. I must add how much I appreciate the three people in my Spring 2010 Black Religious Leaders course. Their book reviews on the early manuscript helped me see my way back into the work.

Two generous and committed organizations made this book possible. I received a dissertation fellowship from the Fund for Theological Education (FTE) in 2006. The money was only part of the support from the FTE that helped me write my dissertation. The relationships that started with our conference at Yale Divinity School have blossomed into a supportive network of friends. That is the FTE way. Thank you, Sharon Fluker and Matthew Williams. In addition, the Louisville Institute funded what I hope will be a book on twentieth-century black Baptists. The grant gave me time to give this book more perspective. This book, then, is also a Louisville Institute project.

Other scholars and organizations invested in this project. Lewis Baldwin and Walter Fluker referred me to a manuscript by Howard Thurman. John Kutsko shared ideas with me about transforming the dissertation into a book. The Lynn E. May Study Grant from the Southern Baptist Historical Library and Archives gave me access to resources that I had not seen. Bill Sumner and Taffey Hall pointed me to key periodicals about black Baptist life. I must also thank my FTE Dissertation Fellowship cohort. Charles Bowie, Warren Chain, Rhon Manigault-Williams, Amanda Mbuvi, Luke Powery, and Andrea White have been partners in this vocation. Our early roundtable conversations made this possible.

I am grateful for my wife and children. Ronda, Raychel, and Alana encourage me to dream big. They also remind me to enjoy the moments that seem to pass by so fast. I cannot repay you, Ronda, for the sacrifices you have made for me. But I will try.

# Abbreviations

**ABC** Abyssinian Baptist Church, Harlem, New York

**CDF** Children's Defense Fund

**L&S** The Letter and the Spirit (column in the *Providence Chronicle*)

*NYT* *New York Times*

**TUCC** Trinity United Church of Christ, Chicago, Illinois

**UTS-PSCE** Morton Library at Union Theological Seminary and Presbyterian School of Christian Education (now Union Presbyterian Seminary)

**VUU** Douglas Wilder Library, Virginia Union University

# Introduction

In his 1972 *New York Times* article, George Dugan gives a fitting description of the new pastor of the Abyssinian Baptist Church of Harlem, Dr. Samuel DeWitt Proctor. Dugan states, "Rugged looking in his black doctoral robe, close to 6 feet tall and weighing 210 pounds, the 51-year-old preacher was an imposing figure in the pulpit."[1] Proctor was a grand presence indeed. Yet there was more to this presence than his physical stature. He was an impressive thinker and an accomplished man. He rose from the depths of a southern racist society in the mid-twentieth century to become a celebrated educator, administrator, Baptist pastor, and author. He served in different government capacities during the Kennedy and Johnson administrations, including stints as an associate director of the Peace Corps and Office of Economic Opportunity. His academic career included presidential posts at Virginia Union University and North Carolina A&T State University, administrative leadership at the University of Wisconsin–Madison, teaching duties at Rutgers University, and lectures at various colleges and seminaries following his retirement. He was the successor to Adam Clayton Powell Jr. at the prominent Abyssinian Baptist Church. Proctor's public ministry spanned six decades. His tale was truly American. He came out of Depression-era Norfolk, Virginia, to the grand stage of the New York church. He was a black youth in the Jim Crow South who became an envoy for presidents. His narrative presents the best and the ugliest of this nation's culture.

Samuel DeWitt Proctor sought to affirm the place of the divine in humanity. M. Shawn Copeland writes, "White racist supremacy seeks to undermine spirituality, to subvert the place of the Divine, the Transcendent in lived human life."[2] Proctor discerned this much and contested it. His Christian faith informed his view of and response to the ethical dilemma of race relations in America. Believing that racism was a primary source of the many problems in the black community, he countered this systemic evil with his faith. His response reflects the historical context in which he situated himself. Racism dominated the social interaction of white and black persons in the United States during Proctor's lifetime. As a Christian preacher, he surmised that God must have something to say about that sad reality. For Proctor, then, the fundamental starting point for constructing a just society in the United States of America was his faith in a simple principle: *all* persons are a part of the human family and, thus, are children of God. The moral attitudes of people and the laws and institutions in society should reflect that equality. Any other response than one that affirms the innate personhood of all humanity would not suffice for Proctor. Such was the message that one could hear from him Sunday after Sunday and in the classroom.

Students and scholars of black Christianity in the twentieth century find in Samuel DeWitt Proctor a deliberate proponent and defender of black humanity as constructed by a black social gospel tradition. He was a well-educated and respected leader. He was a "race man," a member of Du Bois's talented tenth. He is among a group of African American religious figures that is rarely recognized in "scholarly" literature. But research on Samuel DeWitt Proctor and other neglected persons in African American religious history can only benefit scholars and other interested persons. Except for a few texts that list notable leaders and organizations, the academy lacks a comprehensive understanding of the black social gospel. We are more certain of what it looked like than we are of what it said. We are still filling in the spaces in the puzzle of the contexts and content of African American Christianity. This is, therefore, the first major attempt to investigate Proctor's life and thought.

Proctor was a public theologian who attempted to influence policy conversations about racism in America. As a national preacher and public servant, he made it his mission to serve the interests of American life by fighting against racism. Drawing from his social and religious upbringing and theological education—formal and informal—he understood that every human being matters equally to God. His earliest lessons on the inherent dignity of each person came from his family and a black Baptist Christian experience. He received formal language for a black public faith and theology at Virginia Union University, Crozer Theological Seminary, Yale University, and the Boston University School of Theology. As a public theologian, he committed himself to proclaiming a black social gospel faith through changing times and ideological innovation that saw as its goal a genuine community, an inclusive and racially pluralistic global society that confronted racism as the social crisis of its time. He believed that genuine community celebrates the parenthood of God and the kinship of humanity as the basis of human equality and freedom, and the preacher through sermon as literature and theological practice heralds this community by moral suasion.

Proctor understood the sermon to be an effective device for making one's faith claims public and accessible. But the sermon and its message of community had to move beyond the narrow confines of the Christian community to a larger public. Proctor anticipated Linell Cady's ideas about theology and public argumentation. He moved away from "technical, jargon-filled discourse" and held up his experience—his American experience—as an authoritative source for religious truth.[3]

This study argues that Proctor is a type of religious and theological barometer for the black Christian community of the mid- to late twentieth century. He was a participant in black public faith conversations. That is, he had a notion of faith, nurtured within black Christendom, which presented an alternative reality to the pervasive racism in the United States. That notion lived out and articulated in the public sphere honors the inherent dignity of all humanity. I examine the way in which he emphasized his faith in a vision for a racially pluralistic moral-spiritual community in the United States. He did this in spite of the displays of racism from a large segment of the white population and the militancy of a budding black power and black separatist movement in the 1960s and '70s. Yet his upbringing, formal education, and professional experience provided him with a worldview that celebrated the universality of the human experience and championed integration and racial pluralism. His sermons, writings, and talks display a public faith informed by a black church ethic of racial harmony, black social gospel themes, and black middle-class notions of civil society.

The book places Proctor in his historical context. I examine the relationship between his biography and faith claims, arguing that his biography influences his religious outlook. His family, education, and the formative years in an African American community and black religious settings shaped his identity and theology. He also found insights for his ministry in the American liberal theological tradition. He was the product of the black Baptist and liberal Protestant theological traditions. His politically oriented black liberal social gospel responded to the claims of the Religious Right, Protestant fundamentalism, and black liberation strands in theology. At the same time, his black middle-class understanding of American life contributed to his social commentary and ideals of American-*ness*. He considered himself *black*, *Christian*, and *American*, sometimes placing more emphasis on American. These are important ideas within the black public faith that he embodied and proclaimed.

While many American religious historians and historians of the African American religious experience have focused on a few mainstream black Christian thinkers from the twentieth century, they have neglected to examine Proctor and his voice on matters of race and religion. His voice, however, is important. His commitment to a vanishing black social gospel placed him in the middle of the spectrum of black public faith. Proctor also preached and lectured to white audiences extensively during the 1960s and beyond. He had a type of "crossover" appeal that functioned well among white and black audiences. Timothy Tyson's *Blood Done Sign My Name* (the book more than the movie) suggests as much. Proctor's social theology provides some contrasts with the prevailing paradigms of race-conscious theology and social change in his era. He was not a marching activist, social conservative, or black militant. But his ideas embraced or nuanced all of those social postures. He is a celebrated preacher among members of the preaching guild. Yet these authors look at him merely as a model for preaching. Proctor receives no attention in general histories of Christianity in America or in works on African American Christianity in particular. One finds a substantial amount of work on those persons who were *visible* during the civil rights era (c. 1950–1970). Many of these scholars pay attention to only a small group of notable African American religious leaders in histories or anthologies on African American religion. Proctor, who for several years was a black celebrity in the nation's African American newspapers and served one of the most prominent churches in America, barely appears in the representative texts of American and African American religious history.[4]

Another issue related to Proctor's absence from these texts is the use of sermons as sources of religious research—especially sermons in the black religious community. Few historians examine sermons as sources of theology or the ideas of the preachers who preach them. To be sure, not all of the sermons preached will merit the attention of leading scholars. But some preachers' sermons are important documents for historical research. Harry Stout's work on the influence of preaching on colonial New England displays a precedent for the importance of preaching to a community. Stout argues that the theologies in the preachers' sermons display New Englanders' notion of their identity.[5] A study of Proctor's preaching, and the theology in that preaching, will contribute to our understanding of the themes and concerns that shaped dialogues in African American religious life (if only for a sample of African American Baptists). A tacit consensus in modern scholarship holds that preachers in the pulpits do theology until the early to mid-nineteenth century. With the rise of the theological schools in America in the 1800s, some historians examine only the ideas from professional theologians. This point is implicit in the scholarly neglect of persons such as Proctor. His preaching and teaching contained faith claims that yield themes and concepts from a significant tradition within the African American religious experience. Different denominational publishers produce several volumes of sermons each year. Yet these texts lack historical and theological analysis in most cases. This crucial element prevents most preachers' texts from "crossing over" from the seminary classroom into the graduate school. This is unfortunate.

You will discover in this book that Proctor's life experiences and faith claims led him to an inevitable intellectual construct: genuine community. His social locations provided him with a formative home to develop his public faith. This public faith celebrates humanity and presents an alternative to the racist realities of his lifetime. His biography is eerily similar to that of Martin Luther King Jr. But the two men are different. Proctor's intellectual and spiritual path modeled numerous black religious intellectuals whose names may never reach print. To be sure, he fought for an integrated community of persons who embraced love and justice. He made this plain in churches, during commencement addresses, and in closed-door sessions with national and civic leaders. Proctor's legacy measures up to that of any other black preacher, ethicist, and theologian of his generation.

Proctor interrogated racism in American life and fought with an activism of persuasion. He preached at some of the finest universities and walked among "royalty," and his message did not change. He proclaimed a social Christianity that put the ethics of Jesus ahead of notions of respectability and political expediency. He preached with his pen in numerous articles and books. He preached from the Bible, his experience, and American democratic principles. These sources were not mutually exclusive in his mind. In this light, Proctor shows his relationship to prominent African American religious leaders and to the black church. He was a preacher, the rhetorical protégé of a black Christian tradition that affirmed the equality of all persons. He could not address that theme enough throughout his public ministry. But he saw himself as a model for black preachers. He preached and taught the value of a public theology and public ministry. The preacher, he insisted, has the charge and the authority to preach a new world into existence. That is merely a portion of Proctor's legacy.[6]

## Notes

1. George Dugan, "An Imposing Preacher: Samuel DeWitt Proctor," Man in the News, New York Times, July 24, 1972, p. 53.

2. M. Shawn Copeland, "Racism and the Vocation of the Theologian," *Spiritus* 2 (2002): 17.

3. Linell Cady, *Religion, Theology, and American Public Life* (Albany: SUNY Press, 1993).

4. See Peter J. Paris, *Black Religious Leaders: Conflict in Unity*, 2nd ed. (Louisville, KY: Westminster John Knox, 1991); James H. Cone, *Martin and Malcolm and America: A Dream or a Nightmare* (Maryknoll, NY: Orbis, 1992); Anthony B. Pinn, *The Black Church in the Post–Civil Rights Era* (Maryknoll, NY: Orbis, 2002); Albert J. Raboteau, *Canaan Land: A Religious History of*

*African Americans* (New York: Oxford University Press, 2001); Milton C. Sernett, *African American Religious History: A Documentary Witness*, C. Eric Lincoln Series on the Black Experience (Durham, NC: Duke University Press, 1999); and Cornel West and Eddie S. Glaude Jr., eds., *African American Religious Thought: An Anthology* (Louisville: Westminster John Knox, 2003).

5. See Harry S. Stout, *The New England Soul: Preaching and Religious Culture in Colonial New England* (New York: Oxford University Press, 1988).

6. Peter J. Paris, *The Social Teachings of the Black Churches* (Philadelphia: Fortress Press, 1985), 10-11; and Samuel D. Proctor, *The Certain Sound of the Trumpet: Crafting a Sermon of Authority* (Valley Forge, PA: Judson Press, 1994).

# 1

> As global white privilege, racism poses a most dangerous threat to being, to the creation and development of human community, to the flourishing of the Spirit in human lives, to the realization of the body of Christ, to the reign of God. Now inasmuch as theology seeks to understand, to interpret, and to impart the word of God and its meanings in various historical, cultural, and social contexts, it grapples with the conditions and state of culture and society. Racism is one such biased condition in the world order. But, theology can meet its critical exigence only when theologians take up comprehensive analysis and reflection on society and its potential meaning for the realization of a common human good.
> —*M. Shawn Copeland*[1]

The waning years of the civil rights movement produced a flurry of theological activity among clergy and professors within the black Christian experience. That activity, to some extent, carried into the late-twentieth-century writings and sermons of these thinkers. One of the watershed moments that prompted the surge of ideas was Stokely Carmichael's "Black Power" proclamation. The rising sentiment among many young persons in the movement leaned toward ending black political and social gradualism. The June 1966 march in Greenwood, Mississippi, was a boiling point for the leaders of the Student Nonviolent Coordinating Committee (SNCC). This group, among other black civil rights groups, had grown somewhat fatigued with the decision-making tree within the Southern Christian Leadership Conference (SCLC). Younger activists were finding their voice in the struggle for black freedom.

Footage of an interview that graces the scenes of the documentary *Citizen King* shows a debate that took place between Carmichael and Martin Luther King Jr. A journalist interviews both leaders as they march down a Mississippi highway. The journalist questions Carmichael and King on the use of Black Power rhetoric. Carmichael, a young upstart advocate of the term, discusses the merits of including "Black Power" in his civil rights stump speeches. The journalist then turns the microphone to King, the acknowledged leader and veteran of the movement. King agrees with the principles of Black Power but frowns upon the language. The documentary fast-forwards to later in the evening. Police surround the masses of black people who attended the movement rally. The impending sound bites suggest that Carmichael rubbed off on King, if only somewhat. King mounts a stage to calm the crowd and calls for Black Power in their resistance. The black religious conversation was no different. As the long years of the civil rights movement elapsed, alternative notions of a black response to racism emerged. Black theopolitical talk did not take place in a vacuum. A dialogue began that forged lines of debate about the essential character and vocation of black public faith.

Black public faith ideas stem from a long tradition of black preachers, theologians, and ethicists discontented with the social order in America. This black public faith, born out of the African American religious experience of making sense of faith in the public sphere, challenged white supremacy at each turn. Dennis Dickerson argues that numerous black religious intellectuals in the twentieth century developed a theological witness that informed the civil rights movement. Benjamin Mays, Howard Thurman, and lesser-known black religious scholars constructed their ideas in black churches and white seminaries and graduate schools in the early to middle years of that century. Diversity, moreover, exists and existed in this universe of black Christian social engagement. Numerous theological approaches to navigating black life gained notoriety and/or waned into the post-segregation era. The common thread, however, was a singular focus (i.e., contesting racism) born out of a sense of vocation. Participants in the dialogue about black public faith consisted of the varied voices of black religious intellectuals—be they academics or pastoral leaders—committed to improving black life. They weighed into conversations about the nature and character of theology, the failings of white theology, and the theopolitical contributions of the biblical witness. They engaged racism within smaller and larger public spaces. These black theologians, preachers, and religious ethicists challenged "establishment theologies" and debated among themselves about the merits of their respective viewpoints. These representatives meet, in their own ways, M. Shawn Copeland's requirements of the Christian theologian pressed by systemic racism. Copeland argues that the theologian should have a thorough grasp of (black) social and cultural circumstances, attempt to offer responses and challenges to questions that confront faith, and be critical, to interrogate the conditions of researched cultural and social findings.

With time, the post-segregation era produced notable theologians, preachers, and ethicists who took the mantle of black Christian theologies in varied directions. They bore similar themes and notions of racial consciousness, but they also had nuanced positions and different emphases. James Cone's "black theology" had distinctive features that stood out from J. Deotis Roberts's understanding of black theology and its "soul" content. Katie Cannon, Delores Williams, emilie townes, and others in the womanist tradition distinguished themselves quickly from a yet-to-be-defined black religious feminist tradition. To be sure, matters of gender made black theology as articulated by its prominent spokespersons a less-than-viable stand-alone option for many black women Christian thinkers. Some black clergypersons found a home within conservative movements. Few were more visible and vocal than E. V. Hill (1933–2003). His alliances with Billy Graham and Jerry Falwell and his political affiliation with the Moral Majority made him suspect in some black Christian circles. Hill endorsed and campaigned for mostly Republican presidential candidates from the late 1960s forward. Jesse Jackson seems to fall on the other end of the religious-political spectrum. Jackson, Baptist preacher and former presidential candidate, has been avowedly "left" in many social matters. There may not be a more public and political figure than Jackson in recent black religious life except Al Sharpton (Rev. Al of MSNBC).

Although emerging and influential black Christian voices in the post-segregation era flooded seminaries, churches, and television screens, Samuel DeWitt Proctor remained true to the generation that birthed him. He was a "race man" who embraced the social consciousness of the black theological leaders of his time and held fast to the "liberation theology" of his black social gospel rearing. Proctor's vocation and witness provided him the space to measure the changes in society and black public faith. He discerned that his voice was the balance between conservative and liberal strands of black Christian public faith. Proctor's black social gospel theology vied for the universality of the human experience exemplified in the life and teachings of Jesus. Though Proctor differed with some of the ideas that made their way into black Christian thought, he found some common ground on the matter of the vocation of black public faith.

## Racism and the Vocation of Black Public Faith

At the core of the post-segregation black public faith tradition(s) was a sense of call. The essence of that vocation was the desire to fight racism and the many vestiges of white privilege in American society. This call inspired the voices of black Christian preachers, theologians, and ethicists to address racism with the equipment and language of their time. At the foundation of their notions of black public faith was their belief in the inherent dignity of the human being as a God-given birthright. Their paths to affirming black humanity, however, differed. I note that ideological shifts and transitions take place from one generation to the next. I also acknowledge that caution is necessary when presupposing clear lines of distinction between the generations. (Generational gaps often seem to explain some differences in the ways that persons react and/or respond to one another in dialogue and/or debate.) For example, one can trace Samuel DeWitt Proctor's influences to persons such as W. E. B. Du Bois and Booker T. Washington. Du Bois and Washington reinforced some of the terms of the debate about racial uplift. James H. Cone admits to embracing the thought of Malcolm X and Martin Luther King Jr. Katie Cannon and others claim the work their souls must have as bequeathed to them from black "foremothers" such as Ida B. Wells-Barnett, Zora Neale Hurston, and Nannie Helen Burroughs. These are only a few examples that suggest both a contrast and parallel course within the black public faith traditions. But they all sensed and responded to a call to fight racism.

The point of this chapter is to examine some of the key contributions of representative leaders in the black public faith tradition. The following survey is an attempt to distinguish Proctor from the "right" and "left" of black public faith talk. Several visible black leaders in the church, parachurch organizations, and the academy offered theological contributions to that singular vocation. The functions of their thought and presence in their respective locations fall in line with what Robert Gooding-Williams identifies as the genre-defining thematic preoccupations of the Afro-modern political tradition: (1) the political and social organization of white supremacy; (2) the nature and effects of racial ideology; and, (3) the possibilities of black emancipation. In their own way, the ethicists, theologians, and preachers described in this chapter were and are more or less preoccupied with these matters. But they do not all agree on the paths to black social and spiritual emancipation.[2] Their vocation, however, is their common ground.

As a type of theopolitical thinker, Proctor assessed the public faith concepts of black Christian thinkers on the right and on the left and found them inadequate. Proctor believed they did little to prepare people for the inevitability of the kingdom of God and genuine community. That is, he desired a moral-spiritual ideal that affirmed all personhood as displayed and taught by Jesus. Proctor continued to see himself as a bridge figure—a pragmatic harmonizer—who represented the values and beliefs that shaped the civil rights struggles. He carried the banner of the black social gospel tradition into the post-segregation era. He was a part of the black religious intellectual vanguard that carried Du Bois's notions of leadership into mainstream black church pulpits and seminaries. A pulpit that featured the best and the brightest was his ideal. But the social and theological gradualism of Proctor's generation frustrated some of the younger black theologians and ministers. Proctor argued for his theological contribution as a more pragmatic choice in the evolving post–Jim Crow world of black public faith. As the gendered and racialized theological offerings of a late-twentieth-century budding black religious intellectual cadre arose, Proctor found solace in the methodical public faith expressions that brought about the gains that the current generation inherited. Far from content with the social arrangements in the United States, Proctor believed in the founding principles of the nation and the moral power of the Christian social gospel. Others expressed different concerns and beliefs about the conditions in American life.

### *The Discourse of a Black Theological Revolution*

James H. Cone's monumental work *Black Theology and Black Power* helped in solidifying an alternative conversation in the African American Christian experience. Cone was completing his graduate studies while the civil rights movement waned, and his concern was for a public faith that celebrated being black and Christian. Persons such as Martin Luther King Jr., Stokely Carmichael, and Malcolm X influenced Cone's thought. Cone also found himself conversing with members of the National Committee of Negro Churchmen, a group that phrased a racially sensitive commitment to the Christian faith. This group took seriously the language and principles of the Black Power movement. In 1966, these pastors and theological educators expressed their sentiments in a *New York Times* statement on Black Power. Cone did his own wrestling with the sensitive questions of race and faith. The result was a theology that celebrated and affirmed the inherent worth of blackness. It privileged black existence by identifying it with the historical life and work of Jesus. As a part of a larger theological shift during the post-segregation era, Cone's black theology responded to African American critics of Christianity through highlighting the authentic contributions of the black experience. Cone's black theology gave black clergy, primarily seminary-educated black clergy, a mode of discourse through which "black" and "Christian" could make sense to a generation of black people who were witnessing the birth of a changing nation. James H. Cone, among others within the Black Power tradition, identified within theology the goal of self-realization and political autonomy that stemmed from a heightened understanding of black consciousness. For Cone, this self-realization evolved within the black experience of oppression in an inherently corrupt political and social order. This experience paralleled that of the historical Jesus, Cone argues, and his suffering with a downtrodden people.

Cone found himself influenced by the diverse voices of racial uplift that emerged from the civil rights movement. For Cone, Martin Luther King Jr. made theology Christian. Malcolm X, Cone notes, helped make theology black. Both perspectives appealed to Cone. This dialectic aided Cone in hearing the changing tenor of black Christian faith. Carmichael and the emerging nationalist voices within the civil rights struggle provided some cultural space for Cone to retain his Christian beliefs with revisions. Cone writes, "Blackness gave me new theological spectacles, which enabled me to move beyond the limits of white theology and empowered my mind to think wild, heretical thoughts when evaluated by white academic values. . . . Blackness whetted my appetite for learning how to do theology with a black signature on it and thereby make it accountable to poor black people and not to the privileged white theological establishment."[3] Cone experienced the turbulence of the 1950s and '60s and grew up with racism in the state of Arkansas. What Cone later came to label "Black Theology" was a counter to the apparent self-effacing theology within mainstream black Christianity. Black Power, then, was a necessary correlate between African Americans and the power of the Christian faith.

Cone's early work on black theology sought to give the notion of Black Power legitimacy within religious dialogue. In his text *Black Theology and Black Power*, he defined Black Power as the "complete emancipation of black people from white oppression by whatever means black people deem necessary."[4] With freedom as its primary objective, Cone intended that Black Power be a liberating force for black existence. As Cone and others saw it, Black Power ignites the type of self-determination that allows African Americans to free themselves from oppression. Black Power also informs a notion of black humanity that celebrates black being. Cone contends that it is a humanizing force in that it affirms that being, lifts it up as good. He writes, "Black Power, in short, is an *attitude*, an inward affirmation of the essential worth of blackness."[5] Affirming blackness is the path to freedom, Cone maintains. Moving from oppression to freedom means defining for oneself what black means, and affirming it. That is an essential step in the process. What white persons degrade and devalue—blackness—is the essence of black persons' freedom. Without pride in blackness, African Americans are prone to continued power disparity and de facto social-political disfranchisement. Matters such as integration, therefore, required qualifications that Cone sought to address.

Cone did not set out to justify racial separation with his theological construct. The tone in which he wrote his earlier works reflected the anger of many black people in 1960s and '70s America. But one should not confuse the tone with the aim of his public faith. In *Black Theology and Black Power*, Cone states that God did not make humanity to be separate. Cone argues that persons ought not to live with color defining their humanity. But the reality of racism in America beckoned for a corrective. Such was the case, then, that integration needed a clear definition for Cone. If integration meant that blacks would accept the "style" and values of whites to gain entrance into the American mainstream, Cone wanted a new definition. He was suspicious of "white religion." Cone suggests that the "white man" has nothing that blacks should compromise to get. Cone offers, however, a way in which he envisioned integration taking place. Black and white people come together on "equal footing," with no one laying claims to rightness in matters of style and values. This meeting could produce a dialogue that reflects what Cone refers to as the kingdom of God. Seeing that as unrealistic, Cone dismisses integration to reassert the need for pride in blackness: "What is needed, then, is not 'integration' but a sense of worth in being black, and only black people can teach that. Black consciousness is the key to the black man's emancipation from his distorted self-image."[6]

The challenge for Cone, as Peter Paris notes, was to justify Black Power's use in African American faith formation. As Cone saw it, a faith that could translate in the ghetto was the only one necessary for the times in which he wrote. Cone grabbed hold of the revolutionary energy of Black Power proponents and channeled it into an interpretive principle for Christian faith. But this energy found few supporters from the generation of black preachers and theologians who preceded Cone. Proctor was one of those persons who failed to see black theology's enduring worth for public faith. He would maintain that a lasting corrective for theology must come through its ethical contribution. Attaching race to theology, therefore, is a transient fix. But Cone was not the only notable theologian who produced literature that captured that revolutionary tone. "Black theology" perspectives differed, calling for varied emphases that celebrated blackness for Christian faith talk.

### *A Soul Theology of Symbolism and Pluralism*

J. Deotis Roberts entered the black public faith conversation in the post-civil-rights era with what Dwight Hopkins calls a black theology of balance. Roberts received the majority of his theological education in England but concerned himself with the black struggle in America. This led Roberts to produce several works that focused on the political nature of black theology. He writes, "What I am seeking is a Christian theological approach to race relations that will lead us beyond a hypocritical tokenism to liberation as a genuine reconciliation between equals."[7] For Roberts, the country was inconsistent in adhering to the democratic values it stressed. He celebrated Cone and other black theologians' efforts to make theology meaningful for black Americans. Roberts saw black theology as a necessary public faith that could instill the cultural symbols, religious values, and reconciling faith that would affirm black existence. He believed that this soul theology has its place in a white racist society. It balanced what he saw as the need to boost black self-esteem with the symbolism of blackness while aiming for a pluralistic American society.

Roberts's approach to black theology emphasizes the particularity of race. This is a fundamental point of departure for his construct. "Black consciousness or awareness is a realistic foundation for our theological task," he writes. He continues by stating, "When blacks move from color blindness to color consciousness, it becomes difficult to avoid the implications of Black Power." But blackness in America, Roberts argues, is a difficult cultural phenomenon. The "spatial distance" and passage of time between life in Africa and life in America sever much of black people's connection to Africa. And a black person's citizenship in America is contingent upon white temperament and progressive legislation. Roberts, therefore, calls black people a "marginal" people. African Americans are neither fully African nor fully American.[8] A theology of the black experience, therefore, has a unique perspective to offer.

An important part of connecting the Christian faith to the black experience, Roberts argues, is symbol. Lauding Albert Cleage's *The Black Messiah*, Roberts calls for a black savior who appeals to black people. He claims that an Americanized Christ is foreign to the experience of black people. A black Christ, however, is a visual that engenders pride. Roberts notes, "The black person has in the black Messiah a savior. He or she discovers his or her own dignity and pride in a self-awareness that is rooted in black consciousness."[9] Roberts did not claim that the historical Christ was black, but the symbolism of a black Christ sends an important message: black people matter. By no means does Roberts intend for a black Christ to be reverse racism. Roberts sees black theology, through liberation and reconciliation, as a means to reach interracial harmony. The symbol that is the black Christ is a marker for something deeper. A black Christ is a point of entry and departure for the African American. A black Christ is particular inasmuch as a black Christ represents the particularity of the black experience. That Christ is a liberator whose existence frees black people. But Roberts distinguishes the symbolism of a black Christ from the universal functions of the Christ of the gospel. The universal Christ meets people where they are: "A universal Christ will be as 'existential' to red, yellow, and black people as he is to white people," says Roberts. A symbolic Christ becomes the black Messiah for black people. That Christ understands the particulars of the black experience and circumstances that shape black faith. Roberts maintains that struggles of black people in America create a hermeneutic that will allow black people to be authentically Christian. In his work *Liberation and Reconciliation: A Black Theology*, he states that white Christians are "guilty of malpractice."[10] In this way, white Christians have lived an inauthentic existence. Blacks who have followed the Christianity of whites have also failed to be genuine. Theology from the black experience, for black people, remedies this existence. Black theology positions black people to liberate the race. Liberation and reconciliation, Roberts contends, are two central aspects of black theology. The presence of both displays a reality in which blacks and whites relate to each other as equals. This is Roberts's ideal relationship between blacks and whites in America.

With liberation and reconciliation at the core of his theology, Roberts does not desire racial separation. Nowhere is this belief more evident than in his understanding of Jesus as Christ. Roberts writes, "Reconciliation is a more excellent way. Christ the Liberator is likewise Christ the Reconciler. God was in Christ setting us free and God was in Christ reconciling the world unto Himself. . . . Reconciliation has to do with overcoming estrangement, mending fences, breaking down walls of separation between men."[11] Liberation and reconciliation are divine functions of Christ. One does not work without the other, for Roberts. The lack of these theological factors explains the problem with integration in America. On one hand, he suggests, whites have not known the power of reconciliation through repentance. On the other hand, blacks have not realized the power of liberation. African Americans have not known the right conditions to live into the "inner freedom" that is necessary to challenge white hegemonic structures and privilege. This makes integration no more than a sham. The absence of equity and the affirmation of human dignity represent the failures of integration.

Roberts describes human dignity as a divine right and integral to God's desired order for humanity. Roberts writes, "All men are one in the creative purpose—we are made in the image of God. This is the basis of human dignity and equality."[12] Proctor would agree with this assessment. He would question, however, whether Roberts provides a comprehensive public theology. For Proctor, the point of departure (a black theology) represents a compromise of the kingdom of God. White Christian churches and leaders had already made that mistake. For Roberts and others, Black Power and black theology wrest the message of human equality and divine dignity from the hands of racists and white liberal hypocrites. Black theology clarifies this idea and makes it real. Black theology speaks to the black experience, because it was born in the black experience. In black theology, Roberts recognizes a public faith that witnesses to its cultural particularities; it celebrates the dignity of blackness with no apology. Roberts contends, "Soul sums up the black experience, whether religious or secular, better than any other term. . . . Soul theology is Black Theology."[13]

### *Black Women and the Reconstruction of Community*

Closely related to black theology is the womanist tradition. The towering pioneers of womanist thought challenged the dominant categories of theology, ethics, and biblical studies with their writings and presence in the academy. Their advocacy for a theological prism that privileges the experience of black women was a necessary corrective within the emerging post-segregation cacophony of black Christian ideas. Contesting the neglect of their experience within the black and feminist theological traditions, womanist theology and ethics became political and cultural combatants in the public conversation about black life and faith. Womanist thought, through Katie Cannon, Delores Williams, Jacquelyn Grant, emilie townes, and others, created a forum for contesting the racism and sexism that black women face in the United States. These religious intellectuals interpreted the history, experiences, and writings of black women to liberate and empower black women. Intuitively embracing the definition of "womanist" by Alice Walker, they constructed new ways of understanding humanity, community. While interrogating the accepted concepts of white male "universal" theology, womanist thought reframed the issues of race and gender in ways that black and feminist theologians failed to consider. In each of these theological systems, the particularities of race, class, and gender privilege the experiences of their respective authors. Womanist theologians rightly argued for constructs that take seriously the experience of black women. As Stephanie Mitchem argues, "Womanist theology, then, critically draws from the many meanings of faith in the lives of black women in order to assess doctrinal and ecclesial constructions and to begin reconstructions that have relevance, meaning, and power in their lives."[14] To be sure, Katie Geneva Cannon, Delores Williams, and other black womanist theologians and ethicists reconstructed theology and ethics (created a black public faith) with black women at the foundation of their work to push the academy and church toward genuine community.

Katie G. Cannon's explanations of the importance and vocation of the womanist theologian offer insight about this reconstructive process. She set out to challenge the bias that exists in scholarship and in liturgy. Her notable experiences include being the first black woman to earn a doctorate from the Union Theological Seminary in New York and the first black woman to be ordained in the Presbyterian Church in the USA. Positioned to see "life on the inside" of hegemonic structures, she offers this critique: "The accepted canonical methods of moral reasoning contain deeply hidden biases that make it exceedingly difficult to turn them to the service of the best interest of Black women. Universality does not include the Black female experience."[15] The universal that Cannon refers to is the centuries-old constructions of theology and ethics by white male theologians. Biases in theological frameworks are also present in the concepts and ideologies of black and feminist theologies. Their efforts at racial and gender "catchall" theologies lack the complex experiences of black women. Womanist scholarship, then, "moves us toward a fundamental reconceptualization of all ethics with the experience of black women at center stage." Cannon contends that the womanist scholar describes, documents, and analyzes the ideologies and systems that oppress black women. Among these ideologies and systems are gender, class, and race. In turn, the womanist scholar uses the product of this analysis to enhance and support structures of knowledge from which black women can liberate themselves and others.

Cannon's book *Black Womanist Ethics* is a prime example of this reconstructive task. She identified the black woman's literary tradition as a rich source for theological ethics. The folk traditions of black people, she argues, carry rich mother wit and wisdom for everyday living. This tradition is the best "literary repository" of the ethical values of black women, Cannon maintains. In Cannon's view, the need for a turn to this source is obvious: "Seldom in history has a group of women been so directly responsible for exerting indispensable efforts to insure the well-being of both the Black family and the white. At the same time the Black woman is placed in such a sharp disadvantaged position as to accept obligingly the recording of her own story by the very ones who systematically leave her out."[16] After chronicling the moral circumstances of the black woman's life in the United States, she focuses her study on Zora Neale Hurston. Black women writers such as Hurston mine the values and commitments of the black community to frame a narrative that the other races and gender miss. For Cannon, black women writers capture sights and sounds, joys and pains that other groups neglect in analysis. She does not, however, exclude the voices of black men in her constructive work. She ends her text by examining the notion of community as defined by Howard Thurman and

Martin Luther King Jr. She lifts up their ideas as some of the best thinking on the subject within the black church tradition.

Womanist scholars do not seek to exclude persons, especially black men, from their public faith conversation. As emilie townes notes, "Rather than assume the universal claims of traditional theologies, womanist theology acknowledges that all theological reflection is limited by human cultural, social, and historical contexts. These limits are not negative, but merely representative of our humanity. Rather than restrict, these limits can serve as a challenge to explore the particular ways in which any group having similar characteristics (e.g., age, denomination, ethnicity, sexuality) experiences divine activity in life."[17] Delores Williams addresses a similar concern. She sees in womanist theology the mission to build community. And black men are an important part of that goal. Williams states that Walker defines womanist in a way that affirms "black women's historic connection with men through love and through a shared struggle for survival and for productive quality of life (e.g., 'wholeness')."[18] Williams concedes that only one obstacle to sharing community building exists: the violation of women's health.

As an emerging tradition within the post-segregation era of African American public faith, womanist theologians and ethicists have challenged the normative boundaries of theology within the black experience. Their insights have called upon black men in church and academy to take seriously the perspectives of black women as authorities in the shaping of black community. In theory, Proctor understood the necessity of womanist and feminist ideas. He embraced much of the historical-critical models upon which womanist thinkers do their work. In a reaction that resembled his response to black theology, however, Proctor could not see a womanist theology as a viable option for sustaining genuine community. As a "hyphenated" theology, it remained a reflection of the divisive spirit within Christianity. But womanists' collective contribution to black public faith comes in the form of a multilayered social-ethical analysis and methodology. Their work broadens the dialogue in theology along racial and gender lines within church and academy. Their scholarship provides a sounding board for keeping "dominant" groups honest in conversation and/or for calling out political and social structures for their racist and sexist current and past practices.

### *Black Evangelicalism in Conservative Apparel*

Post-segregation-era black public faith formed within pockets of the more "liberal" seminaries and among conservative black evangelical settings and preachers. Edward V. (E. V.) Hill is one example of this conservative faith tradition. Hill was born into extreme economic poverty in rural Texas, and a loving couple, Aaron and Ella Langdon, took him in after receiving permission from his birth mother. In the home of these wonderful people, Hill found faith in Christ. He would speak of this experience with great joy and fervor throughout his career. His preaching ministry started on the college campus of Prairie View A&M University, where he became a ministerial associate for a Baptist convention's campus ministry. He went on to serve as pastor of the Corinth Baptist Church in Houston, Texas. The struggling congregation found a young and spirited leader in Hill. His ministry was instrumental in developing a vibrant congregation that increased in membership. During this time, Hill also joined with the Southern Christian Leadership Conference to fight racism. He even boasted of how he helped elect Martin Luther King Jr. to the presidency of the SCLC. Hill was also proud of his courageous activism, often reflecting on the threats he received from the Ku Klux Klan during those civil rights struggles. The liberal social gospel Christianity of the SCLC would not remain a part of Hill's social-political philosophy, however. He constructed and/or inherited a conservative evangelical focus that promoted a gospel of soul salvation and self-help as the solution to the world's ills. He negotiated this view through a thriving local church social service ministry and leadership within local government. This approach was neither a political compromise nor a surrender to the victors; Hill found in Jesus what he believed was the appropriate response for the racial crisis.

A change of geographical and political scenery came when Hill took over the pastorate of the Mt. Zion Baptist Church in Los Angeles. Hill, who had received the nickname "Hellraiser" for his civil rights work in Houston, claimed that he had left that and his liberal-Democrat tendencies in Texas. Embracing the label of "conservative Republican," he accepted the call to Mt. Zion in 1961. There he found a struggling congregation and a community in political and social turmoil. Believing that there was a simpler way to uplift African Americans from the social problems they faced, Hill turned to a simpler message: save the soul. He argued that people sought salvation in the wrong places, and government was one of those places. Instead, the soul needs a savior who can respond to any need it might have. In this way, Hill gave voice to the disillusionment many black preachers had with the civil rights struggles and strategies. He no longer desired to create the social strategies that would win over society. He believed that Christ had already accomplished that. Hill's job, then, was to ensure that all persons hear the message "Jesus is Lord!"

Hill's alliances with conservative Christian forces did not necessarily mark a distinct shift in theological orientation. Finding allies in Jerry Falwell and

Billy Graham, among others, may have suggested more of a political shift than a theological one. Growing up in a southern rural Black Church experience, Hill heard and preached sermons that emphasized salvation. This was not much different from most evangelicals and fundamentalists. He also had known the oppressive life that racism created in Texas and had come to "hate" white people. He revealed this in a story he shares about a young woman who met with him after a revival.[19] The young woman came at her sister's request. She was becoming bitter with the world and trying to find answers to its problems. One of her questions to Hill was about the effectiveness of Christ on social matters such as racism. Could God deliver her from the burden that was the white man? Hill's response reflected both the fuel behind his previous militant activism and his reoriented position. Hill stated, "No one hated white people more than I did until I was a freshman in college." In an interview with Russell Chandler, Hill credited a part of that transformation to a Baptist Student Union retreat.[20] The state convention's director for the students, Dr. W. F. Howard, drove Hill and some white students from Texas A&M University to the retreat. It was there that Hill saw "regenerated" white people who expressed what God was able to do in the lives of all people.[21] That experience was a part of the "miraculous birth in Christ" that transformed Hill's racial views. As Chandler notes, "Except for the grace of God, Hill might have turned out to be an angry black militant."

Hill was a biblical literalist. It was this understanding of Christianity that helped connect him to Falwell and others in the Religious Right. Hill embraced a premillennial dispensationalism. In his book *A Savior Worth Having*, he argued for the existence of a literal hell. He used the following chapter to state the reasons he did not want to go to it. He stated that this "church age" (one of the markers of a dispensational view of history) has the confusing trait of God's mercy "just being poured out" upon sinners and saints alike. Hill was far "to the right" of most of the other theologians listed in this chapter. But his conservative reading of the Bible was a familiar aspect of black church life in America.

The evangelical tendency in Hill's thought focused on the reality of an afterlife as its end. This focus led Hill to produce *A Savior Worth Having* at the request of Moody Press. The text reflects the evangelical emphasis on the heavenward results of salvation. In his chapter "I Don't Want to Go to Hell," Hill is adamant about the reasons for his perspective. He relies upon an evangelism-tract-like statement of his case. First, hell is a real place. This, he writes, was an early lesson from his mother and an old preacher. Hell is real, and so is the invitation to go to heaven. Hell did not invite anyone, but Christ invited all to heaven. Second, the love of God does not find its way into hell. Third, there is no relief in hell. The discomfort in this world, Hill explained, pales in comparison to what hell will present. Fourth, hell does not have exits. No one will escape from hell. Hill tells a story to support this idea. He mentions the fervent preaching of Dr. Jack Hyles from Hammond, Indiana. Hill stated that Hyles preached as if his life depended on it. Hyles, Hill wroted, told him that his sister had a dream in which she went to hell and witnessed its "desolation." The story is similar to the biblical story of Lazarus and Dives (Luke 16:19-31). Hyles's sister asked one of hell's attendants how long its inhabitants would suffer. He told her, "Forever and ever!" She turned to leave and looked back to see that their father was in hell, suffering with all of hell's residents. Hyles affirmed that their father was in hell and regretted that their father had not chosen Christ. Hyles concluded the story by telling Hill, "I win souls every day so that nobody else's daddy has to go to hell."[22]

Hill's public faith, far from being otherworldly in practice, was influenced by a disdain for black militancy and African Americans' overreliance upon government. His life experiences vouched for an understanding of blackness that highlights the role of community in racial uplift. Knowing the power of a tight-knit black community that seeks the welfare of all its members, Hill did not understand the point of Black Power advocates. In an interview with Russell Chandler for the book *Overcomers*, Hill discussed his frustration with what he called "blackism." Hill described blackism as an "almost idolatrous" focus on skin color that sought to get rights by "any means necessary." Blackism also attempted to replace existing powers with Black Power, substituting corrupt white power with a vengeful and unjust power. For Hill, Black Power was a kind of reverse racism. He even suggested that "blackism" was the product of the maladjustment of African Americans to the progress that society had made on the racial front.[23] In the Watts section of Los Angeles, Hill's approach to race relations only led to suspicion among many young African Americans. Some even threatened Hill's life. Such was Hill's belief in a color-neutral approach to race in America. Poverty and sin were better indicators of the American crisis for Hill.

Hill believed that the government had overreached on many promises to assist the black community. In an interview with Mark Joseph, Hill labeled some government assistance programs "Operation Frustration."[24] Hill argued that, in at least two instances, the government had promised money that the people never saw in communities such as Watts. Once African Americans realized that the government would neglect them, the frustration built up to a boiling point. This is a part of how Hill explained both Watts riots. In this way, he would disagree with Proctor. Proctor cited the lack of moral support from many persons within white evangelical circles as a part of the problem with the failures of the Great Society programs and similar social programs. Hill by that time began to align himself with those evangelical ministers in the Christian Right. He rode those conservative ties to a position of respect within the Republican Party. Hill called it the "Party of Prayer." At the same time, Hill and his church funneled federal money into their community programming. Darren Dochuck writes, "By earning the trust of government officials, Hill gained access to power and money, which he channeled toward social initiatives he thought more effective than federal programs."[25] Some of that money came from the Office of Economic Opportunity (Proctor's employer at one point).[26] Dochuck's description of Hill's work with Los Angeles mayor Samuel Yorty and the social and evangelistic training program that Hill led through Mt. Zion clarify this practice. The program, an intense self-help training endeavor, included Bible study and job training. The work was interracial, seeking to uplift the people in Hill's community. At the height of Hill's ministry, the church offered a halfway house, the Lord's Kitchen feeding ministry, a clothing ministry, and senior citizen centers.

E. V. Hill provides a stark contrast with others in this study, as he identified with conservative political forces within American Christianity. His staunch evangelicalism touted the salvation of the lost soul as its aim. Yet his theological beliefs provided space for political participation and outreach within his community and on a national level. His Los Angeles congregation maintained charitable and social service ministries among the people in the community. In his own way, Hill attempted to fight for the race. He knew well the struggles of black people. He also understood the cultural differences between his role as a black clergyperson and that of his white colleagues. Speaking to his congregants, he distinguished his duties from white clergy by suggesting that white pastors have fewer responsibilities. They merely marry, bury the dead, baptize, and preach. Their boards take care of other matters. The black pastor, he stated, "is considered a community leader, and every aspect of politics, education, civil rights, feeding people, fighting battles, organizing economic opportunities for black people, housing—all of that is considered part of being a good [black] pastor."[27] Hill's alliances and theological commitments, however, would make him a dubious character to most of the theologians in this chapter. Proctor worked on speeches for the Hubert Humphrey campaign. Hill ended up preaching at services in the Nixon White House, the administration of Humphrey's opponent. Hill's political commitments in the 1984 presidential campaign suggest an apparent tension between him and Jesse Jackson. Hill was an avowed Republican from California. He supported Ronald Reagan. Jesse

Jackson was a Democratic candidate for the presidency that year. Hill was a member of the National Baptist Convention, and Jackson had become the head of its civil rights arm under T. J. Jemison, the convention president. Hill was more favored in the convention during Joseph H. Jackson's tenure as president of the convention, Jemison's predecessor. J. H. Jackson also was a Republican.[28]

Hill believed in fighting for a pluralistic world in which African Americans were equals. But he shunned heavy involvement from government and the rhetoric of Black Power, though he used federal money for his church ministries and had a background as a type of race rebel. He rejected any formal theological ideas that complicated a "just Jesus" formula for salvation. A black social gospel was too liberal, and black theology too radical. Hill preferred a Christ of faith, not a historical Jesus. That Christ of faith and the faith in him needed neither a color nor a gender. A gendered theology that elevates black women's narratives and experiences would probably be superfluous to Hill. Preaching the gospel of Christ for salvation meant access to heaven and escape from hell.[29]

### *Black Political Evangelism and the Rainbow Theology*

Jesse Jackson may be the most complex person to identify within the post-segregation era of the African American public faith tradition. There is little evidence that suggests he concerned himself with theological treatises. But evidence does exist that displays his concern for connecting faith with the social circumstances of our time. He preaches a gospel of black economic uplift. He affirms black humanity with his slogan "I am somebody!" And he created multiracial and ethnic coalitions of people through his work with Operation PUSH (People United to Serve Humanity) and the Rainbow Coalition. He is also the product of the evangelical black Protestant stream of Christianity that Martin Luther King Jr. and other black social gospel theologians influenced. Black Power ideas, moreover, found their way into Jackson's beliefs. He maintains a cordial relationship with several social-theological traditions. He has made use of multiple sources to construct his public faith. In the Reverend Jesse Jackson, varied ideas of black public faith find their way into his political evangelistic sermons. His seemingly authentic use of these ideas and beliefs made for a "Rainbow Theology." Nowhere is this more evident than in the scores of black people he brought into the political process during his 1984 presidential run. As James Melvin Washington argues, Jackson's charismatic presence and political rhetoric made him one of the most influential black men in America since Booker T. Washington.[30] Jackson cultivated a political-religious ethos that spoke to the cultural affinities of black publics. Jackson's star has faded some since the early post-civil-rights years. But his contribution to black public faith in America remains a force that requires further study.

Jesse Jackson's rise to public prominence came through his emerging charismatic leadership within the civil rights struggle and through his command of the perceived post-segregation vacuum of visible authority and organization. Jackson's biography reveals his contact with notable black public leaders during his vocational development. Jackson was a student at North Carolina A&T State University during Proctor's time as president of the institution. Jackson was student body president and had access to the president's ear. Proctor had some influence in Jackson's life. He had a hand in getting Jackson to enter seminary upon completing his undergraduate studies. Proctor cautioned Jackson by stating that Martin Luther King Jr. needed prepared leaders to work with him. This advice led to a brief stint at Chicago Theological Seminary for Jackson. Already a Baptist preacher, Jackson admitted that he was frustrated with all of the seminary theology talk that had no grounding in the real world. He withdrew from seminary and signed on full-time with the SCLC. The established civil rights organization found room for this gifted and socially conscious minister. Jackson quickly found favor among the leaders of the organization. King assigned Jackson leadership of the northern effort through Operation Breadbasket.

The SCLC declined in the years following King's death, but Jackson's public profile grew. He would take control of Operation Breadbasket and use it to begin his own organization, Operation PUSH. With this political organization in place, Jackson had the autonomy to establish his political agenda. The agenda would take him across the world in numerous political and religious capacities. Newspaper clippings, television broadcasts, books, and articles all testify about the extent of Jackson's visibility—or fame. Absent from most of these accounts is his theological legacy.

Jackson's rhetoric of black economic and social uplift grew out of the influence of Black Power rhetoric and action. Jackson's public faith absorbed some of this content. For example, he speaks of God in the language of power during the early post-segregation period. Jackson claims that God is creator and ruler of the moral order. God is the power that humanity appeals to for the good in life. In doing so, humanity acknowledges that there is no power above God. In a 1970 speech, "Christianity, the Church, and Racism," Jackson offers these words: "We relate to God and bow to him because he's power. If God didn't have power, we would disregard him. It is precisely because God is the maker and the giver of every good and perfect gift and the Creator and the sustainer, the one who made the valleys and made the mountains and made all of the resources and who controls them and who can apply justice and who can grant mercy or grant grace . . . . Our basic relationship to God is a power relationship."[31] For Jackson, there would be no worship of God if not for God's power to create and control creation. Jackson admits that the church has power and that it wants more power to wield its influence. What separates the church from "ordinary people" is its attempt to apply its power justly, by seeking a fair distribution of resources and wielding moral authority. Jackson stops short of giving God a race/color. He argues that God is an experience and a revelation. One relates to God, and God reveals God's desire for love and justice. It is only fair, then, that African Americans be able to demand reparations, or compensation for years of unpaid labor. Neglect of such ideas by the leaders in the Christian church led Jackson to be critical of seminaries. He accuses them of using phrases "to death" without action that reflects the gospel.[32] Seminaries (white), he contends, will not use black banks or invest in black communities. The white supremacy in the country, economic disparities among the races, and theological inconsistencies of the white power structures led Jackson to embrace Black Power themes.

Jesse Jackson has blamed the church for its lack of a prophetic voice during the early post-segregation-era events. He identifies a portion of the confusion that exists in much of American Christianity in the poorly crafted merger of nationalism and the Christian religion. Some persons combine notions of hyperpatriotism with a misguided Christianity, Jackson maintains. This troubled him during the Vietnam War period. He was concerned that so many young men volunteered to join the war effort. That, Jackson argues, was a moral-spiritual failure of clergy. Clergypersons, Jackson claims, need to make clear to American Christians the problems within the American social and political structures. Economically, a privileged few control the economic fate of masses. Politically, American leaders can destroy more lives "with the wave of a finger"[33] than churches can heal through years of baptism and evangelistic work. This makes the work of the church even more important. Faith, he claims, provides believers with hope and fulfillment. Jackson argues that black churches give believers hope but lack fulfillment. While praising the ministries of King, Adam Clayton Powell, and Nat Turner, Jackson states that the black church has let its white counterpart off the hook on such matters. Blacks still live under the pall of racial inferiority. White people, therefore, can maintain their status as racially superior. (White churches, he maintains, give their people neither hope nor fulfillment.) Jackson argues that the "American presupposition" of such things as wealth, race, labor, and religion need revision. In his address "In Search of a New Focus and a New Vision," Jackson states that the nation's structure is faulty and its purpose requires a new definition. African Americans are a necessary part of this re-envisioning and redefining. For Jackson, black people have a special mission in America. The race has a divine purpose in this land.

Within Jackson's public faith is a black messianic understanding of the African American experience. On at least two separate occasions, Jackson states the divine mission of black people in America. In the 1970 address on Christianity, to what must have been a predominantly white audience, Jackson states, "America has built upon our shoulders. We can help determine its destiny. And that's why I plead with Black people not to hate you, not to try to run away from you. God was operating at his providential best when he sent us here to be saviors of the human race not as slaves of white men."[34] At another event, his address "Liberation and Justice" struck a similar chord. Jackson claims, "We're not slaves brought here to serve white folks. We're God's children sent here to save the human race."[35] While Jackson is not the first African American leader to embrace such a view, his messianic understanding of the black race is significant in light of his national campaigns for the presidency. But Jackson holds that the "economic generation" he fights for cannot come without the participation of the black masses. His rhetoric has as its aim spiritual renewal and political education. Jackson attempts to connect the political to the spiritual in all of his sermons and addresses.

Jackson is a political revivalist/evangelist. While aided some by his theological formation in seminary, Jackson draws from several streams of black faith from the dawn and twilight of the civil rights era. While mastering none of them, he constructed a political evangelism that sought to educate African American people about their divine and social rights. Jackson adapted within what James Melvin Washington calls the three cultural strands of political praxes in black Christendom: folk, bourgeois, and urban. These strata find expression in revivalistic, pastoral, and prophetic political functions. At their best, these cultural strands fight white supremacy. Jackson merges them to do just that. He expressed his public faith through black political revivalism. Washington writes, "Black political revivalism includes the use of sermonic folk discourse and a complex of cultural praxes that are all rooted in the distinctive spirituality of black Christianity."[36] Manning Marable echoes that thought in his description of Jackson's 1984 presidential campaign: "The campaign throughout retained both the character of a Black religious revival, and the special idealism which motivated desegregation efforts of the 1960's."[37] Washington argued that Jackson displayed his political ingenuity by reforming the techniques of black political revivalism. That reform helped Jackson transfer a primarily southern movement to northern urban areas without losing the movement's southern agrarian ethos.[38]

Washington highlights another key component of Jackson's public faith. Citing Jackson's continued membership in the National Baptist Convention USA (NBCUSA), Washington labels Jackson's theology "conservative" and "evangelical." Jackson remained a member of the denomination after the infamous split between black Baptists who started the Progressive National Baptist Convention (PNBC) and the leadership of the NBCUSA. Joseph Harrison Jackson, the NBCUSA president, at the time of the split sought to discredit Martin Luther King Jr. and his form of activism. J. H. Jackson was convinced that the civil rights movement displayed Communist tendencies. He also embraced some conservative social policies and supported Richard Nixon's presidential bid. Jesse Jackson, moreover, made a deliberate choice in his denominational affiliation. King was a part of the group that formed the PNBC, but Jackson remained with the NBCUSA. Washington writes, "Despite Jesse's fierce ideological disagreements with Reverend Joseph Harrison Jackson, he never left the National Baptist Convention. One explanation for this is Jackson's basically conservative evangelical theology, which was evident, for example, in his initial opposition to abortion and homosexual rights. The convention's powerful black folk spirituality, its traditional evangelical theology, and, from a historical viewpoint, its atypical political conservatism—thanks to Joseph Jackson—vied successfully for Jesse Jackson's allegiance."[39] Washington's claim has merit. But Jackson's conservative evangelical beliefs are just a part of his public faith. His tendency to grab from the varied offerings of black Christian beliefs undercuts a clear label outside of his function as political revivalist.

### *Pragmatic Harmony of a Black Social "American" Gospel*

Samuel DeWitt Proctor saw himself as the theological bridge between his black social gospel theology and the emerging voices of black conservative ideology, black and womanist theologies, and the black Christian political and economic uplift traditions of public faith in the post-segregation era. With the common ground being a vocation that seeks to contest white supremacist practices in their varied forms, Proctor appealed to a universal Christ whose life and ethical teachings meshed well with a class-conscious black middle-class ethos of Proctor's generation. Proctor was a bridge between black theological traditions. His understanding of the Christian gospel was a type of pragmatic middle ground of black public faith. His race-conscious approach to theology eyed the uplift of black humanity and the gradual social-moral unification of humanity. This black social gospel included a race-conscious but universal public faith that fought racism for the sake of genuine community.

Proctor grew up with the hope of the integration of the races. His "black world" made space for few interactions with white persons, and boundaries were seldom crossed. But Proctor's family embedded within his psyche no need of a "black" theological system. Everything was already black, mostly. He mastered the black bourgeois education that he received from his parents. They were graduates of a post-Reconstruction denominational home mission college. As Evelyn Brooks Higginbotham notes, these schools sought to make good citizens of black students by assimilating them into white culture.[40] Preparation for citizenship looked a lot like modeling the value systems and "style" of white people. This was a part of Proctor's education. The new world of his adulthood, therefore, validated the findings of his rearing. If one were to live into a life of respectability that came with the cultivation of the black bourgeois ethic, one could enter a mainstream America that made room for the one who prepared. He had faith in this America. He was the recipient of a white benefactor for seminary. He interacted with white people within the Northern (later American) Baptist Convention. He was a part of a second wave of black religious intellectuals who gained access to graduate theological education. He also worked for the United States government. Proctor comes close to embracing what James Melvin Washington calls the doctrine of integration.[41] Proctor's experiences do not justify this claim alone. But the experiences shaped his response to racism. A 1967 *Chicago Defender* article, "Some 'Soul Culture' Must Go if Integration Wins,"[42] reported that Proctor cautioned his audience about what was needed to integrate into mainstream American society. Speaking "correct English" and learning algebra are a part of that assimilation. Proctor presupposed a desire by *the* black community to integrate. But he is a generational and ideological bridge.

In Proctor, the reader has an opportunity to see the influence and legacy of the black liberal theological tradition. His approach to the theology had the tint of Rauschenbusch's social gospel ideas. The reader encounters in Proctor an intentional focus on the kingdom of God as the social-spiritual ideal. This is what Jesus taught, Proctor would tell you. His belief in the historical-critical approach to the Bible helped him see that. But the black liberal theological tradition had a focus on solving the racial problem, making *community* its goal. There remained in this tradition a hope in or naïveté about the inherent good of the American political structure. America needed the proper social and political education and interaction with the best and brightest of the Negro race to see the problems in the social and political systems. The black social gospel tradition positioned itself on the front line to violate unjust laws and transgress, sometimes unsuspected, the boundaries of society. But while Proctor's views remain unchanged, perceptions of them have, so that he is now considered a moderate rather than a liberal. Other, more visible theological expressions gained steam to the right and left of him. More, however, on the specific expressions of Proctor's thought will follow.

## Common Enemy, Diverse Trajectories

The evolving race consciousness and radical nature of the Black Power movement challenged the presuppositions of the civil rights struggle. The incident between Carmichael and King is one instance of this fact. White backlash reinforced the "mythic" nature of black bourgeoisie claims to integration and called for a restatement and reinterpretation of the theology that existed in black Christianity. A "soul theology" became a necessity for African Americans who saw through the patronizing programming of white liberal theopolitical agendas. Cone is one example of the development of a theological system that sought to appreciate blackness for what it is. This would concern Proctor, however, due to a perception problem. "Black" became a volatile term in the post-segregation period. Proctor appreciated blackness. But he was concerned about a celebration of blackness and gender leading to a type of chauvinism that lacked pragmatic value to larger black Christian audiences.

Proctor differed from the womanist and black traditions in several ways. Proctor questioned the viability of a political and/or public theology that was just for African Americans. Although diplomatic in his critique, he maintained that black theology lacked the schematics and infrastructure of a movement and seemed somewhat isolated to conversations within the classrooms of mainline seminaries. The real substance of his challenge was a question of character. Is the gospel as narrow as a black theology would represent? While Proctor used experience as a primary locus of his theology, he believed in theology's universal nature. He once testified that he thought "all theology was liberation theology."[43] He wrote, "There is nothing angelic about being Black. Much of general theology applies to *all* Black people, as it does to everyone else."[44] He conceded that black and feminist theologies had good intentions. But he also questioned whether they were committed to going out of business when society catches up with their aims. That is a part of what Proctor called the "metes and bounds" of black theology. When it has run its course, "Black theologians should be the first to rejoice to see their witness become irrelevant and the 'metes and bounds' of Black theology get lost and erased in a new emergence of strong and convincing movement toward a genuine community in the world."[45] Proctor would have levied the same criticisms against womanist theology.[46] Incidentally, one may observe that Cone's work questions the inherent justice in American democracy. Cone's theology is a call for restructuring the social order. The American social structure is evil and produces racism. Proctor believed in the intrinsic fairness of American democracy. Its stage players, however, need moral reform.

Proctor was ambivalent about the value of black theology. He understood why theologians such as James Cone and J. Deotis Roberts wrote on the topic. Yet this did not persuade him of the authority of their claims. Proctor saw black theology as a contextual and transient discipline in theology. He accepted the aim of black theology, a theology that addresses the oppression and racial marginalization of blacks. But he argued that its major problem was its penchant for separatism. This comes across in the way he designates it "a hyphenated brand of theology."[47]

Proctor cherished the idea of an integrated community of races. His upbringing made the racial lines fluid to him in some ways. He navigated "white worlds" rather easily in his adult life. This may be a reason for his support of integration. Proctor discerned the type of concerns that labeling something black could create among whites. His response to black theology is not much different from the responses the term *Black Power* received from black integrationists and liberal white persons in its heyday. Proctor argues that the word *black* triggers the memory of a separated reality: "It is understandable that the term 'Black theology' would cause some apprehensiveness, because none of us enjoys these reminders of our scandalous separations in America. Hence it is embarrassing to admit that even theology reflects this separation. Blacks see God through the lenses of their experience."[48]

A 1969 article in the *Negro Digest* reveals that these sensitivities about the separation of the races were not new for Proctor.[49] In the article, he responds to the Black Manifesto's call for a black university. He reasons that the racial signifier *black* was "associated with the riots and four letter words." Although he did not understand why, Proctor claimed that using *black* as a modifier signaled violence to a larger audience. He did not diminish the value of having a black university, but he believed that the same objective could come through other means. Such was the case for his commentary on black theology. He did not deny a need for its existence but thought it could lead to further separation in an area of life that was universal—theology.

Proctor saw clear limits to black theology. For him, its "metes and bounds" lie in its praxis. When persons begin to address the issues that black theology covers, there will no longer be a need for it. He staked his claim on his optimism. This was an optimism drawn from the content of his experiences. His hope was that there would no longer be a need for black theology. In addition, persons who are black and those who are not black experience similar issues. And "black" does not necessarily define one's existence. Proctor argued that the experience defines the theology. Nonblack persons, therefore, can move vicariously and empathetically into the experience of African Americans, and vice versa. Proctor contended that persons have the ability to transgress and transcend the limits of their experiences and enter into group, class, and racially oppressive circumstances. They are able to enter the portals of another person's experience.[50] Proctor's background in the social gospel tradition may be another reason why he did not take to black theology. Proctor cared less about the color of the theology and more about what the theology addressed.

Other issues remain as points of contention between Proctor and the theological and political positions of E. V. Hill and Jesse Jackson. Proctor would call into question the value of Hill's Jesus and Hill's religious circle of friends. Proctor found the behavior of those persons and groups to be inconsistent with the witness of Jesus. Proctor would be concerned about the wisdom of siding with the same religious forces that created "Christian" academies to keep white children from attending integrated schools with black children. Theologically, Hill's personal evangelism displayed a Jesus who was too heavenly for Proctor's taste. Hill's Jesus lacked the power of the ethical religion of God. The focus on a heavenly Jesus negates the saving power of the historical person. Hill's literal reading of the Bible could not produce the kind of consistent ethical insight that years of science and human progress have manifested. Proctor quotes Adam Clayton Powell Jr. on such black conservatives: "I'll never forget when he spoke in our college chapel in 1941, shortly after his election to the city council. 'I can't stand conservative Negroes,' he said. 'They don't have a damn thing to conserve!' I have never forgotten how vehement he was when he said that."[51]

Proctor would temper Jackson's black messianic vision. Always cautious about misrepresenting the black experience to larger audiences, Proctor would rather provide evidence of the social import of the black American contribution to the United States. Jackson was one of Proctor's protégés, but Jackson's confrontational approach to politics was not a part of Proctor's playbook. The "rainbow" of theological ideas that Jackson espoused would also concern Proctor. Proctor could quantify his contribution in social victories and theological heirs. Jackson is one of them.

The vocation of black public faith in the post-segregation era remained and remains the fight against racism in American life. The changing dynamics of the religious conversation in this period evinces this singular vocation in the thought of many black public faith advocates. Each of the persons listed in this chapter attempted and/or attempts to combat racism from his or her vantage point. All of their positions reflect critical points of departure for considering both the nature of black religious response traditions and their interactions. Their fight against racism, their vocation binds together these post-segregation-era voices. Be it the search for black solidarity or genuine community, the celebration of black women's experience, the quest for black political and economic freedom, or soul salvation—in all of these endeavors, racism challenged these black public faith advocates to respond. Copeland's keen insight about racism and the vocation of the theologian calls for action. Faithfulness to the aforementioned tasks that Copeland sets out equips the theologian for the work of truth telling. That truth has been necessary for black existence and remains necessary for the American experience. She writes, "In the twilight of American culture, telling the truth about white racist supremacy is a theological obligation, no matter how cauterizing these truths may be."[52] Proctor taught and preached these truths.

## Notes

1. M. Shawn Copeland, "Race and the Vocation of the Christian Theologian," *Spiritus* 2, no. 1 (2002): 21.

2. Robert Gooding-Williams, *In the Shadow of Du Bois: Afro-Modern Political Thought in America* (Cambridge, MA: Harvard University Press, 2009), 3.

3. James H. Cone, "Looking Back, Going Forward: Black Theology as Public Theology," in *Black Faith and Public Talk: Critical Essays on James H. Cone's Black Theology and Black Power*, ed. Dwight N. Hopkins (Waco, TX: Baylor University Press, 2007), 251.

4. James H. Cone, *Black Theology and Black Power* (Harper & Row, 1969; repr. Maryknoll, NY: Orbis, 1999), 6–7.

5. Ibid., 8.

6. Ibid., 17–18.

7. J. Deotis Roberts, Liberation and Reconciliation: A Black Theology, 2nd ed. (Louisville, KY: Westminster John Knox, 2005), 9.

8. J. Deotis Roberts, *A Black Political Theology* (Philadelphia: Westminster, 1974), 53–55; see also Dwight N. Hopkins, *Introducing Black Theology of Liberation* (Maryknoll, NY: Orbis, 1999).

9. Roberts, *Liberation and Reconciliation*, 72–73.

10. Ibid., 7.

11. J. Deotis Roberts, "Black Theology in the Making," in *Black Theology: A Documentary History*, vol. 1, *1966–1979*, ed. James H. Cone and Gayraud S. Wilmore (Maryknoll, NY: Orbis, 1993), 120.

12. Roberts, "Black Theology in the Making," 121.

13. Roberts, *Liberation and Reconciliation*, ix.

14. Stephanie Y. Mitchem, *Introducing Womanist Theology* (Maryknoll, NY: Orbis, 2002), 46.

15. Katie G. Cannon, "Hitting a Straight Lick with a Crooked Stick: The Womanist Dilemma in the Development of a Black Liberation Ethic," in *Black Liberation Theology: A Documentary History,* vol. 2, *1980–1992*, ed. James H. Cone and Gayraud S. Wilmore (Maryknoll, NY: Orbis, 1993), 301, 305.

16. Katie G. Cannon, *Black Womanist Ethics*, American Academy of Religion Academy Series (Atlanta: Scholars, 1988), 75.

17. Emilie M. Townes, "Womanist Theology," *Union Quarterly Review* 57, no. 3–4 (2003): 159.

18. Delores S. Williams, "Womanist Theology: Black Women's Voices in Black Theology," in *Black Liberation Theology: A Documentary History*, vol. 2, *1980–1992*, ed. James H. Cone and Gayraud S. Wilmore (Maryknoll, NY: Orbis, 1993), 268.

19. E. V. Hill, *A Savior Worth Having* (Chicago: Moody, 2002), 95.

20. Russell Chandler, *The Overcomers: Outstanding Christians Share the Secrets of Successful Living* (Old Tappan, NJ: Fleming H. Revel, 1978), 54, available at http://www.ccel.us/overcomers.ch4.html.

21. Hill, *A Savior Worth Having*, 98–99.

22. Ibid., 91–92.

23. Chandler, *The Overcomers*, 60.

24. Transcript of interview of Pastor E. V. Hill by Mark Joseph, 1994, MJM Entertainment Group, http://www.mjmgroup.com/Transcripts/EV_Hill.htm, accessed July 10, 2012.

25. Darren Dochuck, *From Bible Belt to Sun Belt: Plain-Folk Religion, Grassroots Politics, and the Rise of Evangelical Conservatism* (New York: W. W. Norton, 2011), 289.

26. Richard V. Pierard, "Religion and the 1984 Election Campaign," *Review of Religious Research* 27, no. 2 (1985): 104; and transcript of interview of Pastor E. V. Hill by Mark Joseph, 1994.

27. "Time Has Told the Story: E. V. Hill," *Fundamentalist Journal* 7, no. 2 (1988): 22–23.

28. Erin Curry, "E. V. Hill Remembered as Conservative African American Pastor, Civil Rights Leader," *Baptist Press*, February 26, 2003, http://www.bpnews.net/bpnews.asp?id=15322.

29. Hill used the celebration of the fortieth anniversary of the Little Rock high school integration ceremony to emphasize this point. Billy Graham followed Hill by inviting the audience to accept God's gift of forgiveness. See Russell N. Dilday, "Little Rock 40th Anniversary Puts Focus on Reconciliation," *Baptist Press*, September 26, 1997, http://www.bpnews.net/printerfriendly.asp?ID=4086.

30. See James Melvin Washington, "Jesse Jackson and the Symbolic Politics of Black Christendom," in *African American Religious Thought: An Anthology*, ed. Cornel West and Eddie S. Glaude Jr. (Louisville, KY: Westminster John Knox, 2003).

31. Jesse Jackson, "Christianity, the Church, and Racism," *Religious Education* 65, no. 2 (March–April 1970): 92–93.

32. Ibid., 93.

33. Ibid., 94.

34. Ibid., 97.

35. Jesse Jackson, "Liberation and Justice," in *Straight from the Heart*, ed. Roger D. Hatch and Frank E. Watkins (Philadelphia: Fortress Press, 1987), 62.

36. Washington, "Jesse Jackson and the Symbolic Politics of Black Christendom," 924.

37. Manning Marable, "The Rainbow Coalition: Jesse Jackson and the Politics of Ethnicity," *Cross Currents* (Spring 1984): 26.

38. As migration studies will show, numerous residents in the urban north had southern agrarian backgrounds. One key to Jackson's success may have been familial connection between northern and southern black people. Many black people in the north could sympathize with their southern family through psychic and social experiences, past and present.

39. Washington, "Jesse Jackson and the Symbolic Politics of Black Christendom," 932.

40. Evelyn Brooks Higginbotham, *Righteous Discontent: The Women's Movement in the Black Baptist Church, 1880–1920* (Cambridge, MA: Harvard University Press, 1994).

41. James Melvin Washington, ed., *Conversations with God: Two Centuries of Prayers by African Americans* (New York: Harper, 1994), xlvi. Washington wrote, "The doctrine of integration argued that African Americans needed to become as close to perfect copies of white people as possible."

42. "Some 'Soul Culture' Must Go if Integration Wins," *Chicago Defender*, January 14, 1967, 33.

43. Samuel D. Proctor, "The Rich Young Ruler," sermon presented at the Union Theological Seminary, Richmond, 1980, UTS-PSCE.

44. Samuel D. Proctor, "The Metes and Bounds of Black Theology," *Journal of Theology* 96 (1992): 39.

45. Ibid., 41.

46. Proctor did not acknowledge womanist thought. His theological bibliography shrank after his graduate school days.

47. Proctor, "The Metes and Bounds of Black Theology," 34. Proctor writes, "It appears that other theological labels somehow seem to belong: process theology, liberation theology, neo-orthodox theology, personalism, existentialism, Calvinism, mysticism, and fundamentalism; but Black theology has yet to earn its legitimacy. It does not quite make the canon."

48. Martin Luther King Jr., *Where Do We Go from Here? Chaos or Community* (Boston: Beacon, 1968), 30. See also Proctor, "The Metes and Bounds of Black Theology," 35.King reasoned with leaders of the Student Nonviolent Coordinating Committee (SNCC) that the issue with Black Power is one of semantics.

49. Samuel D. Proctor, "Symposium: Black Educators Respond," *Negro Digest* 18, no. 5 (1969): 71-73.

50. Proctor, "The Metes and Bounds of Black Theology," 39. Proctor gave the example of white missionaries who live among and relate to indigenous peoples. They may experience discrimination from any number of groups, including the native groups.

51. Samuel DeWitt Proctor, *The Substance of Things Hoped For: A Memoir of African-American Faith*, with a foreword by Marian Wright Edelman (New York: G. P. Putnam's Sons, 1995), 148.

52. Copeland, "Race and the Vocation of the Christian Theologian," 22.

# 2

# On the Making of a Public Theologian

## *Proctor's Cultural Roots*

Samuel DeWitt Proctor was a prominent Baptist minister, college president (of two historical black colleges), and former associate director of the Peace Corps during the Kennedy-Johnson administration—among other things.[1] Yet Proctor's beginnings were humble, as an African American growing up in a segregated community in Norfolk, Virginia. He lived under Jim Crow restrictions and knew the hardship of living through the Depression with a single-wage-earner family. The social conditions, nevertheless, were small obstacles in hindsight. He was almost destined to become a "race man," considering the moral-spiritual investment that people made on his behalf. Proctor was the product of a loving home, a Baptist congregation that connected theological and racial consciousness to moral and social achievement, and a formal theological education that prepared him for his unique vocational challenges. His upbringing was centered in these three communities: family, church, and school. Proctor's life and thought consist of the confluence of persons, places, and events that shaped his sensibilities to racism and prepared him for a public ministry that would combat notions of black inferiority.

The three social-religious communities of Proctor's formative years nurtured him. These interwoven spaces, integrally connected, created in him a morally developed sense of responsibility for the African American race and a theological foundation for responding to the crisis of racism in the United States. Peter Paris observes that these three communities have been an important part of the ethical development of African Americans in the recent past: "In earlier times and in societies simpler than our own, the family, school, and church shared a common moral ethos."[2] He notes that the circumstances of racial segregation in North America and other parts of the world prompted African Americans in these communities to respond to white hostility with an intentional sense of moral purpose. Black parents, teachers, and preachers set the moral tone for their communities and the children they raised. In this way, they created a legacy of "moral integrity" that united the black communities against the white world that sought to destroy them. This was the case in Proctor's life.

## Proctor's Early Years, 1921–1937

Proctor grew up in a stable and nurturing environment that provided for him a spiritual-ethical basis for judging the segregated environment in which he lived. The confidence to succeed in life was a part of the Proctor upbringing. The racist messages transmitted in a southern city like Norfolk could not contend with the loving care of a family that preached "somebodiness." He learned from his grandmother that all of God's children matter—equally. His education in the segregated Norfolk public schools and in his African American Baptist experience emphasized and affirmed that message. Proctor learned, therefore, how to face a world in which being black could disqualify persons from the type of vocational accomplishments that he achieved. His parents, moreover, instilled in him a Protestant ethic that made family, religion, and education the keys to prospering in the United States.

### *Proctor's Youth: Family, Church, and Education*

Samuel DeWitt Proctor was born on July 13, 1921, to the union of Herbert Proctor and Velma Hughes. The couple had six children in all. There were five boys and one girl. The family lived in a district of Norfolk, Virginia, known as Huntersville. Proctor called it "a small dusty bottom" in that city. On another occasion, he referred to the urban district as the "black center" of Norfolk.[3] The family house was located at 918 Fremont Street. Proctor's maternal grandfather, William Hughes, built the home. Proctor's grandfather worked with Hampton Institute (now Hampton University) students through an internship program with African American builders in the area. They built the home at 918 Fremont Street during the summer of 1919. In this "nine-room frame structure" home, Proctor stated, was little money but a lot of love. This love prepared Proctor for what he would face in a segregated society steeped in racist attitudes and practices.

Racism was a part of life in Norfolk, Virginia, and it was something Proctor faced in his childhood and adolescence. He acknowledged that such was the case. Norfolk, like many other cities in the south, was a segregated city. Segregated schools, churches, and neighborhoods were among the cultural practices that defined life in Norfolk. In an interview for a city-sponsored history of Norfolk, he recalled having to enter the local river ferry on whatever side was inconvenient for blacks.[4] When white persons boarded the ferry, blacks needed to make room by moving across the ferry—if necessary. Ferry officials allowed white persons to board where there were no black persons standing. The white-sponsored Norfolk newspaper used words like *pickaninnies, darky*, and *dusky* to label African Americans. In 1914, the city passed and enforced an ordinance to keep neighborhoods segregated.[5] In 1923, "eighty to one hundred armed whites" forced an African American family out of a home that was too close to a white neighborhood.[6] A "reborn" Ku Klux Klan appeared in Norfolk in June of 1921. Six days after Proctor was born, the Klan held a public rally. In the following years, the Klan held recruiting events at Norfolk's Fairmount Park fairgrounds. In July 1925, thirty-five thousand people attended a Klan-sponsored event in the city. To be sure, the Klan's presence contributed to the racism that plagued Norfolk. The presence of the white supremacist group, however, did not paralyze many members in the black community.

Poll taxes kept many African Americans in Norfolk disfranchised. Blacks, therefore, had little to no voice in Norfolk's electoral politics.[7] The Depression amplified this problem for many members in the black community. Limited earnings were a factor that discouraged more than a few persons from paying the poll tax. The lack of political power was evident. Most blacks had problems voting. Thomas C. Parramore and others observe, "Of nearly fifty thousand Norfolk blacks in the mid-1930s only about seven hundred were registered and few of them could count on voting."[8] Without real political power working on behalf of African Americans, the city managers lagged behind on important issues for African Americans. Blacks went without sites for recreation throughout most of the 1920s. Deliberation over the matter of a park for black citizens began in 1923. They were not granted a park until 1926, as the city leadership stalled during the process of deciding what to do about the problem. Earl Lewis summarizes the irony of the circumstances. Lewis states that it should not have been difficult to provide African Americans with space for recreation in Norfolk, "for it is surrounded by beachfront on almost all sides." Lewis states that the debates about how the city would address the *Plessy v. Ferguson* decision's separate-but-equal mandate displayed both Norfolk's entrenched racism and the desire of blacks to make their life better.[9] Even after the council decided on the locations of the segregated parks, the disparities among whites and blacks remained apparent.

The lack of political and economic opportunity created an environment that was ripe for groups such as Marcus Garvey's (1887–1940) Universal Negro

Improvement Association (UNIA) and the Communist Party in America. Garvey appeared in Norfolk in 1922 at the Crispus Attucks Theatre, the entertainment center for African Americans, encouraging them to build a new nation in Africa. The social emphasis for many African Americans in Norfolk, however, was on creating a better Norfolk for their children.

For the most part, Proctor remained protected from racism by living in an insulated world. Within his family circle, loving parents, siblings, and a grandmother created spaces of positive affirmation that combated the racist themes of the larger society.[10] Proctor's paternal grandfather, George Proctor, was a barber. He died at a young age, leaving behind a very young family. Proctor's paternal grandmother, Hattie Ann Virginia Fisher Proctor, was a slave born around 1855. She was raised on the Fishers' tobacco plantation around Chesterfield County in Virginia (an area that is now a part of metropolitan Richmond, Virginia). Proctor noted that she was good at sewing and stitching, so the Fisher family provided her with work in the "big" house. While working in the Fisher home, she received an education from the Episcopal priest who taught the Fisher children. As a result, she learned to read and write; many slaves did not have this kind of opportunity. The Fishers eventually sent her to the Hampton Institute, where she graduated in 1882. Incidentally, Samuel Proctor hung her degree in his study, long after she died. At some point after emancipation, Hattie Ann's family moved to Norfolk. When she graduated from Hampton, she returned to her family. In Norfolk, she taught in a segregated school.

After returning to Norfolk, she met and started a family with George Proctor. The two were married and had eight children. A believer in education, Hattie Ann made sure that all eight of her children completed high school. All of them, moreover, received some education beyond high school. Samuel D. Proctor was proud of the fact that all of Hattie's children played an instrument as well; his father played the piano, violin, and clarinet. Proctor noted in an interview that Hattie Proctor became a traveler's aide later in life. She would meet the boats and trains "at the end of Brooke Avenue."[11] He remembered going to the terminal with his grandmother. She maintained an active life in her older years and provided an example for her children and grandchildren.

Hattie Ann Proctor was a fixture in the Proctor family home of Samuel Proctor's youth. She taught her grandchildren Bible lessons and, he remembered, would correct him and his siblings when their grammar was less than perfect. Proctor stated in his memoirs that he could not imagine how this woman could have been a slave. This was a woman, he observed, who was "highly refined and poised." Just as important was one of the lessons she passed on to her grandchildren regarding racism and segregation: "Grandma's intrepid confidence rested on a single uncomplicated notion: God created all people; any inequalities among us were due to unequal opportunity. From her we learned that hatred and vindictiveness were always destructive. 'No use fretting or crying,' she would say. 'If you do your part, God will do the rest.'"[12] Hattie Proctor's "uncomplicated notion" stayed with Samuel Proctor for the rest of his life. Education and religion were mainstays in Proctor's family. His grandmother passed that along to her children.

Herbert Proctor, Samuel's father, is a sparkling example of this fact. He worked at the Norfolk Naval Yard while his wife, Velma, worked at home. To supplement the family's income, the senior Proctor would do odd jobs like writing obituaries for the local papers. About his father, Samuel D. Proctor stated, "Well, now, my father was a lucky one. He went to Norfolk Mission College, and it is very apparent, very clear to me, that he must have been an extraordinarily good student because he was excellent in writing and poetry, and music. He was a very cultivated man."[13] He also made time to participate in the Norfolk Philharmonic Glee Club, a group of African American men who performed choral selections for an integrated—mainly white—audience. Herbert Proctor met Velma Hughes at the Norfolk Mission College.[14] The United Presbyterian Church founded the college in 1883 by order of the General Assembly. Concerning the curriculum at the Norfolk Mission College, Ruth Rose reports that it was "rigorous and comprehensive."[15] Along with the basics (writing, reading, and arithmetic), students learned Greek, Hebrew, and Latin. The young men learned basic skills in carpentry along with printing and "chair caning." The young women took courses in sewing and cooking. Rose writes that the instructors designed the curriculum to educate students for a trade or profession. The balance of the classical education with more practical labor skill reinforced the curriculum's goals. Before settling in at the Norfolk Naval Yard, Proctor's father worked as a truck driver and chauffeur. He eventually worked at the latter job for about 40 years. (The Naval Yard was where most persons in Norfolk found steady work during and after World War I.)

The Proctors secured their home with love. Proctor reminisced about how his father made toys for him and his siblings and how his mother baked "goodies."[16] The Great Depression hit during Proctor's early years of life, but Herbert and Velma Proctor did not let their children feel its effects. Proctor wrote, "As children we were unaware of the full impact of the Great Depression. We never felt severely impoverished, and our parents imposed a strong sense of security around us, just as their parents had done for them.

There was never enough of what we wanted, but always enough of what we needed."[17] Such was probably the case that the Proctors did not experience fully what other persons experienced during that difficult period in America. Many of the naval yard workers had steady jobs, which provided a steady income. Others were not so fortunate.

Proctor's mother, Velma, also a Norfolk Mission College graduate, managed the household. Her duties were domestic. Although she had received a similar education to her husband's, Proctor's mother attended to the details of the household. Proctor's stories about her may lead one to believe that one of her main roles was being the conscience of the household and the community. He observed that she cared about the misfortunes of others. She did so to the point that she often cried—a lot—for persons who were disadvantaged for whatever reason.[18] In his sermon "Mr. Sceva and His Seven Sons," Proctor said his mother was like a social worker or unpaid guidance counselor. Proctor noted that she would sit on the porch in the morning while children passed by, going to school. There were occasions on which she would groom the children whose hygiene or appearance was not in order.[19] Proctor commented in that same sermon that some of those same children came to pay their respects at her funeral. The Proctor family, moreover, could not hold Velma Proctor's funeral in the family's church, Bank Street Baptist, because the sanctuary could not seat the large crowd that attended.

The Proctor family held education in high esteem. All of Herbert and Velma Proctor's children went to college; three of the children earned graduate degrees. The grandmother, Hattie, was a Hampton graduate, and Proctor's parents received a comprehensive education from the Presbyterians at the Norfolk Mission College. To be sure, there existed within this household, within this family, an emphasis on learning.

The Proctors' focus on education was in accord with many African Americans' notions of racial uplift. The moral and social development of the race relied, in part, upon a cultivated mind. Many persons, white and black, therefore thought that African Americans would attain some level of respectability in society once educated. In Proctor's schooling, he received an education that prepared him for the racist environment in which he lived. To be sure, black educators felt obligated to affirm the personhood of African Americans in their schools. Proctor stated that the teachers in the Huntersville schools prepared the students for the social barriers and racial constructs they would face: "For whatever reason, our Huntersville schools saved us from a sense of futility and prepared us to hold our heads high in the midst of the daily insults. Our education was so grounded in religious faith and practice that the flavor of the gospel was laced through all our schooling."[20] In another statement, Proctor commented that the teachers insulated the black children from segregation and worked to ensure a future for the students that did not include such obstacles. He had memories of the segregated schools he attended and the quality of the materials in them. He referred to the hand-me-down textbooks his school used as "tattered," and he remembered that the school building had outdoor toilets. Proctor did not, however, discredit the education he had received. He cited, for example, how he learned from Miss Edith Green about Tennyson's sonnet about a flower in a granite wall. Proctor makes a reasonable case for the contribution and influence that Norfolk's African American teachers had upon their students in his generation.[21]

The black public schools in Norfolk had progressive African American leaders who worked on behalf of the race.[22] Before Proctor entered high school, the Norfolk Mission College was turned into the city's only public high school for black students, Booker T. Washington High School. Proctor benefited from the school's achievement program, wherein some eighth-graders who did well on a placement test skipped the second term of the eighth grade. He graduated, therefore, from high school at age sixteen. Winston Douglas, who was named the high school's principal in 1927, established the second high school National Honor Society chapter in Virginia. In addition, he was a key person in bringing about the formation of Norfolk State University. He wrote several letters to different colleges asking for their assistance in offering college courses to the African Americans in Norfolk. The president of Virginia Union University responded to Douglas and set in motion the process that founded Norfolk State.

Douglas was not the only progressive leader with whom Proctor came in contact. Aline E. Black, a science teacher at Booker T. Washington High School, pushed for equal pay for black teachers. In 1938, she petitioned the Norfolk city school board for a salary equal to that of her white counterparts at Maury High School in Norfolk. According to the *Chicago Defender*, her lawyers, J. Thomas Hewin, Thurgood Marshall, Charles Houston, and Leon Ransom (lawyers from the NAACP), brought a mandamus action against the city.[23] She was Proctor's biology teacher. Although Proctor did not remember the date, he did remember that she had been fired for taking such action. In his memoir, he noted that black teachers' salaries were 30 percent less than their white counterparts' salaries, although many black teachers had better credentials. Aline Black's actions were indelibly etched in Proctor's mind. Her case, as suggested by the national attention, made her somewhat of a celebrity.[24]

These educators were among the examples that Proctor had in his youth. It is not hard to see that Proctor had progressive examples of how to respond to racism. In short, Douglas and Black expected that the same types of opportunities afforded to white Americans extend to African Americans. Proctor's beliefs in equality and the elimination of the racial divide existed in his education in the public school and in the church school. He stated that many of his public school teachers were also Sunday school teachers at the Bank Street Baptist Church.[25]

The local Baptist church was an important part of Proctor's formation. The Proctor family was the initial unit in which the idea of the significance of Christian community found its home. On Sundays, the Proctor family would tune in to "Glenn T. Settles and the Wings over Jordan Choir" radio broadcast out of Cleveland.[26] The family would put on its Sunday best, and Herbert Proctor and the children would be among the first to enter the church on Sunday mornings. Samuel Proctor would later joke about how you could not fake being sick in order to miss church. If you said you were sick on Sunday, Grandmother Hattie would make you take castor oil to heal you. Samuel Proctor also shared that learning Scripture verses and practicing for the Sunday school orchestra were a normal part of the Proctor household routine.

The Christian experience was a part of both sides of Proctor's family—maternal and paternal. His maternal great-grandfather, the Reverend Zechariah Hughes, founded two Baptist churches in the city of Norfolk. Four of Proctor's uncles were Christian pastors. Proctor's aunt was a "local hero" who played organ at several churches in the city. Proctor joined the church at age twelve. He would join the church (by way of the altar call or invitation to discipleship), but he joked that he would turn up missing on the days that the church baptized its candidates for membership.[27] His great-uncle, Everard Hughes, who later gave Proctor counsel about the ministry, was a graduate of the Oberlin Graduate School of Theology.[28] Proctor was entrenched in an Afro-Baptist experience. This early experience found expression in the Bank Street Baptist Church. Hattie Proctor's mother had "carried her" to the Bank Street Baptist Church when Hattie arrived in Norfolk. Herbert Proctor and family had also settled in that church.

Earl Lewis described the Bank Street Baptist Church as one of the congregations that "led most others in membership and community prominence."[29] He also claimed that the membership consisted of both working-class and "elite" African Americans. The earliest members of the church came out of the First Baptist Church Bute Street, an integrated congregation. This new congregation called itself the First Colored Baptist Church. The members purchased the "old Presbyterian church" on Catherine and Charlotte Streets in 1840. The congregation changed the name of the church when Catherine Street was renamed Bank Street sometime between 1862 and 1872. As with many African American churches in the antebellum period and even during the Civil War, the First Colored Baptist Church employed the services of a white minister. This changed, however, in 1862, when the congregation called the Reverend Thomas Henson. The Bank Street Baptist Church's historical statement described him as "a college and seminary trained man from Boston." From that point on, every pastor of Bank Street has been college and/or seminary educated.[30]

Bank Street continued to reflect its belief in education with its ministerial charges and cultural attitudes. Proctor grew up listening to the Reverends C. E. Long Sr., G. W. Watkins, and D. C. Rice. When referring to the preachers that Proctor had heard during his time at the Bank Street Church, Proctor stated, "You never had an uneducated pastor there. All the ministers had gone to college in some kind of special theological training since I was a boy. I don't ever remember having an ignorant pastor standing up in front of me Sunday morning."[31] Moreover, many of the members at Bank Street were Norfolk Mission College graduates. They applied their education to the work in the church. Concerning this, Proctor observed that the members "did everything in good order." The worship at Bank Street may have leaned toward a more formal approach. Not a lot of religious revivals took place at his home church. He went to revivals at other churches (Lindenwood, Mt. Olive Baptist, and other places) to experience a different style of worship. In environments such as his home, his schools, and the Bank Street Baptist Church, Proctor was being equipped for success. To be sure, the next step along the way was to further his formal education.

### *Virginia State College and Virginia Union University*

Proctor left Norfolk in the fall of 1937 to begin college in Petersburg, Virginia. He won a music grant to attend Virginia State College by playing Schubert's "Serenade" on his clarinet. He paid for his housing with a National Youth Administration grant. He began college with the intention of becoming a lawyer, but he would leave Virginia State College with a completely new direction in life.[32]

Proctor's time at Virginia State College and later at Virginia Union University was not without persons and experiences that would shape him. One of the notable figures on the Virginia State campus was Dr. Luther P. Jackson (1892–1950), a historian who researched and wrote about the histories of African Americans and local black communities.[33] Jackson graduated with a Ph.D. from the University of Chicago in 1937. Proctor remembered that he and his friends would watch and imitate Jackson. They were impressed by the presence of and stature of this "Chicago Ph.D." Jackson became an associate of Carter G. Woodson, a famous black historian and founder of Negro History Week. Jackson also became the state coordinator for the Association for the Study of Negro Life and History (ASNLH), a Woodson brainchild. Jackson valued black history and heritage and used his awareness of their narratives to inform his teaching and activism. Michael Dennis writes, "Historical consciousness, black voter registration, and the equalization of African-American schools merged in Jackson's work beyond the campus."[34] Jackson promoted the necessity of the black vote. He used his teaching and writings as a way to argue for the importance of blacks in American society.

Luther Jackson fought to engender racial pride among blacks. He traveled all over the state of Virginia to collect resources to write about the histories of African American communities and to register voters. Proctor remembered Luther Jackson vividly. Proctor recalled:

> My professors believed in the future. They were committed to service and never stopped to question whether they would be personally rewarded. I can see my history professor, Luther P. Jackson, wearing his one blue suit, his arms filled with papers, hurriedly walking toward his beat-up old Plymouth, getting ready to set off for some small town in rural Virginia to organize a voter registration drive. When he wasn't registering voters, he was bringing young black men together to form glee clubs. He worked constantly and never looked back.[35]

Proctor appreciated his time on campus but did not leave Virginia State on good terms. At some point during his sophomore year at the school, he joined a fraternity. At the initiation stage, the fraternity members hazed Proctor. The hazing entailed receiving a beating with a "four-foot oak board." [36] He made up in his mind that he would not tolerate anyone participating in another initiation in which such hazing occurred. He threatened his fraternity brothers to discontinue the activity or he would report them to the proper authorities. When the fraternity continued committing acts of hazing, Proctor reported the group. He tacitly credited Providence for the events that led to his testimony against the fraternity. One Sunday morning after the hazing, he attended the Zion Baptist Church, where he heard a stirring sermon from a "short West Indian preacher named Reverend Brown" that promised God's presence in the midst of his courage.[37] The sermon came from a passage in the book of Joshua:

"As I was with Moses, so I will be with you; I will not fail you or forsake you. Be strong and courageous" (Josh. 1:5-6a).

The events that took place during that school year led him to decide upon the course of his future. Proctor labeled his time at Virginia State as "turbulent." He became a social outcast. He even received the silent treatment from his girlfriend. That process, however, led Proctor down his "Damascus Road." His time of crisis led to the introspective process by which Proctor began to hear God's call upon his life. Before he left the school, he sought counsel from Dr. Harry Roberts, a sociology professor and Methodist minister.[38]

Proctor did not return to Virginia State College in 1939. Instead, he went to work in the Norfolk Naval Yard. But his time back in Norfolk was not wasted. He received counsel from his Bank Street pastor, D. C. Rice. Rice, a graduate of Virginia Union University and Union Theological Seminary in New York, helped Proctor discern the direction his life would take.[39] It was during that brief stint at home that he accepted a call to the Christian ministry and transferred to Virginia Union University in 1940. At Virginia Union, John Malcus Ellison (1889–1979), among Proctor's other professors, provided for Proctor an environment that further prepared him for ministry in the local church and critical engagement in the theological academy.

Virginia Union University, a small historically black college in Richmond, Virginia, established for itself a reputation for educating African American clergymen. One finds the origin of the school in the American Baptists' (Northern Baptist Convention) desire to provide education for the "freedmen" during and after the Civil War.[40] The school is the product of the merger of Wayland Seminary (Washington, D.C.), Richmond Theological Institute, and later, Hartshorn Memorial College for women (all three schools were Baptist-related institutions). Ralph Reavis states that the goal of the school "was to train leaders to teach, preach and guide African-American men and women of the Negro race."[41] From its beginnings, the school was dedicated to providing top-notch facilities and faculty members for its students. This is the place where Proctor would complete his studies. At Virginia Union, he encountered persons such as Dr. Joshua Baker Simpson, who drilled in him the basics of Latin and Greek. This is also where his relationship with Dr. John Malcus Ellison began. Ellison was a teacher at heart, whose scholarship drew him little national acclaim. He completed his undergraduate studies at Virginia Union University (1917); he earned a master's degree from the Oberlin Graduate School of Theology (1927) and his doctorate in sociology and Christian education at Drew University (1933). He was a churchman and educator, serving pastorates in Washington, D.C., and Richmond, Virginia. During his professional career,

Ellison founded and was the principal of a high school in his native Northumberland County, Virginia. His time in the academy included posts at Howard University, Virginia State College, and Virginia Union University. He succeeded William John Clark as the president of Virginia Union University in 1941. Ellison was the first alumnus and the first African American to preside at the school. After resigning the presidency, Ellison settled into his post as professor and chancellor at Virginia Union.

Ellison published several books and was adamant about preaching and writing. The list of his publications includes *Tensions and Destiny* (1953), *They Who Preach* (1956), and *They Sang through Crisis* (1961). He also published several pamphlets and books for local Baptist state conventions and ministerial organizations. Ellison credits his pastor, the Reverend Levi Reese Ball at the Shiloh Baptist Church in Washington, D.C., for setting a high example of ministry for him. Ball admonished Ellison not to emote during the sermon. (This lesson would stick with Ellison throughout his teaching and preaching career.) Ball prepared his sermons in manuscript form, and this practice rubbed off on Ellison. Concerning this, Ellison stated, "In my early ministry I began writing my sermons each week, endeavoring for correctness in composition and excellence in diction. My pastor, fortunately, was a man of fine education whose literary attainments appealed to me."[42] Seminary and graduate school probably cemented this practice for Ellison. The emphasis on writing translated well into Ellison's career. Many of his books consisted of his sermons. In his preaching manual, *They Who Preach*, Ellison dedicated a whole chapter to the idea of developing the sermon in written form. One reads a brief portion of the chapter to understand Ellison's emphasis on writing and preaching. Ellison argued that writing challenges a preacher to be careful about his wording and intentional about the way she/he structures a sentence. This allows the preacher to produce a polished sermon with deeper insights and a "keener" interpretation.[43]

J. M. Ellison's sermons and writings were more than pious expressions of his evangelical faith. In an article entitled "The Problem of Community in America Today," Ellison argues that the race question was a pressing concern for black people. He states, "The minority group for whom the phrase 'equal opportunity' has less meaning than any other is the American Negro."[44] In other sermons, Ellison included passages of famous literature and concepts from philosophy and psychology, and he combined his background in sociology with his understanding of God. He stated that the Apostle Paul's more excellent way (1 Cor. 12:31) requires the acknowledgment of "the dignity of human personality."[45] I am not sure if one can directly connect Ellison's emphasis on writing and writing the sermon to Proctor's practices and thoughts. The indirect influence is very clear, however. Reavis argues that Ellison did have the ear of the preachers who sat in his classroom: "Dr. John M. Ellison influenced as many young ministers as any other clergyman of his day."[46] Proctor was within that sphere of influence.

Samuel Proctor's relationship with Ellison began early in Proctor's professional development. Bessie T. Proctor, Samuel D. Proctor's wife, observed that he and Ellison had a wonderful relationship dating back to Samuel Proctor's time in college. She noted that Proctor spent time with Ellison during those days. Proctor was Ellison's chauffer.[47] Ellison was serious about the craft of preaching, and it is likely that Proctor looked to him for guidance. Later correspondence between the two show that Proctor continued to look to Ellison as a mentor.

Proctor was active on the campus of Virginia Union, and his extracurricular activities probably led Ellison to take note of this budding giant. In Proctor's senior year of college, he participated in a number of activities. A look through the school yearbook displays his busy itinerary. Proctor was band director, YMCA and NAACP advocate and participant, Pan-Hellenic Council member, president of the student government, vice president of the J. E. Jones Lyceum (the undergraduate ministers' group), honor student, and a member of the campus's Kappa Alpha Psi fraternity. He was not hard to notice on the small black college campus of Virginia Union University. Ellison, moreover, seemed to follow Proctor's academic and professional pursuits with interest. (Proctor sent Ellison regular updates on his progress in graduate school and at his church.)

The Reverend Dr. Richard McKinney was another influence in Proctor's Virginia Union experience. McKinney, a preacher and educator who completed his doctorate at Yale University, took time to mentor Proctor during his time as professor at Virginia Union. McKinney also served as pastor of the Pond Street Baptist Church in Providence, Rhode Island, and served later as president of Storer College in West Virginia. It is probable that Proctor's relationship with McKinney led to his nomination as the pastor of Pond Street in 1945.[48]

These prominent figures in Proctor's life were examples of educated black leadership. They exposed him to the possibilities that existed for persons to equip themselves intellectually in service to humanity. When the opportunity to attend seminary at Crozer Theological Seminary in Chester, Pennsylvania, was presented to Proctor, theological education in the north was a logical step in his vocational development.

## Formation in the American Liberal Theological Tradition, 1942–1950

Proctor continued his education in schools that were influenced heavily by liberal theological traditions of the late nineteenth and early twentieth centuries. He completed studies at Crozer, pursued the Ph.D. at Yale Divinity School, and graduated with a Doctor of Theology degree from Boston University School of Theology. Proctor left Virginia Union well equipped to enter the next phase of his academic career. A white Baptist pastor from Norfolk and trustee at Crozer, Dr. Sparks White Melton, assisted in Proctor's transition by securing a scholarship that paid all of Proctor's tuition. With a solid intellectual foundation from Virginia Union and social-spiritual foundation from home, Proctor was ready to engage the social gospel tradition, historical-critical methods of biblical research, and racist attitudes at these formidable theological institutions.

### *Crozer Theological Seminary*

In 1942, Proctor matriculated at Crozer Theological Seminary. Crozer was associated with the Northern Baptist Convention (now American Baptist Churches USA). As Jeffrey Paul Straub notes, Crozer and several other Northern Baptist seminaries—including the University of Chicago Divinity School—came under pressure for their embrace of the modernist impulses in theology during the early 1900s.[49] A stress on the social aspects of Christianity, an embrace of the scientific trends, and a turn to the historical-critical methods of biblical research found their way into the curricula of these schools. Such was the case at Crozer. In an article on Martin Luther King Jr.'s time at Crozer (1948–1951), Clayborne Carson describes some of the professors that Proctor would have encountered in his day. James Bennett Pritchard relied heavily on historical and archaeological findings when teaching his Old Testament course. Morton Scott Enslin, who taught New Testament courses, was a "Harvard-trained expert in the history of early Christianity." And George Washington Davis, a Northern Baptist educated in a Northern Baptist–sponsored seminary, was a disciple of Walter Rauschenbusch and the social gospel thought.[50] These men are some of the persons with whom Proctor spent time in dialogue. His description of the school may shed more light on the nature of its study of the Bible:

> The seminary was so radical in its approach to the Bible that it actually ruined the religious beliefs of some of my classmates. We were shocked to discover that Bible study included learning the history and geography of the Near East. . . .

> My professors taught that certain books of the Bible reflected different types of literature; some were written like poems or long parables to make a serious point. The teachers showed us how Bible stories had been revised by various writers at different times, and taught us how to look at biblical events in a larger context. Indeed, by giving a deeper interpretation of the Bible, the Crozer theologians showed us how religion could have social and ethical application in the modern world.[51]

The theological path that Proctor traveled at Crozer presented some new challenges for him. The "liberal" education at the seminary was different from his biblically conservative roots in the Black Baptist tradition. He also had to deal with the issue of racism. Crozer may not have been as progressive on that issue as Proctor would have liked. Proctor, expecting the racial attitudes of educated northern white theologians to be different from the ones he experienced from white persons in the South, learned that racist practices existed among the educated classes of the North as well. He was the only black student on the campus during his first year. One of his most memorable experiences was the new-student orientation. The students were given jobs to complete around the school, because the war (World War II) left Crozer short on staff. When the students gathered, the faculty supervisor, Dr. E. E. Harkness, announced all of the clerical and custodial assignments except for Proctor's work. He was the last person to receive a job. Proctor's responsibility was kitchen duty, and he "instantly aged ten years" when he learned of this task. Mrs. Moitz, the woman supervisor in food services, was ashamed of what had taken place and apologized to him. Proctor noted that it was then that he realized he was going to learn more about Jesus from the little old woman in the kitchen than he would from the professional theologians in the classroom. Mrs. Moitz and some other persons helped Proctor navigate the academic and social terrains of seminary life.[52]

An important person who must receive some attention when listing Proctor's intellectual mentors is the Reverend J. Pius Barbour.[53] Proctor sought refuge from and answers for the seminary experience in the Barbour home. Barbour, the pastor of the Calvary Baptist Church in Chester, Pennsylvania, from 1933 to 1974, was the first African American graduate of Crozer Seminary. Proctor spent time with Barbour, working through the "issues" he had during his years at the seminary. Proctor attended Calvary during his time at Crozer, and as Lewis V. Baldwin states, he became a "son" of the church.[54] (His service to the church probably included an occasional Sunday-morning sermon and responsibility for one of its ministries.) In other words, the members adopted him as one of their own. Proctor described Barbour as a "scholarly man" who loved to participate in theological debates. Barbour was a conscientious person as it pertained to the matter of race in America, but his was not an activism of protest as much as it was mediation between the races. In examining Barbour, Richard Lischer notes that Martin Luther King Jr. appreciated the way in which Barbour used the Hegelian dialectical method of preaching. Barbour was "skillful" with his use of the triadic movement of thesis, antithesis, and synthesis. Lischer argues that Barbour combined erudition with a folksy delivery.[55] The extent of Barbour's influence on Proctor is evident but immeasurable.

With Barbour as his mentor, Proctor remained immersed in the Black Church preaching tradition. Barbour later sought out opportunities for Proctor's voice to be heard among the members of the National Baptist Convention, USA. He wrote a letter to Proctor, inviting him to write an article for the *National Baptist Voice*. Barbour said he wanted to dig Proctor "out of oblivion."[56] In Barbour, Proctor remained connected to a person who understood preaching as a prophetic voice on matters of race. Proctor's relationship with Barbour was important during his Crozer period. Lischer acknowledges Proctor's place among the students Barbour mentored: "Of all the preachers who passed through the Barbour parlor over the years, Martin was the most promising, save perhaps for Sam Proctor, who would eventually succeed Adam Clayton Powell at Abyssinian Baptist Church in Harlem."[57] Proctor's time in Chester was important.

Two events from Proctor's time at Crozer should be acknowledged. In 1944, he married his college sweetheart, Bessie L. Tate of Fredericksburg, Virginia. In that same year, they returned to Chester and accepted a job as live-in employees for the new president of the seminary, Dr. Edwin E. Aubrey (1896–1956) and his family. Aubrey succeeded Dr. James H. Franklin and kept Crozer entrenched in the liberal theological tradition. Aubrey was a student of the University of Chicago and its empirical approach to theological studies. He earned the Master of Arts, Bachelor of Divinity, and Doctor of Philosophy degrees at Chicago and taught at the school from 1929 until 1944. He served Crozer from 1944 to 1949. Proctor's interactions with Aubrey included theological discussions and studying the Aubreys "as though they were in a museum."[58] Proctor kept in contact with Aubrey, seeking his guidance in revising his dissertation to submit to publishers.

### *The Appeal of Harry Emerson Fosdick*

Proctor experienced a quandary when he arrived at the seminary: How does one pull together a conservative to fundamentalist black Baptist tradition of theology and a liberal theological education? The curriculum in the liberal Crozer Seminary, he suggested, began to overwhelm him. He had to "put his Bible back together" after sitting in the seminary classroom. For Proctor, it was a question of how one could go out and preach what was left of the Bible after yielding it to the historical-critical methods. His sacred Bible was "assaulted" by the physical sciences, anthropology, and the study of languages. His beliefs about the origin of the world, the Jews as the chosen people, and the order of the biblical books all came under question. The works of Harry Emerson Fosdick played a role in resolving Proctor's dilemma:[59]

> In order to get through it all, I leaned heavily on the sermons and writings of Harry Emerson Fosdick. He did not run from the new insights or from the political threats hurled by so-called defenders of the Word. He let the light of history, science, physics, archaeology, and psychology come shining through. I ended up with a Bible better understood and a warmer faith in that God who was the source of *all* truth, from wherever. And I found Jesus more real; with a more lasting trust and devotion he was my Savior.[60]

Harry Emerson Fosdick (1878–1969) was a Protestant minister whose renowned ministry made an impact on many persons. He was at the heart of the liberal theological debate against fundamentalism and became the liberal theological movement's most visible figure. Fosdick's ministry at the Riverside Church in New York made him well known to the religious public. His books and his radio program catapulted him into a nationally known phenomenon. From this post, Fosdick became one of the most venerated preachers in American history. Gary Dorrien states that Harry Emerson Fosdick was the "greatest public figure" of the American liberal theological tradition.[61] Fosdick's appeal to Proctor, therefore, is not surprising. Fosdick was known as the "pastor" of the liberal tradition during Proctor's time in seminary. The controversy over biblical methods loomed large in the Northern Baptist Convention, of which Proctor was a member, and Fosdick was the most visible and prominent figure in the early years of the conflict. As Proctor struggled with the notions of biblical criticism, he stated that he was often encouraged by Fosdick's words: "On his weekly radio programs Dr. Fosdick went after persons just like me. There was nothing superficial or simpleminded about his message.

... He probed into my doubts with penetrating thoroughness. He swept every corner of doubt and confusion clean with wide, strong strokes from the witness of literature, history, biology, astronomy, and the Bible."[62]

With help from Fosdick and others, Proctor graduated from Crozer with a Bachelor of Divinity in 1945. After leaving Crozer, Proctor began a part-time pastorate at the Pond Street Baptist Church in Providence, Rhode Island. He also received a Crozer fellowship to study for a Ph.D. in social ethics at Yale Divinity School. These stops were next on his vocational journey.

### *Called to the Pastorate: Pond Street Baptist Church*

Before Proctor left Crozer, a providential intervention shaped the direction of his early career. He worked many jobs during his time at Crozer, and one of them was in the seminary bookstore. Proctor wanted to serve in a congregation but received no offers during his time in the seminary. As he moved closer to graduation, the only option seemed to be a graduate education at Yale Divinity School. On one occasion, while he worked a shift at the Crozer bookstore, a man approached Proctor with an offer to serve as the pastor of a small Baptist church in Providence, the Pond Street Baptist Church. Proctor accepted the position and was off to balance a pastorate and his studies at Yale.

The Pond Street Baptist Church extended a call to Proctor on July 12, 1945, after the deliberations of a "well attended" business meeting. The call came just a day before his twenty-fourth birthday. Proctor succeeded the Reverend W. C. Wynn as the pastor of the church. (Wynn left to become the chaplain at his alma mater, Florida A&M University.) Proctor began his duties on September 1, 1945. Bessie Proctor arrived later to a reception from the members of the church. They resided in an apartment above the home of a "senior family in the church."[63] He remained at the church while completing his doctoral studies.

Proctor entered doctoral studies to focus on Christian social ethics at Yale University in 1945. He studied with notable professors Liston Pope, H. Richard Niebuhr, and Roland Bainton. Socially, the white students at the school ignored Proctor and four men of African descent along with a woman student. Proctor remembered Niebuhr's contribution to his social experience at Yale: "The special efforts of two white professors made a striking contrast to the attitude of the students. Professors Richard Neibuhr [sic] and Liston Pope took the initiative to make sure that I was fully engaged and included in every aspect of the program."[64]

Proctor's time in New Haven did not last long. He and his wife had their first child, Herbert, who was born with a congenital heart defect known as blue-baby syndrome. He transferred to Boston University to be closer to his residence in Providence.[65]

Proctor transferred from Yale to Boston University School of Theology in 1947. He enrolled in the Doctor of Theology program, which Richard Morgan Cameron describes as "greater scholarly preparation for the pastoral ministry."[66] He received credit for his Yale work and finished his coursework and exams in two years. Proctor, however, did not say much about his time in Boston in his writings. The social-ethical emphasis of the Boston school of thought attracted Proctor. He split his time at Boston between his studies, his duties at the church in Providence, and the care of his first child. The Boston experience, therefore, might have been a blur.

Based upon several studies of the school at that time, we do know that Boston University was known for a philosophical-theological system called Personalism. Concerning a definition of this system, Paul Deats, a student of the tradition, writes, "Personalism is a philosophical perspective for which the person is the ontological ultimate and for which personality is the fundamental explanatory principle."[67] The father of Boston Personalism was Bordon Parker Bowne (1847–1910), and several students carried on the tradition. Among those students were well-known philosophers Albert C. Knudson, Edgar S. Brightman, L. Harold DeWolf, and Walter G. Muelder (these men were professors during Proctor's time at the school). The degree to which Boston Personalism shaped Proctor's thought is unclear. His degree work focused on New Testament studies, so his interaction with the personalist philosophers in the school might have been limited. Inasmuch as Personalism was a part of the mood of the liberal age, however, he clearly absorbed some of the tenets of Boston Personalism. For Proctor, personhood or the inherent dignity and divinity of the person is the fundamental point of departure in theology and philosophy. To skip that starting point was a violation of being. In what ways this belief is a by-product of personalist thought is unclear.

Proctor completed his degree in New Testament in 1950. His dissertation chronicled the denominational debate between the "fundamentalists" and "modernists" in the Northern Baptist Convention.[68] Proctor's work was a history of interpretation that described the controversy that took place within the Baptist convention in the early 1900s. It was an apology for the modernists' emphasis on the historical-critical approach to the study of the Bible. He believed he had a position that was amenable to fundamentalists and liberal theologians. He argued that Baptists should determine under what methodology they would operate when using the New Testament as the sole authority on matters in the church. A normative approach, he believed, would create an environment that fostered serious dialogue to further Christian missions. Dr. Edwin P. Booth directed the dissertation. Cameron states that Booth believed that a person should study the New Testament by way of the "historical route."[69] The other dissertation reader was Dr. Donald T. Rowlingson, who had just arrived at Boston from Candler School of Theology in 1950. Proctor's dissertation showed his interest in the Bible, the historical-critical methods, and the life of the denomination in which he participated as a pastor.

## Moving from the Theory of Faith to Practice, 1945–1960

Proctor's professional career entailed a trajectory that placed him among the "talented tenth" of the black community.[70] His rise to leadership within the race was indicative of the religious and academic guidance he provided in his various posts. He served the Pond Street Baptist Church in Providence, Rhode Island, for a brief time and was a budding leader at Virginia Union University for over a decade. His drive fueled his desire to remain connected to the areas of his vocation, teaching and preaching. He tied his successes closely to his belief in the power of the classroom and the church to overcome the racial problems in America.

### *Pond Street Baptist Church, Providence, Rhode Island (1945–1949)*

Not long after arriving in Providence, Proctor grew in favor and stature among the clergy and people in the city. He preached sermons with titles such as "The Third Dimension of Christ," "Second Degree Converts," and "Giving Christ the Benefit of the Doubt." He even had a "stump" sermon that he preached at least twice in a period of five years, "Long Cords and Strong Stakes."[71] He participated on a civic panel to talk about the fair-employment practices in Providence. The Rhode Island Council of Churches invited him to speak on the radio during Interracial Week. In 1948, he was elected president of the Roger Williams Association of Churches (an interracial group of churches affiliated with the Northern Baptist Convention). In 1949, he was elected president of the African American pastors' group, the Providence Minister's Alliance. Persons called upon him to preach at joint worship experiences, including the "Inter-Racial, Inter-Faith Thanksgiving Service" and the Passion Week services at Bethel Church. Upon that occasion, a reporter remarked that Proctor's sermon "aroused the congregation to great enthusiasm and kept their hearts ablaze with the unction of the Holy Spirit."[72]

Proctor was instrumental in working with the clergy of Providence to rally for fair-employment legislation. About this, Proctor recalled, "One night, soon after I had begun in Providence, all the black ministers and their followers met at a big rally in the black community center. 'We're going to organize a movement here for fair employment practices in this state,' one pastor announced, 'and Reverend Proctor will lead it.'"[73] Proctor saw this as a key moment in which he was to put his faith and theological education into action. Still in his twenties, he became a visible advocate of fair employment opportunities for African Americans in the Providence community. He worked closely with the Providence Urban League on those matters related to racial uplift and provided a platform at his church for persons who sought reform. Such was the case when his former professor, Richard McKinney, came to speak at Pond Street about passing the fair-employment legislation.

Proctor demonstrated progressive leadership during his tenure at the church. He had the privilege of leading the congregation during a period that saw its membership increase. He had a vision for Pond Street and for ministry in the Providence area. He led the congregation to acquire a larger building (the former Stewart Street Baptist Church). Around the same time, he helped initiate a conversation about a possible merger between the Pond Street Church and Congdon Street Baptist Church. Congdon Street was without a pastor at the time. Proctor stated publicly that the combined congregations could offer ministries that had not been available in Providence. The merger efforts failed, however. The Congdon Street members voted to discontinue the talks with Pond Street. That did not stop Proctor from leading an aggressive building campaign to renovate the Stewart Street facilities.

Proctor's ministry work received attention from wider audiences. In 1947, Proctor began writing a weekly column for the *Providence Chronicle*. He would retain that space in the newspaper for almost two years. Moreover, the Northern Baptist Convention kept a close eye on the Reverend Proctor. They sponsored his attendance at several conferences and secured his services to teach at others, and commended him and the church on their work in Christian missions. The convention offered him a position in the summer of 1947. But he turned down the denomination, feeling that his ministry at the church remained incomplete. There was also interest from his alma mater. John Malcus Ellison followed Proctor's emerging career from a distance and invited him to return to Virginia Union University.

### *ELLISON CALLS*

Dr. Ellison began talks with Proctor about teaching at Virginia Union University at some point in 1948. In a letter dated September 10, 1948, Proctor accepted the offer made by J. M. Ellison to return to Virginia Union as a member of the faculty. The agreement simply stated the salary, his teaching and other responsibilities, and his vacation and research needs. (His starting salary was $3,600 a year.) An enthused Proctor stated, "I am proud of the chance to return to my Alma Mater and I hope to render competent, devoted service." He returned to his alma mater in 1949 to teach religion and philosophy. Within a year of his employment, he earned the Doctor of Theology degree in New Testament from the Boston University School of Theology. Within five years of his graduation, he became vice president of Virginia Union University and dean of the seminary before being promoted to president of the university in 1955. He quickly became a prized member of the faculty at the small historically black college.[74]

Persons at the school and across the country made use of Proctor's teaching, preaching, and administrative gifts. Not long after Proctor became a part of the VUU faculty, Ellison promoted him to the rank of professor. Later, he was promoted to dean of the School of Religion and vice president of the university. His duties in the classroom included preaching and Bible courses for the Bachelor of Divinity degree students, as well as philosophy and religion courses at the undergraduate level. Among his many students were the future governor of the Commonwealth of Virginia L. Douglas Wilder, civil rights activist and pastor Wyatt T. Walker, and Walter Fauntroy, churchman and former U. S. representative from the District of Columbia.

Quickly becoming an ambassador for the school, Proctor made appearances at churches and schools across much of the country. He continued his relationship with the Northern Baptist Convention. The denomination called on him to teach at regional and national workshops. The National Baptist Convention president, J. H. Jackson, called upon Proctor to speak at various meetings. Proctor's lecturing and preaching garnered for him a measure of renown among black and white preachers and churchgoers in America.[75]

It was apparent that Proctor had the confidence of the president of the university, John M. Ellison, and the university trustees. Upon Ellison's resignation, the voting body of the university moved to make Samuel D. Proctor the school's fifth president. The inaugural was held on November 4, 1955, with an address by Proctor entitled "Lengthening Our Cords and Strengthening Our Stakes." He was the second alumnus and African American to preside over the affairs of the school.[76]

Incidentally, in 1955, Martin Luther King Jr. invited Proctor to present a series of lectures on "The Relevance of the New Testament to the Contemporary Situation" at the Dexter Avenue Baptist Church in Montgomery, Alabama (King's first pastoral charge). The two men had met at an alumni function at Crozer around 1950–1951, when King was a student there. After becoming president of Virginia Union, Proctor envisioned King becoming the dean of the seminary at the university. Proctor had to look elsewhere, however, as King was immersed in battles for civil and human rights in Alabama. Benjamin Mays (1894–1984), the Morehouse College president, convinced Proctor that King probably would not make the move to the academy.[77]

During his tenure, Proctor oversaw renovations to the college chapel, the building of a women's dormitory, and an increase in the student population. He was a risk taker who wanted to strengthen Virginia Union and create opportunities to grow the university. Private correspondence displays his role in the merger of Virginia Union University with Storer College in Harpers Ferry, West Virginia. Storer was closed in 1955, and Proctor, as he had done in the case of the Congdon Street merger, envisioned what the two learning communities could offer with shared resources. The merger, however, took place after Proctor was well into his tenure at North Carolina A&T State University.

Although the campus afforded Proctor an insulated racial environment, the world around him was changing for the better. In 1954, the *Brown v. Board of Education* ruling opened the doors for Proctor to talk further about integration. To be sure, his inaugural address included statements regarding the problems of race in America. He stated, "The recent discussions on school integration have exposed a deep, swift, current of stubborn racism, based on perverted sociology, spurious political philosophy, and anachronistic racial stereotypes."[78] The scholarly community, Proctor stated, bore some of the onus in educating the world about the "American dilemma" of race relations. Reminders would crop up, however; a cross was burned on the school lawn while Proctor was president at Virginia Union. In a 1987 sermon, Proctor attributed the cross burning to his work to integrate the public schools in Richmond.[79]

## An Emerging Leader: Proctor's Global Awakening, 1960–1968

The subtle tension of leading the faculty members who had taught him, among other considerations, led Proctor to seek employment at North Carolina Agricultural & Technical State College. He resigned his position at Virginia

Union in 1960 and accepted the appointment as president at A&T on April 19. Calling upon the school to consider the "formidable frontiers" that it faced, he adopted a global perspective. His inaugural address listed several challenges the institution faced as a center of learning for African Americans: transitioning "the Negro" out of economic adolescence to economic maturity, empowering the socially and politically impotent African American, and nurturing an environment of social and political responsibility. This speech was also the platform for global concerns. Proctor remarked, "We are 12,000 miles away from the center of the surge toward freedom and dignity in Africa and Asia, but what happens there will determine the future for our children."[80] Acknowledging the students from Africa and the West Indies, he stated, "We recognize that we cannot become obsessed with the quest for our own happiness and security, while so much of the world bleeds and hungers. . . . We can never become so involved in applied science that we forget applied faith. And our faith is that every single human being lays a claim upon our energy, our intellect and our genius." Proctor moved to build upon the strengths of the school.

Proctor's interaction with students at A&T and other institutions would not allow him to avoid issues of race in America. Proctor accepted the position just months after the Greensboro Four, a group of African American college students, staged a sit-in at the Woolworth lunch counter in the city's shopping district. While Proctor was still president at Virginia Union, he attended a meeting of the Collegiate Interscholastic Athletic Association (CIAA) presidents to determine the schedule for the conference football activities. When his A&T predecessor received a phone call about the sit-in, the rest of the presidents returned to their campuses to oversee the reactions to the event.

To be sure, Proctor's preaching and lecturing schedule often put him in front of black and white audiences. He remained at home in the pulpits of black churches in the south, but he was also asked to present ideas about the issue of race in America to white audiences. The talks to white audiences followed a basic outline:

> All of my speeches followed the same pattern: I first presented the anti-thesis: Here is the kind of America we are creating—a huge underclass, an embarrassing jail population, illiteracy at 15 percent and poverty at 35 percent. Minorities are locked into low-paying jobs and minority students have low expectations. . . .

> Then I presented the thesis: We can change this. We can start recruiting and training bright young women and minorities. We can encourage colleges to recruit them and offer scholarships.[81]

Proctor's audiences at these events questioned him about his ideas for integrating schools and workplaces, but he held fast to the belief that African Americans could perform as well as any race of persons. To express this idea, he borrowed a phrase from Victor Hugo: "The Power of an Idea Whose Time Has Come." Leading a college and representing the race were all a part of the tacit job description. Related to this matter was Proctor's practice of taking students with him to the churches and schools where he spoke. The Reverend Dr. Jeremiah Wright, retired pastor of the Trinity United Church of Christ in Chicago and former Proctor student at Virginia Union and United Theological Seminary, rode with Proctor for one of these trips. Jesse Jackson, the student body president, was one of Proctor's A & T students. He traveled with Proctor on occasions, as Proctor shared life and preaching lessons with him. Both men grew into race-conscious advocates for civil rights in America.

### *Proctor and Politics*

In March 1959, then-Senator John F. Kennedy met Proctor at a United Negro College Fund event. Proctor spoke at the event, and Kennedy was impressed with the college president. He approached Proctor through Belford Lawson and asked Proctor to join his presidential campaign. Proctor turned down the offer, but he remained on the Kennedy radar. This initial contact was the basis for a working relationship with Kennedy and later Lyndon Johnson that lasted for almost a decade.

Sargent Shriver and Bill Moyers kept Proctor on the short list of the persons they called to get things done. In 1962, Shriver asked Proctor to take a leave of absence from A&T to direct the Peace Corps in Nigeria. Proctor received permission from the governor of North Carolina to vacate the presidency at A&T for a short period. I address Proctor's time in Nigeria later in this chapter. After serving in Nigeria, Proctor returned to A&T only to join Shriver again; this time he went to Washington to become the associate director of the Peace Corps. A few years later, he joined Shriver in the Office of Economic Opportunity (OEO) as an associate director (1965–1966). Proctor spoke highly of Shriver and later wrote an article to praise Shriver's work on behalf of the country.

Proctor continued with various roles in the Johnson administration. Members of the administration invited Proctor to head the Institute for Services to Education (ISE) from 1966 to 1968. Proctor took advantage of his administrative positions to serve underprivileged youth. For example, following his direction, the OEO and ISE committed to funding higher education for about 1,100 young persons. These positions, Proctor noted, created job offers from various employers. Former vice president Hubert Humphrey called upon Proctor to produce campaign speeches for him when he ran for office in 1968. Proctor also gave several commencement addresses as a stand-in for President Johnson. And Proctor found time to reflect upon what he learned in these positions in his book *The Young Negro in America, 1960–1980* (published in 1966).[82]

### *The Peace Corps: Nigeria*

Proctor had international experience prior to his involvement in the Kennedy and Johnson administrations. Through his connections to the Northern Baptist Convention (American Baptist Foreign Mission Society), Proctor traveled throughout Europe and visited India, Syria, Lebanon, and Jordan, among other places, as an emissary for the Baptist body in 1953. His duties included preaching missions among German students, talks to student groups in India, and meetings with American soldiers. He joined a group of missionaries for a tour of the former Soviet Union in 1958, on behalf of the Baptist World Alliance.[83] He broadened his view of the world at an early stage in his career. His Peace Corps stint in Nigeria might have left the more telling impression of his commitment to the black freedom struggle in America.

The Peace Corps initiative began during the Kennedy-Johnson administration. The idea stressed America's responsibility as a world leader to serve developing nations. In Nigeria, the Peace Corps was off to a bad start. A volunteer wrote home about what she felt were poor conditions. Her note never made it to the post office. Nigerians found the note, and it quickly became a public relations disaster for the Kennedy administration. Proctor came into the picture as a possible candidate to take over the Peace Corps in Nigeria. In 1962, Sargent Shriver, the director of the Peace Corps, invited Proctor to take the position. The governor of North Carolina promised to hold Proctor's position at the college while he was in Africa. After serious consideration, the Proctor family agreed to move to Nigeria for a brief period. He saw this as his way to contribute to the changing world: "My reluctance was overcome by guilt feelings. During World War II, I had been a deferred seminary student, and dozens of my boyhood friends never returned from Anzio Beach and the Pacific Islands. I owed them something. More to the point, as a college administrator throughout the civil rights protests, I had done good work, but not on the front lines. I had never been shot at, beaten, thrown in a dirty jail, or chased by police dogs. I called Shriver back and told him I would go."[84]

Nigeria exposed Proctor to a world he had never known. The nation was reconstructing its identity after winning its independence from British rule in October 1960. Proctor arrived in Lagos amidst this new national energy. To be sure, this experience raised Proctor's awareness of race consciousness and America's aloofness toward developing nations. He also saw this as an opportunity to contribute to solving the complex issues of race at a global level. For Proctor, racism in Africa was related to issues of race in America. He wrote, "Soon it became clear to me that the black struggle in America was a vanguard to rebuilding the tremendous damage colonialism had wrought in Africa," noting that "segregation was the absolute rule" in Lagos.[85] The remnants of colonialism in Nigeria would not allow Proctor to forget what African Americans experienced.

A time of reflection and "probing" took place once Proctor settled into his life in Nigeria. During his time in the country, he recalled seeing visions of a young African snatched away from the coast. The visions were of an African being taken into slavery. This vision helped raise his awareness of being black and American. He felt he was unaccepted by Nigerians because of his status as an American. He knew he would not receive equal treatment in America because of his race. Concerning this, Proctor wrote, "As a black man I lived a marginalized life in America, and in Nigeria I was a stranger. Was I in Nigeria as an American visitor, or as a child come home?"[86] Issues of race did not elude Proctor, even thousands of miles from America.

Another event highlighted Proctor's time in Nigeria. He was especially impressed with a Yoruba chief, Oyrinde, who had graduated from Virginia Union in 1911. Although the chief had graduated from the school, he went back to his native land and lived in relative obscurity. The chief was a classmate of Proctor's great-uncle, and Proctor was excited about and humbled by this encounter. Proctor had to process how a person who had lived in America could go back to Nigeria and live a life of such simplicity. Proctor also questioned why he had not learned more about his African heritage during all of his years of schooling. His time in Nigeria was a period of awakening that helped Proctor confront himself.[87] He returned to America in 1963.

## The Preacher and Teacher, 1969–1997

After a brief stint with the National Council of Churches in 1964, Proctor returned to the two fields of ministry in which he had started: preaching and teaching. When the hurry and high-paced life of the Washington Beltway no longer appealed to Proctor, he settled into the last stages of his career. The end of his career represented the transition to the two places behind which his gifts had been most apparent, the classroom lectern and church pulpit.

In 1968, at the age of forty-seven, Proctor took a post at the University of Wisconsin in Madison. This job was going to be his last, but the reception he received from the students on campus would not allow him to settle into this job comfortably. As the University Dean of Special Projects, Proctor had a catchall title to handle tasks related to increasing the enrollment of minority students. He remarked in an interview that he "went to Wisconsin to spend the rest of my life in Madison."[88] This situation did not turn out the way he had envisioned. To go along with the problems presented by the students, the school fired the administrator who had hired Proctor. Proctor left after one year. This led him to consider simultaneous offers from Harvard University and Rutgers University. He chose a tenured position at Rutgers in 1969, as it provided him with a platform free from administrative duties. The position was in the School of Education, and he used it to create opportunities for African American graduate students. He remained at Rutgers for nearly twenty years, retiring from the full-time post in 1984.

### *Abyssinian Baptist Church: Harlem, New York*

In 1972, Proctor was called to pastor the Abyssinian Baptist Church, located in Harlem, New York. The call was the culmination of a long relationship between Proctor and the church. A 1962 *Chicago Defender* newspaper story stated that Adam Clayton Powell Jr. (1908–1972) had resigned and selected Proctor to follow him as pastor of the Abyssinian Baptist Church. The story suggested that Powell had resigned abruptly to give his full attention to the congressional seat he held. Proctor was in Nigeria, but speculation grew. In fact, Powell did not resign, at least not for any real length of time, and Proctor stayed on with the Peace Corps. That did not keep the *Defender* from gossiping about such a move for Proctor. Indeed, this article was a harbinger of this impending relationship. It expressed what many Abyssinians already knew—Powell liked Proctor.[89]

Proctor had met Powell in 1941, as he picked Powell up from the train station in Richmond. This was merely the beginning of their relationship. Powell's father, Adam Sr. (1865–1953), was an alumnus of Virginia Union, and Powell Jr. supported the school. Proctor wrote that Powell had once offered him a position to run a social agency in Harlem. (This offer was the one the *Defender* mistook for the pastoral selection of 1962.) The faith that Powell had in Proctor was on display, as Proctor was "often asked to fill the pulpit in Powell's absence."[90] The two men were a contrast in leadership styles, yet they fought for the same goal—economic and social uplift for blacks in America.

By 1972, Proctor had made his home in a small community in New Jersey. With his family tucked away in New Jersey, he was close enough to Harlem to preach at Abyssinian Baptist Church on Sunday mornings. He preached there often, so the church's members were familiar with the kind of preacher they selected. When Powell left the church due to failing health, there were questions about who would replace him. But those questions did not linger among the Abyssinian family. Powell died in 1972, and the church called in Proctor to eulogize him. Proctor preached "A Warrior for Justice" to honor Powell's life.[91]

Shortly after the funeral, the church would not take long to narrow its pastoral search and call Proctor to the position. From a field of three candidates—Proctor plus the Reverends Morris Lee and C. Henry Gregory III—the church selected Proctor on July 14, 1972. He preached his first sermon as pastor-elect on July 23, 1972, before a congregation of 1,500 persons. At Abyssinian, Proctor had taken his place in one of the premiere pulpits in the African American Christian experience. He was in the Mecca of twentieth-century black preaching. Gardner C. Taylor graced the pulpit of the Concord Baptist Church in Brooklyn; Sandy F. Ray led the Cornerstone Baptist Church in Brooklyn, and William A. Jones served at the Bethany Baptist Church in Harlem. These men were some of leading preachers in the African American Baptist experience, and Abyssinian was one of the most visible black churches in America. Powell's fame, moreover, placed Proctor and the church under a microscope.

In accepting the position at Abyssinian, Proctor returned to his vocational roots. The *New York Times* called Proctor an "imposing preacher."[92] He had had preaching assignments throughout his time as an educator and administrator. Yet this was his first pastoral charge since his time in Rhode Island. He would go to work assessing the church's documents and outlining a vision for the congregation. He looked to the ministers who were in place and to Union Theological Seminary in New York for clergy staff members. Proctor and the membership agreed that he would continue to teach at Rutgers. This meant he would need a capable staff that would see to the daily issues of the church. He found those persons in Marvin McMickle (now president of Colgate Rochester Crozer Divinity School) and Calvin Butts (Proctor's successor as pastor of the Abyssinian Church), among others. During his time at Abyssinian, Proctor preached sermons entitled "Pressing toward the Mark" and "Standing on Holy Ground."[93] He sought to organize the church fiscally and by way of polity. He helped Abyssinian align its denominational ties with the American Baptist Churches. As pastor, Proctor also presided over the funerals of notable performers, Moms Mabley, Mahalia Jackson (at an Episcopal church), and Count Basie. He sought to promote a renaissance of the arts in Harlem by inviting the New York Philharmonic to perform at the church. Another impressive achievement was the renovation of the sanctuary and purchase of a $250,000 pipe organ to enhance the music in worship. His leadership was a change of pace from the controversial Powell.

While many of the ministers Proctor hired moved on to other charges, one minister remained through Proctor's time at the church. The Reverend Calvin O. Butts III came to Abyssinian the same year as Proctor. Proctor showed confidence in Butts by delegating more and more responsibility to him as the years progressed. When Proctor retired in 1989, Butts was the logical choice to succeed Proctor. Proctor went before the church, requesting that the members name Butts as his successor to forward the work of the church.[94]

### *Semiretirement*

Seminary, college, and conference planners across the United States regularly called upon Proctor to give lectures, sermons, and keynote addresses. His service to humanity and to education, moreover, earned him over fifty honorary doctorates. (He joked that schools gave him honorary doctorates in lieu of a decent honorarium for his speeches.) In the early to mid-1990s, he spent time teaching at Duke and Vanderbilt (1990–1991) divinity schools and returned to teach a course at the School of Theology at Virginia Union University. The Yale University Divinity School invited Proctor to give the 1990 Lyman Beecher Lecture.[95] He created a Doctor of Ministry program at United Theological Seminary in Dayton, Ohio, around 1992. At United, he helped educate over one hundred students in that program. His courses focused on social ethics in order to prepare black church leaders for the context in which they did ministry.[96] He lectured at the Hampton University Minister's Conference on several occasions and spent time preaching to attendees at the annual Children's Defense Fund gatherings. Pastors and former students secured Dr. Proctor's service for several Sunday mornings a year. They all wanted to hear him preach the gospel. For Proctor could not let go of the preaching ministry. Above all, he was a preacher.

Race was a concern for Proctor throughout his career. He felt that the gains made by affirmative-action programs were being thrown aside by the Reagan and Bush administrations in the 1980s. At the Hampton Minister's Conference on the campus of Hampton University in 1990, his lecture "What the Law

Cannot Do" reminded his audience that racism still existed.[97] Other sermons and lectures from those years are filled with references to circumstances in news that signaled the need for more work to be done on racial matters. He used such stories as examples of how far America had come or fallen behind on matters of race. He included in his sermons several illustrations that expressed his concern for African American people. I will say more about Proctor's evolving notions of racism in chapter 3.

Proctor was able to put on paper what he practiced in the pulpit late in his career. Abyssinian published a small volume of his sermons early in his tenure as pastor. Once he became pastor emeritus, however, he published even more. Within a span of seven years (1989–1996), he produced four books on preaching, one on the pastor's work, and two autobiographical works. He had always found time to write in the earlier stages of his career. But many of those articles or essays were reproductions of his speeches at education conferences. These later books marked a fruitful period in which he dedicated himself again to empowering preachers. He wanted to be concise about how to address congregations on the important issues of the day. He produced preaching manuals that delineate the sermon preparation method he used throughout his ministry. He had come full circle, as he wrote most of the books for Judson Press, the American Baptist publishing house.

Proctor's life was an example of the influence of the essential aspects of his formation on his ability to thrive in a racist American environment. His family, education, and religious upbringing contributed to his sensitivity to the struggles of black people in the United States. For Proctor, the family remained the key element in introducing persons to education and religion. Without the family, the rest of the model was in danger. His early education in the home and in the Norfolk public school system, his religious instruction, and theological education produced a preacher-teacher who fought against the racist currents of the culture.

Proctor's wife and four sons mourned his passing in May 1997. He suffered a heart attack while giving a talk at Cornell College in Mount Vernon, Iowa. Dr. Gardner C. Taylor, Proctor's colleague and friend, preached at the funeral, hailing Proctor's faithfulness as a servant of God. He lauded Proctor's indefatigable service to humanity: "But Sam Proctor never gave up. Be thou faithful—faithful in the lectern of the academy—faithful in the pulpit of Christendom—faithful as he walked among us—faithful in his encouragement—faithful in his confidence about our black destiny in America and faithful about the nation's capacity to rise up to its fullest potential. Faithful! Faithful! Faithful!"[98]

# Notes

1. For biographical information on Proctor, see Samuel DeWitt Proctor, The Substance of Things Hoped For: A Memoir of African-American Faith, with a foreword by Marian Wright Edelman (New York: G. P. Putnam's Sons, 1995); Samuel D. Proctor, Samuel Proctor: My Moral Odyssey, with a foreword by Bill Moyers (Valley Forge, PA: Judson, 1989); and Marvin A. McMickle, "Proctor, Samuel D.," in An Encyclopedia of African American Christian Heritage (Valley Forge, PA: Judson, 2002). Proctor published many books, mostly pastoral in nature. He published numerous books on preaching, and though his earliest text, The Young Negro in America: 1960–1980 (New York: Association Press, 1966), would probably be considered by most as outside of the theological genre, it reflects his practical theology. His contribution extends to the field of education as well. He published several articles in education journals. Yet his popularity is somewhat limited to the African American tradition. This may be the product of his time in historical black colleges and universities, his time on the black "preaching circuit," and his work in seminaries with African American church leaders.

2. Peter J. Paris, "Moral Development for African American Leadership," in *The Stones That the Builders Rejected: The Development of Ethical Leadership from the Black Church Tradition*, ed. Walter Earl Fluker (Harrisburg, PA: Trinity, 1998), 28.

3. See Proctor, *My Moral Odyssey*, 21–22; Proctor, *Substance of Things Hoped For*, 14; and Samuel D. Proctor, interview by Tommy Bogger, June 15, 1991, transcript, History of Norfolk Project, City of Norfolk, Norfolk, Va., 11. I received the transcript from the City of Norfolk.

4. Proctor, History of Norfolk Project, 6.

5. Earl Lewis, *In Their Own Interests: Race, Class, and Power in Twentieth-Century Norfolk, Virginia* (Berkeley: University of California Press, 1991), 67, 69.

6. Thomas C. Parramore, Peter C. Stewart, and Tommy L. Bogger, *Norfolk: The First Four Centuries* (Charlottesville: University of Virginia Press, 1994), 313.

7. Parramore et al., *Norfolk*, 305–6; and Lewis, *In Their Own Interests*, 85.

8. Parramore et al., *Norfolk*, 328.

9. Lewis, *In Their Own Interests*, 83.

10. Parramore et al., *Norfolk*, 312–13; Proctor, *Substance of Things Hoped For*, 9; and Proctor, History of Norfolk Project, 3–4.

11. Proctor, *The Substance of Things Hoped For*, 9, 15.

12. Ibid., 2.

13. Proctor, History of Norfolk Project, 7.

14. Proctor, *The Substance of Things Hoped For*, 20.

15. Ruth Rose, *Norfolk, Virginia* (Charleston, SC: Arcadia, 2000), 55.

16. Proctor, History of Norfolk Project, 15; Proctor, *My Moral Odyssey*, 22.

17. Proctor, *The Substance of Things Hoped For*, 18.

18. See Parramore et al., *Norfolk*, 321; and Proctor, *My Moral Odyssey*, 28–29. Parramore states, "For much of Norfolk's population, the Great Depression was little more than a temporary inconvenience. With the news media full of stories of soup kitchens, mass underemployment, and suffering elsewhere, Norfolk in the crisis years of the early 1930s fared relatively well. Partially insulated from national economic woes by its military and other federal facilities and the government's million payroll, its seaborne trade still fairly strong, Norfolk was weathering the tempest better than most."

19. Samuel DeWitt Proctor, "Mr. Sceva and His Seven Sons," in *The Samuel DeWitt Proctor Institute For Child Advocacy and Ministry* (Washington: CDF, 1996), 6. In this same sermon, Proctor told the story of Crazy Ida. All of the other children called her by that name, but Proctor's mother would not allow him to do so. His mother told him about Ida's past and admonished him to value her personhood.

20. Proctor, *My Moral Odyssey*, 44–45.

21. Proctor, *The Substance of Things Hoped For*, 17.

22. Gary Ruegsegger and Linda S. McGowan, *The History of Norfolk Public Schools, 1681–2000* (Norfolk, VA: Norfolk Public Schools, 2000), 44–45; and Isaac Deveraux Faulkner, "A Study of the High School Achievement of a Group of 225 Negro Boys and Girls Admitted at the End of the First Term of the Eighth Grade as Compared with the High School Achievement of a Group of Pupils Admitted at the End of the Second Term of the Eighth Grade during 1933–1936, Inclusive, in the Booker T. Washington High School, Norfolk, VA" (thesis, Hampton Institute, 1937), 1.

23. "Va. Teachers Salary Fight up April 20," *Chicago Defender*, March 25, 1939, p. 5.

24. Proctor, *The Substance of Things Hoped For*, 27. Proctor placed the date of this event in 1935. Aline Black brought the suit in 1938; she was notified of her dismissal on June 14, 1939.

25. Ibid., 22. Proctor wrote, "Incidentally, my Sunday school teachers were also my public school teachers. All week long they shouted at us in the name of algebra and Shakespeare, and on Sundays, with a little more perfume, more makeup, nicer clothes and higher heels for the women and a blue suit for Mr. Newsome, they shouted at us in the name of Moses and Jesus."

26. Glenn Settles formed the first full-time African American gospel choir in 1938, in Cleveland, Ohio. His radio broadcast was carried on local CBS stations and then on CBS affiliates throughout the country. For more information on Glenn T. Settles and the Wings over Jordan Choir, see Madeline Olivia Trigg Price, "'Wings over Jordan' and American Radio: 1937–1947" (Ph.D. diss., University of Southern Mississippi, 1995); and Samuel Barber, "The Choral Style of the Wings over Jordan Choir" (Ph.D. diss., University of Cincinnati, 1979).

27. Proctor, History of Norfolk Project, 16–19. As a matter of fact, one of Dr. Proctor's brothers held membership in that church as late as 1988. See also Proctor, *The Substance of Things Hoped For*, 15–16; and Samuel D. Proctor, "Sermon on John 19:38," sermon presented at the Abyssinian Baptist Church, New York, April 1987, audiotape.

28. Proctor, *The Substance of Things Hoped For*, 38.

29. Lewis, *In Their Own Interests*, 71. See also Bank Street Baptist Church, *Bank Street Memorial Baptist Church, 1840–1985* (Norfolk, VA: Bank Street Baptist Church, 1985).

30. Albert Paul Brinson, "Ministering to the Black Middle Class" (D. Min. diss., United Theological Seminary, 1990), 21.

31. Proctor, History of Norfolk Project, 17. Incidentally, this was probably in contrast with other religious communities in the Norfolk area. One in particular was led by Bishop Charles Emmanuel Grace (1881–1960), better known as "Sweet Daddy" Grace. He led ministries up and down the East Coast. In Norfolk, he led the Norfolk House of Prayer. For more information on Grace's ministry in the Norfolk area, see Lewis, *In Their Own Interests*, 151; and Proctor, *The Substance of Things Hoped For*, 23–24. Proctor talks about Grace, without naming him, in his memoir. He refers to him as a "Cape Verdean charismatic preacher from New Bedford, Massachusetts."

32. Proctor, *My Moral Odyssey*, 56; and Proctor, *The Substance of Things Hoped For*, 34. At some point during his time at Virginia State, Proctor would earn money by playing in a jazz band with a musician, Billy Taylor, who became well known for playing jazz music. They called themselves the Virginia State Trojans. See Samuel D. Proctor, "The Call of Isaiah: When God Gets His Man," sermon presented at the Trinity United Church of Christ, Chicago, 1992, audiotape.

33. For more information on Luther P. Jackson, see Michael Dennis, "A Community Affair: Luther P. Jackson and Historical Consciousness," *Journal of the Historical Society* 3, no. 2 (Spring 2003): 249–76; and, Michael Dennis, *Luther P. Jackson and a Life for Civil Rights* (Gainesville: University Press of Florida, 2004).

34. Dennis, "A Community Affair," 250–51, 253–54. Proctor mentioned in more than one sermon how impressed he was with Luther Jackson.

35. Proctor, *The Substance of Things Hoped For*, 35. Proctor also had an uncle at Virginia State, Tommy Carter. He taught in the French department. Later, he worked as a Peace Corps administrator in Senegal and Morocco.

36. Proctor, "The Call of Isaiah."

37. Ibid.

38. Proctor, *My Moral Odyssey*, 58–59; and Samuel DeWitt Proctor, "Joanna: Doing What You've Got to Do," in *The Samuel DeWitt Proctor Institute For Child Advocacy and Ministry* (Washington, DC: CDF, 1995), 6.

39. "Jersey Pastor at Pond Street," *Providence Chronicle* (Providence, RI), November 22, 1947, p. 7. The paper does not list the dates in which Rice matriculated at Union Theological Seminary. At the time of the article, Rice was the pastor of the Union Baptist Church in Montclair, New Jersey. He was the guest preacher for the Pond Street Baptist Church's 117th-anniversary celebration.

40. For more information on the history of Virginia Union University, see John M. Ellison, ed., "A Century of Service to Education and Religion," *Virginia Union Bulletin* 65 (June 1965): 4–107; Miles Mark Fisher, ed., *Virginia Union University and Some of Her Achievements: Twenty-Fifth Anniversary, 1899–1924*, (Richmond: Virginia Union University, 1924); Cecil Raynard Taliaferro, "Virginia Union University: The First One Hundred Years, 1865–1965" (Ph.D. diss., University of Pittsburgh, 1975); and Ralph Reavis Sr., "Black Higher Education among American Baptists in Virginia: From the Slave Pen to the University," *American Baptist Quarterly* 11, no. 4 (1992): 357–74.Several passages of Taliaferro's book come straight from Ellison's work on the history of Virginia Union University. Passages read word for word and lack the appropriate citations.

41. Reavis, "Black Higher Education among American Baptists in Virginia," 369.

42. John Malcus Ellison, to James H. Croushore (?), Archives and Special Collections, Douglas L. Wilder Library, Virginia Union University, Richmond, VA (VUU); and John W. Kinney, "John Malcus Ellison: Narrated and Interpreted, 1980(?)," photocopy, 7–8. Kinney interviewed Ellison for his research; the interview gives more detail about Ellison's relationship with Reverend Ball.

43. J. M. Ellison, *They Who Preach* (Nashville: Broadman, 1956), 81.

44. John M. Ellison, "The Problem of Community in America Today" *Journal of Religious Thought* 1 (1943): 13.

45. John Malcus Ellison, *Tensions and Destiny* (Richmond: John Knox, 1953), 126.

46. Reavis, "Black Higher Education among American Baptists in Virginia," 370.

47. Mrs. Proctor shared this information in an informal telephone conversation with me on March 21, 2006.

48. "Interrace Body Hears M'Kinney," *Providence Chronicle*, February 1, 1947, p. 1.

49. Jeffrey Paul Straub, "The Making of a Battle Royal: The Rise of Religious Liberalism in Northern Baptist Life, 1870–1920" (Ph.D. diss., Southern Baptist Theological Seminary, 2004), 4.

50. Clayborne Carson, "Martin Luther King Jr.: The Crozer Seminary Years," *Journal of Blacks in Higher Education* 16 (Summer 1997): 124.

51. Proctor, *The Substance of Things Hoped For*, 47–48. See also Proctor, *My Moral Odyssey*, 64. In *My Moral Odyssey*, Proctor writes, "The ultimate test of my freedom was the challenge to view the Bible differently. I was bound intellectually and spiritually, by loyalty to tradition and by emotional satisfaction, to cling to the Bible as the literal, inerrant word of God without further debate."

52. Proctor, *The Substance of Things Hoped For*, 45; see also Samuel D. Proctor, "Turning the World Upside Down," sermon presented at the Trinity United Church of Christ, Chicago, 1992, audiotape. See also Samuel D. Proctor, "Meeting the Challenge," *Selections* 14, no. 3 (1998): 54–55.

53. For more information on Barbour, see Lewis V. Baldwin, *There Is A Balm in Gilead* (Minneapolis: Fortress Press, 1991); Richard Lischer, *The Preacher King: Martin Luther King, Jr. and the Word That Moved America* (New York: Oxford University Press, 1995), 67–71; Kirk Byron Jones, "King Had a Mentor in Chester" *Delaware County Daily Times* (Philadelphia), January 16, 1989; Kirk Byron Jones, "The Activism of Interpretation: Black Pastors and Public Life," *Christian*

Century 106, no. 26 (1989): 817–18. We probably learn more about what took place during these visits from a survey of the research done on Martin Luther King Jr. As it relates to King studies, Barbour continues to appear as an important figure during King's time in Chester, Pennsylvania. Barbour worked with many of the African American students who came through the seminary. Proctor is among that group of students. He says little, however, in his writings about this experience. In Proctor's sermon "Taking Care of Unfinished Business," he mentioned that there were preachers who aided him in his journey. Moreover, he said that he asked the publisher of his book *Preaching about Crises in the Community* to list the names of those preachers—Joseph Pius Barbour, John Malcus Ellison, and John Bennett Henderson. See Samuel D. Proctor, "Taking Care of Unfinished Business," sermon presented at the Abyssinian Baptist Church, New York, 1987, audiotape.Barbour and Proctor maintained a good relationship after Proctor's seminary days. Barbour was the editor of the *National Baptist Voice*, the official publication of the National Baptist Convention, USA. In a letter dated 1954, he invited Proctor to write an article for the periodical. Proctor dedicated his book on preaching about crisis in the community to Barbour. It is not clear how Proctor was introduced to Barbour. Based upon findings in the archives at Virginia Union University, it would not be a stretch to suggest that John M. Ellison alerted Barbour to Proctor's presence on the campus. Barbour and Ellison had a cordial relationship as well. In a letter to Ellison dated 1951, Barbour portended Proctor succeeding Ellison as the president of the Virginia Union. Barbour was about fifteen years off on his prediction.

54. Baldwin, *There Is a Balm in Gilead*, 167.

55. Jones, "The Activism of Interpretation," 817; and Lischer, *The Preacher King*, 67–69. It is not clear if this was the preaching model that the Crozer preachers were taught. King is said to have been a practitioner as well. Proctor employs the same method and includes a "relevant question" to prepare listeners for the application of the truths that he presents in the thesis.Lischer interviewed Proctor for his section on Barbour's influence on King during the Crozer years. When reading this section, one cannot help but believe that Proctor describes some of the activities that took place during his time with Barbour.

56. J. Pius Barbour, to Samuel D. Proctor, November 1, 1951, Archives and Special Collections, VUU, Richmond, VA.

57. Lischer, *The Preacher King*, 70.

58. Proctor, *The Substance of Things Hoped For*, 49, 51.

59. Before making a case for Fosdick's influence on Proctor, it is important to note that Fosdick had a cross-cultural appeal. In addition, Fosdick is one voice among many of the persons who influenced Proctor. One must not mistake, however, Proctor's use of some of the features of Fosdick's preaching method with Proctor wanting to be Fosdick or "borrow" his material. Lewis V. Baldwin does well by pointing to the deficiencies in Keith B. Miller's study on the liberal white preachers who had some influence on the thought of Martin Luther King Jr. To be sure, persons such as Walter Rauschenbusch, Harry Emerson Fosdick, George Buttrick, Paul Scherer, and Ralph Sockman were well-known preachers. However, Proctor and King are equally, if not more, indebted to the African American traditions in which they were raised. African American preachers like Proctor, John Malcus Ellison, Benjamin Mays, Howard Thurman, and King were influenced by their liberal theological education. In attending liberal theological seminaries from the 1920s to 1950s, they read or heard models that were mainly the works of British and white American preachers. As Baldwin and others note, the larger, more pressing influence was determined by their understanding of race in America and how God addressed that problem. We can trace that concern directly back to the Black Church and its development in America. Moreover, how these black preachers delivered their messages make clear their cultural heritage.Proctor, as noted earlier in this chapter, was influenced by great black preachers. He was a child of the Black Church, and his preaching reminds us of this fact. I pay attention to Proctor's relationship with Fosdick because Proctor includes a note about him in most of his books. Therefore, it would be impertinent for me to do cultural-intellectual biography without including Fosdick. See Proctor, *The Certain Sound of the Trumpet*, 29.See also Proctor, *"How Shall They*

*Hear?" Effective Preaching for Vital Faith* (Valley Forge, PA: Judson, 1992), 8. Proctor writes, "It was Harry Emerson Fosdick who towed me safely through the churning waters of my seminary days. I clung to his books, and I raced to my radio every Sunday afternoon to be there when he began, 'Behold, I stand at the door and knock; saith the Lord.' And with my faith lying like scraps on the floor, I stuck with him as he guided me in picking up the pieces, bit by bit, and organizing a belief system once again with joy and sweet surrender." To attest to Fosdick's cross-cultural appeal, William B. Lawrence wrote that his grandfather, in northeastern Pennsylvania, would tune the radio to hear Fosdick after attending men's Bible class and worship at the Methodist church. Lawrence labeled his grandfather as undereducated and black-collar, noting that various persons listened to Fosdick. See Lawrence, *Sundays in New York: Pulpit Theology at the Crest of the Protestant Mainstream, 1930–1955* (Lanham, MD: Scarecrow, 1996), ix.

60. Proctor, *My Moral Odyssey*, 65. Proctor mentioned on other occasions that he turned to books like Fosdick's work on the Bible. See Harry Emerson Fosdick, *The Modern Use of the Bible* (New York: Macmillan, 1924, 1947).

61. Dorrien, *The Making of American Liberal Theology: Idealism, Realism, and Modernity, 1900–1950* (Louisville: Westminster John Knox, 2003), 9. See also L. Susan Bond, *Contemporary African American Preaching: Diversity in Theory and in Style* (St. Louis: Chalice, 2003), 47. Bond notes that Proctor's preaching concern for practical living and the problems of the "ordinary believer" is similar to that of Fosdick's method. She does not say much more about that relationship.

62. Proctor, *My Moral Odyssey*, 75.

63. "Pond Street Calls New Pastor," *Providence Chronicle*, July 21, 1945, p. 8; "Rev. Wynn Heads Liberian School," *Providence Chronicle*, February 2, 1946, p. 1. The pulpit committee also invited the Reverend Henri M. Deas of Boston, a doctoral student at Harvard, to participate in the applicant pool. I believe that Dr. Richard McKinney, one of Proctor's undergraduate professors, might have had a hand in this process. McKinney was also a former pastor of the Pond Street Church. There is, however, no evidence—as of yet—to support this claim.Proctor's time in Providence is well documented in the *Providence Chronicle*, the local black weekly newspaper. In 1947, the *Providence Chronicle* hired him to write a weekly column on religious topics called "The Letter and the Spirit." There was not much about black life in Providence that was not recorded on the pages of this weekly.

64. Proctor, *The Substance of Things Hoped For*, 59. Incidentally, Proctor mentions being impressed by the writings of the other Niebuhr, Reinhold Niebuhr (1892–1971). Specifically, Proctor enjoyed Niebuhr's *Moral Man and Immoral Society* (1932).

65. Proctor, *The Substance of Things Hoped For*, 58; Proctor, History of Norfolk Project, 21; and Proctor, *My Moral Odyssey*, 93. Informal conversations I have had with one of Proctor's Doctor of Ministry fellows, Dr. James Harris, at Virginia Union University suggest that Proctor wanted to be in a program that he could complete in a shorter period of time.

66. Richard Morgan Cameron, *Boston University School of Theology, 1839–1968* (Boston: Boston University School of Theology, 1968), 78.

67. Paul Deats and Carol Robb, eds., *The Boston Personalist Tradition in Philosophy, Social Ethics, and Theology* (Macon, GA: Mercer University Press, 1986), 2.

68. Samuel D. Proctor, "New Testament Interpretation within the Northern Baptist Convention" (Th.D. diss., Boston University School of Theology, 1950).

69. Cameron, *Boston University School of Theology*, 79.

70. This term stems from W. E. B. Du Bois's belief that a class of educated black leaders—approximately a tenth—would/should lead the black masses to social, economic, and political freedom in the United States. Proctor bought in to this idea.

71. The *Providence Chronicle* listed the sermon titles each week. Concerning the sermon "Long Cords and Strong Stakes," it probably became the basis for his inaugural address as the president of Virginia Union University. He took the text for this sermon from Isa. 54:2.

72. "Over 400 Hear Rev. Proctor at Bethel Church," *Providence Chronicle*, April 2, 1949, p. 1.

73. Proctor, *The Substance of Things Hoped For*, 54.

74. John M. Ellison to Samuel D. Proctor, September 14, 1948, Archives and Special Collections, VUU, Richmond, VA. Ellison was so motivated by Proctor's acceptance that he attempted to endow the Chair of Biblical Studies for Proctor. See also Proctor, *The Substance of Things Hoped For*, 75; "Dr. Proctor Named Virginia U. Dean," *Chicago Defender*, September 30, 1950, p. 1; "University President Named," *NYT*, May 12, 1955, p. 31; and "Elect Proctor New Prexy of Virginia Union," *Chicago Defender*, June 4, 1955, p. 5.Although no publishers accepted Proctor's early manuscripts for publication, during his time at Virginia Union, he revised and submitted his book to be considered by publishers at Harper, Prentice-Hall, Broadman Press, and Judson Press. He did publish an article on John C. Bennett in 1955. See Samuel D. Proctor, "The Social Philosophy of John C. Bennett," *Journal of Religious Thought* 11, no. 2 (Spring–Summer 1954): 93–104.

75. Letters and program bulletins at the archives at Virginia University's L. Douglas Wilder Library display the numerous sites where Proctor preached and lectured. For example, see Lois J. Anderson to Samuel D. Proctor, November 22, 1955, Archives and Special Collections, VUU, Richmond. Proctor was the American Baptist Convention representative on the television show "Lamp unto My Feet," which aired on CBS. For other invitations, see Adam Clayton Powell Jr. to Samuel D. Proctor, November 22, 1955, Archives and Special Collections, VUU, Richmond; and M. L. King Jr. to Samuel D. Proctor, November 18, 1955, Archives and Special Collections, VUU, Richmond.

76. Samuel D. Proctor, "Lengthening Our Cords and Strengthening Our Stakes," inaugural address presented at Virginia Union University, November 4, 1955, Archives and Special Collections, VUU, Richmond.

77. Clayborne Carson et al., *The Papers of Martin Luther King, Jr.*, 3:129. In a letter to King dated February 16, 1956, Proctor writes, "After my conversation with Dr. Mays a few weeks ago in Atlanta, I think that I had better fix my hopes somewhere else for a Dean of our Seminary."

78. Proctor, "Lengthening Our Cords and Strengthening Our Stakes."

79. Ellison, "A Century of Service to Education and Religion," 42; and Samuel D. Proctor, *Maintaining Our Christian Courage*, sermon presented at the Abyssinian Baptist Church, New York, November 1987, audiotape.

80. Samuel DeWitt Proctor, "Inaugural Address, 1961," (photocopy), F. D. Bluford Library Archives, North Carolina Agricultural and Technical State University, Greensboro.For more on Proctor's move to North Carolina, see "Name New Prexy at A & T College," *Chicago Defender*, May 7, 1960, p. 16; and "A & T to Install Dr. Proctor," *Chicago Defender* January 28, 1961, p. 22.

81. Proctor, *The Substance of Things Hoped For*, 91.

82. The *New York Times* monitored his career. The paper paid close attention to him from the time he joined the Peace Corps in 1962. See, for example, "Negro in Peace Corp Post," *NYT*, December 10, 1962, p. 2; "Teachers Taught about the Negro," *NYT*, December 5, 1965, p. 138; and M. S. Handler, "Negroes Advised to Aid Their Poor," *NYT*, February 21, 1966, p. 45. The African American newspaper *The Chicago Defender* kept a closer watch on him. See "Proctor Named to High Post," *Daily Defender*, December 10, 1962, p. 4; "A & T Prexy Denies Rumors He Quit College," *Daily Defender*, January 31, 1963, p. 11; "Reports Solid, Rapid Progress in Nigeria," *Chicago Defender*, March 30, 1963, p. 19; Samuel D. Proctor, "Former Peace Corps Worker Rates Shriver Tops as Boss," *Chicago Defender*, November 14, 1964, p. 9; and "300 at A&I College Hear Shriver Aide Blast Middle-Class Apathy," *Chicago Defender*, October 22, 1966, p. 9. Proctor received de facto leadership status in black newspapers and in the black community because he was a black academic with an earned doctorate. When he became president of Virginia Union, he solidified this role by virtue of his vocation and title. He seemingly became a black "national" leader in the view of the white press when he came on board with Shriver and the Peace Corps. After that, he was a newsworthy item in the *New York Times*. There even came a point at which rumors began to appear in an African American newspaper about Proctor being promoted to ambassador and other posts. He could barely make a move without it appearing in a newspaper of

some national scope. This speaks to both the nature of the events in which he participated and the status that he attained as an African American leader.On his time as president of the Institute for Services to Education, see Proctor, History of Norfolk Project, 23. Proctor stated, "That was designed to help black colleges strengthen themselves. Lyman Brooks helped put that together with me, and I was the head of that for a couple of years."

83. Proctor reported on his American Baptist trip in the National Baptist's periodical. He began at an early stage in his career to see some of the racial problems created by white Christian missionaries in foreign countries. Persons in India, he wrote, were skeptical of interacting with a black missionary. They were told or given the impression that the African American missionary was not competent. See Samuel D. Proctor, "Dean Proctor, Virginia University, Reports on Trip to India," *National Baptist Voice* 26, no. 10 (1954): 1, 13. I am sure that coincidence was not involved in Proctor's being selected for the Baptist World Alliance missionary tour. A Virginia Union trustee, Dr. Theodore F. Adams (1898–1980), also pastor of the First Baptist Church, Richmond, Virginia, served on the executive committee of the alliance from 1934 until his death. He held the position of vice president (1947–1950) and president (1955–1960) during his time on the committee. Dr. Adams held Proctor in high esteem. See *Religious Leaders of America*, 2nd ed., s.v. "Theodore Floyd Adams." See also "College Prexy Tours Europe," *Chicago Defender*, August 2, 1958, p. 19.

84. Proctor, *The Substance of Things Hoped For*, 98.

85. Ibid., 100–101.

86. Ibid., 105.

87. Ibid., 104–106. During the middle years of the 1960s, Proctor began to question the dedication of the black middle class to lower-class African Americans. He was skeptical of the way in which middle-class blacks forsook the lower-income members of the race. Proctor had always recognized the responsibility of the more advantaged members of the race. Whether this came from his trip to Africa is not clear.

88. Proctor, History of Norfolk Project, 23.

89. The *Defender* might have been misled by word of a message being sent to Proctor in Nigeria. The offer was for Proctor to run an antipoverty social agency in Harlem. Proctor wrote that the date of this offer was in 1962, around the same time as the *Defender* story ran. The *Defender*, clearly, received the wrong information but predicted the future. See "Powell Picks Dixie Educator as Heir," *Chicago Defender*, December 8, 1962, p. 1.Esther McCall served as membership secretary and administrative assistant during the Powell and Proctor eras. She mentioned to me that "Adam" would tell the staff to call "Sam" if Powell could not preach on a certain Sunday. Proctor's relationship with Powell Jr. began with Proctor hearing Powell preach in the chapel at Virginia Union University. Powell's father was a graduate of Virginia Union University, so the Powells had a relationship with the school. John Malcus Ellison may have assisted in deepening the ties between Powell Jr. and Proctor. Pictures in the Abyssinian display cases show John Malcus Ellison posing with Powell Jr. during a ceremony at the church.

90. Proctor, *The Substance of Things Hoped For*, 147.

91. Samuel D. Proctor, "A Warrior for Justice," *African American Pulpit* 4, no. 1 (2000–2001): 69–74.

92. George Dugan, "An Imposing Preacher: Samuel DeWitt Proctor," *NYT*, July 24, 1972, 53.

93. I gathered these titles by listening to the audiotapes of these sermons at Abyssinian.

94. Adolphus Clarence Lacey, "Congregation as Community Developer: A Socio-Historical Reading of the Social Ministry of the Abyssinian Baptist Church" (Ph.D. diss., Northwestern University, 2002), 68. Lacey writes, "To many Proctor was a radical departure from the canonical norm established by the Powells. . . . Yet upon closer examination, we discover that Proctor continued in the same activist tradition through a slightly different means. He was a public policy advocate, not a politician. He dealt with the product of politics, not politics *per se*. Faced with police brutality, instead of leading a protest to stop it, Proctor would convene a quiet meeting

with the principals to hammer out a solution that was based upon consensus."The Abyssinian archives are being reorganized at the time of this writing. Kevin McGruder was kind enough to share with me some of the documents from Proctor's tenure as pastor. Within the collection are documents in the archives that reveal aspects of the pastoral search process and Proctor's approach to overseeing the ministries of the church.

95. Proctor turned the lecture into a book on preaching. Proctor, "*How Shall They Hear?*"

96. Proctor remained concerned about the work of the Black Church. A listing of his courses at United includes African American Church in the 21st Century; Mission of the African American Church into the 21st Century; and Advanced Mission of the African American Church into the 21st Century. See *United Theological Seminary Bulletin*, 1992–1994, Archives and Special Collections, United Theological Seminary, Dayton, OH. Among that group of graduates is the Reverend Dr. Suzan Johnson Cook, current Ambassador-at-Large for International Religious Freedom.

97. Samuel D. Proctor, "What the Law Cannot Do," sermon presented at the Hampton Minister's Conference (Hampton, VA: Hampton University, 1990), audiotape.

98. Gardner C. Taylor, "A Mighty Oak Fallen," *African American Pulpit* 4, no. 1 (2000–2001), 79.Obituaries marking Proctor's passing appeared in several newspapers across the country, particularly the New York papers. See Eric Pace, "Samuel Proctor, 75, Dies; Led Abyssinian Baptist Church," *NYT*, May 26, 1997, p. 29; Peter Steinfels, "Crowds Fill Harlem Church to Honor and Remember the Rev. Samuel Proctor, Master Teacher and Preacher and Example," Beliefs, *NYT*, May 31, 1997, p. 25; and J. Zamgba Browne, "Hundreds Bid Final Farewell to Dr. Samuel Proctor," *New York Amsterdam News*, June 7, 1997, p. 7.

# 3

# On the Making of a Public Faith

## *Proctor's Intellectual Roots*

Samuel DeWitt Proctor's faith provides insight into understanding his concerns about racism in America. His understanding of those doctrines or faith claims that make up the Christian witness is an amalgam of his experience as an African American and his theological education (local church and academic). He was a bridge figure or pragmatic harmonizer. His was a theology that made theory praxis. In his experience as an African American, he witnessed and encountered segregation firsthand. Proctor, moreover, was a black Baptist who processed the Christian religion through that theological lens. There is no doubt that his experience as an African American Baptist shaped his worldview and impressed upon him the importance of valuing all persons as children of God—a lesson he learned as early as his childhood.[1] His religious notions were formed by an Afro-Baptist context and by principles and language appropriated from his formal theological education—notions that informed his desire to transform the racist environment of American public life while diplomatically rejecting ideas of the Black Power movement and black liberation theology.

As noted in chapter 2, Proctor received his formal theological education in a Baptist college, a theologically liberal northern Baptist seminary, and prominent northern universities. He learned the principles of the social gospel theology and matriculated at the center of the Personalist school of theological and philosophical thought, the Boston University School of Theology.[2] The confluence of a racially conscious Christian upbringing and socially oriented education in theology led to the formation of a black public faith that sought to transform society for African Americans and other marginalized persons in the world. The ideas that Proctor published early in his career did not always reflect his social thought. The religious principles at the foundation of his early thought, however, anticipate his public theology and its response to racism.

This chapter and the next one are dedicated to what that thought looks like in his writings and sermons. I examine his sermons and writings to piece together his Christian beliefs. Later chapters will examine the aims of Proctor's religion.

A focus on Proctor's Christian faith requires some basis by which one approaches it. As a Christian preacher, on most Sunday mornings, Proctor used one of the main sources of theological reflection: the Bible. Before examining some of Proctor's religious notions and tendencies, we should take an in-depth look at the intellectual and spiritual concepts that shaped him. Proctor was a black Baptist preacher who was also a product of the twentieth-century liberal theological tradition in America.

Since Proctor spent a large portion of his career expressing his beliefs from the pulpit of an African American Baptist congregation, it follows that his sermons would provide insight into his religious thought. In addition to his writings, I rely heavily upon Proctor's sermons as sources of theology. Research on sermons from twentieth-century preachers, especially black preachers, is a neglected area of historical research. But his sermon catalog is rich with theological material. He fits into the larger context of the Baptist faith and the liberal theological tradition. I cannot here describe in detail the varied practices and beliefs that exist among Baptists and the numerous theological suppositions of the "liberal" theologians of the period.[3] But the following discussion is an effort to summarize general religious beliefs among these groups, aimed at a better understanding of Proctor's development within his historical and theological contexts.

## Proctor the Black Baptist

As a product of an Afro-Baptist theological tradition, Proctor embraced the tenets of the Baptist faith. Because of the limited resources available from Proctor's childhood, I rely on a general understanding of the Baptist faith. The calendar of high and holy days in the Black Church tradition probably produced several Easter and Christmas recitations from the Proctor children. Sunday school was the norm for Proctor. The Baptist church was the home of his faith. Something held Proctor in the Baptist tradition. He was an ordained Baptist preacher. He served as the pastor of two Baptist congregations. To be sure, certain links to the larger Baptist tradition are evident in his thought.

As a Baptist, Proctor grew up with an evangelical faith that leaned on the Bible as its primary source of God's revelation to humankind. In the Bible, Christians (of which Baptists are one tradition) embrace the life, death, and resurrection of Jesus as the pinnacle moments of salvation history. The Baptist emphasis on the witness of the Bible and the existence of the Trinity were foundational elements that pervaded the polity and literature of Proctor's spiritual development. A closer look at Baptist beliefs and the beliefs of black Christians may show the reasons for his commitment to Baptist polity and practice.

Bill Leonard's work *Baptists in America* lays a foundation for *some* of what the larger Baptist family believes. His caution to readers holds true for this overview of Baptists as well: "Beyond a core of distinctives, Baptists themselves often differ as to doctrinal definitions and approaches to ministry."[4] Several beliefs make up a part of *most* Baptist belief systems. Leonard argues that Baptists are Trinitarian in their belief of God. In addition, Baptists see Jesus Christ as the Son of God, savior of the world, Word of God incarnate, born of a virgin, sacrificed for the sins of humanity. They see a personal experience with Christ as a prerequisite for baptism, and they see the Bible as the special revelation from God and authoritative source for all matters.

Anthony Pinn highlights a similar list of Christian beliefs that the Black Church has embraced in its existence. Pinn focuses on the importance of a Trinitarian God, the salvation experience, the Bible and its interpretation, and worship and music. Pinn, moreover, argues for the place of the Bible as the *main* source of Christian theology for many African Americans. Pinn states that Scripture is important to black Christians because they consider it to be the word of God as God's self-revelation. He goes on to write that some black Christians believe that persons should accept the literal meaning of its content as infallible, inerrant, while other black Christians argue that its inspiration requires a study of the historical and cultural contexts to interpret its meaning.[5] To be sure, the Bible was and is the foundation upon which many African American Christians built and/or build their faith. Black Baptists are no different in this way. Many African American Baptist Christians profess their belief in the Bible as the word of God. This belief, then, informs these Christians' notions about Jesus the Christ.

Speaking from experience in the black Baptist context, the evangelical faith of most African American Baptists holds that Jesus is the Son of God. This faith is evangelical in that it is a faith of the word (the Bible), believed and preached. Historically, these Baptists profess that Jesus as the Christ died for humankind, that the sins of humanity might be washed away "in the blood of the Lamb." A duty of the black Baptist Christian, as for other Baptists, is to tell the world of the savior's love. The Sunday school literature of Proctor's time would have expressed these beliefs. James Tyms examined this literature and came to several conclusions. He argued that African American Baptists produced curriculum that expressed a concern for saving souls. The writers of black Baptist Sunday school literature exhibited in these lessons their concern for racial uplift, Christian nurture, and evangelism. Tyms noted that many of the lessons encouraged students to model the personality of Jesus. Traditional Baptist emphases suggest that Christ is the focus of the religion. The Bible leads the believer to this point. Many Baptists, then, affirm that Christ is the fulfillment of the book—Christ is God.[6]

The available sources do not reveal, other than what Proctor said, how his beliefs shifted or morphed once he arrived at Virginia Union and Crozer Theological Seminary.[7] The writings he produced during his career show that he remained Baptist in practice and thought. As with much of Baptist theology, Baptists seem to emphasize and articulate more their confessions about God and Jesus as Christ than a doctrine of the Holy Spirit. The Baptists do not hold to creeds. And the sacraments (ordinances in the Baptist faith) have no saving power; they are symbols of the sacrifice that Jesus made on the cross. All accounts show that Proctor affirmed most Baptist beliefs. His early religious ideas were shaped by what he considered a literal approach to the Bible in his upbringing. He had a different experience of the Bible, though, in the seminary and graduate school. His educational environments challenged the traditional doctrines he embraced. The tension between the inerrant and the "almost irreverent" approaches to the Bible were at work in several church-sponsored (Baptist) seminary classrooms. He experienced a type of second conversion at Crozer Seminary.

## Proctor the Modernist Pastor-Theologian

The American liberal theological tradition, or what Proctor called modernism in his time, weighed heavily in Proctor's development. He called himself a son of the social gospel thought of Walter Rauschenbusch. And Proctor's doctoral dissertation displayed his bias toward the historical-critical methods of biblical studies that were prominent in the liberal theological seminaries of his generation.[8] One can see by his choice in graduate education (Yale Divinity School and Boston University School of Theology) that he remained among those thinkers who strayed away from the "orthodox" views and dogmas that the biblical literalists and the self-proclaimed fundamentalists embraced.[9]

Several prevailing features characterized this liberal theological tradition. Borrowing from Henry P. Van Dusen, liberal theology claimed (1) a fidelity to truth; (2) deference to science and the historical-critical studies movement; (3) tentativeness as to metaphysical certainty; and (4) an assumption of continuity with the Christian tradition. William R. Hutchinson, in his book *The Modernist*

*Impulse in American Protestantism* (1976), poses similar yet distinct characteristics. He argues that modernist thought consisted of (1) a self-consciously intended adaptation of religious ideas to modern culture; (2) a belief that God is immanent in human cultural development and revealed through it; and (3) a belief that human society is moving toward the realization of the kingdom of God.[10] Liberal theology emphasized heavily the historical-critical methodology in its biblical studies and moral Christianity in its theological system.

Concerning the claim that the liberal theology of the modern age was loyal to truth, one must consider the grounds on which that claim lay. The new methods of biblical studies wreaked havoc on certain mainline denominations. The liberal seminaries that taught the historical-critical methods, for the most part, were attached to these denominations. For many theologians in this age—fundamentalists and modernists—the issue became one of authority, mainly the authority of the Bible and the "authority" of the historical-critical method. Historical-critical approaches to the Bible grounded their notions in reason and empirical data. The theologian, then, validated the truth in Scripture by examining the evidence available and making sense of it based upon his or her experience. Gary Dorrien writes, "The essential idea of liberal theology is that all claims to truth, in theology as in other disciplines, must be made on the basis of reason and experience, not by appeal to external authority."[11] In this case, that external authority is the Bible. For biblical literalists and fundamentalists, the Bible was *the* source of truth. One could not find truth if not affirmed by the biblical text. Van Dusen argues that liberal theologians aspired to "intellectual honesty and personal integrity."[12] They wanted to make Christian theology—even the Bible—accountable to the findings of science. Daniel Sommer Robinson called this type of theology progressive. Concerning this area of thought in liberal theology, Robinson argues that the theologian undertakes a constant process of doctrinal revision. New discoveries beckon the theologian to make theology consistent with scientific findings. Robinson maintains, "More accurately expressed, he must ever strive to make his interpretations of inner religious experience consistent with the scientist's interpretations of outer perceptual experience."[13] This, Robinson maintained, makes theology "progressive." A practical example of this fidelity to truth is apparent in Harry Emerson Fosdick's *The Modern Use of the Bible* (1924). Fosdick wrestles with this idea in explaining how biblical miracles were not consistent with the thinking of the modern mind. Fosdick made a case for a "law-abiding" world that serves all rather than a Christianity of miracles that serves a few on special occasions. Liberal theologians attempted to make sense out of the seeming contradictions between the Bible and modern science.

The liberal tradition in Christian theology was known for its openness to the findings of scientific exploration. Liberal or modernist theologians saw in science an aid to religious reflection, not an opponent. By showing deference to scientific discoveries, persons such as Fosdick sought to make Christianity credible to the modern seeker of truth. Van Dusen contends that the historical method rescued Jesus of Nazareth from the tradition that held him hostage. Science and the tools of historical research were giving theologians the equipment to demythologize the biblical text. Once free from the garb of literalist Christian doctrine, modernist theologians were free to see Jesus as an ethically relevant human being with a divine purpose. This made Jesus a reality to be interpreted for salvation, not adored for his place in a dogmatic theological system. In other words, one could glean from his teachings and his life those things that exemplify what it means to live in harmony with God. One then proved the veracity of those teachings and that life by reason and experience.[14] Modernist theologians believed that reason and experience are authoritative in matters of theological clarity. They viewed the Bible as one among many sources for verifying the truth of a theological claim. This is what Van Dusen argues in stating liberal theology's tentativeness as to metaphysical certainty. Charles A. Briggs summarizes this point when he explains that "scriptures are not the only source of Christian theology."[15] Briggs held that the Bible does not answer every question of religion. It is, nonetheless, a source for enlightenment. Modernist theologians saw the Bible as an authority, but not *the* authority. Concerning this thought, Dorrien states, "Christian Scripture may be recognized as spiritually authoritative within Christian experience, but its word does not settle or establish truth claims about matters of fact."[16] This is an important aspect of liberal theology. Experience is how one judges truth in this system of thought. One uses the content of one's experience to develop, challenge, and critique theology. These theologians moved the conversation away from the abstract and theoretical.

The Bible was considered an aid to religious reflection, as was science, but experience was the hermeneutic linchpin of liberal Christian theology. Religious experience verified a liberal theologian's belief in God's immanence. This belief led to the modernist's optimism of the age. The kingdom of God could be present on earth, and the world would be better. Contrast that to many conservative Christians' belief that the world is only getting worse. Progress became an important idea in the liberal tradition. The evidence of this progress was in all aspects of life. Through dialectical and/or organic stages, some modernists argued, one could see God improving society.

A final category to consider is Van Dusen's assumption of the continuity of liberal theology with the Christian tradition. Liberal theologians were connected to the Romantic tradition of Schleiermacher and the pragmatism of William James. As beneficiaries of German scholarship, modernist theologians argued that they were making sense of the history Christians inherited. Despite the harangues of the fundamentalists, modernists saw themselves in line with the tradition. They believed themselves to be the rightful heirs of Jesus' teachings, for they understood what to do with those teachings. The focus on the Jesus of history made this emphasis easier. God as an ethical being was on display in the person of Jesus. To follow Christ is to follow ethical principles, not dogmatic beliefs. Kathryn Lofton remarks, "Finding Jesus—a Jesus historically constituted, rigorously researched, and scrupulously interrogated—was the central practice of modernist Christianity."[17] Jesus as the central figure of Christianity is what linked modernism to the church of ancient and medieval times. Jesus is also where Proctor could find common ground with the Christian communities that nurtured him.

The Black Church—specifically, the Afro-Baptist tradition—and the liberal theological tradition are the theological environments in which Proctor developed. A God who is "closer than mother and father" in the rich experience of African American Christianity was comparable to the immanent God taught at Crozer and the personal God of Boston University. A God who acts on the behalf of the "least and left behind" was the God whose kingdom shall come in the social gospel theology. While these categories are general, they suffice to show the intellectual-theological landscape from which he developed his thinking. However brief, these generalities sketch the contour of Samuel DeWitt Proctor's thought.

## The Bible as Spiritual Resource for Life

Without question, the Afro-Baptist and liberal/modernist theological traditions were important sources of Proctor's religious beliefs. He was adept at wedding the Bible and preaching. And his understanding of biblical texts displayed traces of modern biblical scholarship. His dissertation, completed in 1950, provides evidence of his stance toward the Bible and commitment to Baptist life:

> The writer's approach to the study of the Bible in the Church is critical-historical, accepting data without bias or theological preference with the presentation of the fact as it stands and with an earnest effort to present opinions as nearly accurate as the writer's ability and honesty will allow.

> Finally, the writer shares a deep sympathy with the fellowship of Northern Baptists, was educated by their philanthropy and is now engaged in teaching New Testament in an institution founded by Northern Baptists to train minds of black men in the liberal arts and religion so that they may walk in their new freedom unafraid and competent.[18]

Earlier statements in his newspaper columns exhibit the same acceptance of this approach to biblical studies. To be sure, Proctor was not willing to remove the Bible as a canon and authority for the Christian faith. The Bible was a main source for religious reflection, especially ideas birthed out of the life and teachings of Jesus the Christ. He believed that seeing the Bible through the lens of the historical-critical perspective was the "ultimate test" of his intellectual and spiritual freedom.

Like other modernist theologians, Proctor received the text with a critical appreciation. Proctor, therefore, would not vouch for the historical veracity of certain biblical characters and accounts. It is evident whose side Proctor took in the debate between the "literalists" and the "modernists" over the approach to the Bible. Proctor labeled the seminary approach to the Bible as "the most significant development" for the Northern Baptists and their approach to the Bible. He interpreted the benefits of this development: "The seminaries were deliberate in their conviction to present the Christian message in historical, scientific terms and in giving their students a moral, psychological interpretation of Christianity for today."[19] Although Proctor attempted to argue from a neutral point of view, his dissertation amounted to an apology for the modernist approach to biblical studies. Acknowledging the practical side of his concern, Proctor asked if the modernists' Bible could preach. His answer was yes, and he found his example in the popular radio preacher Harry Emerson Fosdick.

Proctor maintained throughout his public career that the Bible has in it the experiences of a people who believed in God. Proctor wrote on numerous occasions that the Bible is a record of the human encounter with God. The pages of Scripture are replete with the writings of persons in ages past who sought, attempted to understand, and believed in God. Revelation, as far as the Bible was concerned, could be a matter of how one views history. The Bible is that "slice" of human history that details God's relationship with humankind. Scripture, then, is a spiritual history or "holy history" that examines the way in which a group of people understood how God works to redeem humankind from its sin. Proctor understood that some biblical ideas about sin were tribal, contextual.

Proctor was not without his evangelical understanding of the Bible's role in Christianity. He did believe in the biblical concept of salvation from sin. But his approach to salvation was different from that found in popular Christian tracts produced by "conservative" and "fundamentalist" groups and denominations. Proctor touted the potential of humankind. He used the Bible to promote human potential, not highlight human sin. Proctor argued that the preacher receives from the Bible a sense of where the "human spirit" began and how far it can go. He noted, "When we look for a witness on the subject of human nature and its possibilities, no matter wherever else we may turn to find that hidden, persistent propensity towards goodness, to find the total fulfillment of our finest human capacities, and to see the flow of history toward something better, our task is incomplete until we turn to the book that has kept notes on this subject since Abraham came out of Ur of the Chaldees."[20] That "flow of history" did not come without its imperfections. The process was organic for Proctor.

The Bible developed over time, Proctor held, and its greatest revelation came in the record of the life and ministry of Jesus. L. Susan Bond examines this aspect of Proctor's thought and argues that he placed the Bible at the center of theological discernment. This judgment may be hasty, as it is not the sole source for deliberation. Proctor embraced the historical-critical methods to the point in which the biblical writings were suspect to him, considering some of the theological judgments that it made.[21] He did maintain that the Bible is *a* record of the "self-disclosure" of God. Proctor saw in Jesus the greatest expression of this revelation of God in history. Proctor believed that the content of the faith of Israel developed over time. He stated that the eighth-century bce prophets moved the conceptual model of the Jewish faith from a narrow ethnocentric view of religion to an inclusive one that heralded God's welcoming love. Proctor argued that the perceptions of God in the Hebrew Bible were incomplete. They did not express fully the merciful God revealed in Jesus. The value of the Scriptures is in the "encounter" of humankind with God. That encounter grew with time and experience. The prophets were better equipped than their ancestors were to speak about God. Jesus, moreover, was aware of prophetic literature and could base much of his teachings upon the prophets. Proctor could not accept the fundamentalist understanding of scriptural authority. He placed value upon a historical, organic understanding of biblical authority:

> The Bible has an intrinsic authority that is more significant than any claims of literal, plenary inspiration. It is hard to believe that the God who was revealed in Jesus Christ commanded all of that killing in the Old Testament, but the Bible is the book that records God's reach for humanity and humanity's reach for God. It is the encounter that makes it a book of religious authority; it traces our spiritual ascent from crude human sacrifice and using women as property to the revelation of God in Christ and all persons as precious in God's sight.[22]

His later writings show that Proctor was concerned about the way in which preachers and parishioners used the Scriptures. He disliked the issue of division over theological doctrine derived from the Bible. He argued that people should not "haggle" over the small things that arise from the Bible. Proctor believed that some persons saw in the Bible what they wanted to see to justify their petty theological concerns. He saw the Bible as a resource that provides the preacher with a "moral and spiritual orientation" for human relations. But Proctor was aware of how persons exploited others using the Bible. In a 1987 sermon entitled "Taking Care of Unfinished Business," Proctor mentioned a documentary on South Africa that he watched. He told the congregation that some white children told the film crew that the Bible said that they were superior to blacks. Proctor did not see the Bible as an answer book. The Bible is a source for wrestling with the issues that present themselves to humankind.[23]

Proctor, troubled by a type of bibliolatry in the religious practices of some Christians, encouraged preachers to discover the Bible's real value. He worried that people were worshiping the book rather than the God of the book. Proctor noted that God existed before the Bible. Jesus lived and died before the gospels were written about him. The focus for preachers, therefore, should be on the encounter between God and humankind found in the pages of Scripture. While Proctor desired that preachers place a stronger emphasis on the Bible, he preferred that they adhere more to the substance of the Bible. Proctor did not believe that every practice that took place in ancient times could translate into twentieth-century life. He did feel that the ethical posture of Jesus is relevant in all times. In the hands of a competent preacher, the Bible could be a foundational source for resolving pandemic issues.[24]

Proctor continued to develop and articulate the biblical concepts and ideas that had their foundation in his religious journey. The historical-critical approach to the Bible did not hinder him from seeing in the Bible the God taught to him by his grandmother. Yet Proctor took from formal studies a

God who made sense in his experience. Proctor encouraged his congregation to read the Bible, telling them that it is a marvelous "spiritual resource." At the same time, he stated that there are times when people have to imagine "certain details" until the Holy Spirit fills in the information that the Bible does not cover. Proctor the preacher understood that the Bible was at the heart of the African American religious experience. He knew that it was a guiding document for the Black Church. His faith was not based upon the historical-critical methods alone. He built his faith within the nurturing home of Velma and Herbert Proctor, at the Bank Street Baptist Church in Norfolk, Virginia, and in his educational journey.

## God as Partner with Humanity

Further evidence of Proctor's religious-intellectual heritage exists in the writings and ideas that African American Christians expressed in the generations preceding him. While social gospel ideas and principles seem to be the more accessible language in Proctor's written work, African American Christians provided him with ideas that predated the formal social concepts he employed. Proctor was a liberal theist. Consider, as well, the racial environment in which Proctor lived. Benjamin Mays in his book *The Negro's God* exhibits the racial concerns in the theology of the "classical" writings of African Americans after 1914. Mays argued that black preachers and social commentators wrote about a God of equality. Their writings promoted an awareness of their racial identity—blackness—and discredited any claims about the inferiority of African Americans. Proctor embraced ideas and concepts that were prominent in the spirituals (e.g., the omniscient, omnipotent, omnipresent God). Without receiving the same label, many of the moral-ethical religious ideas in the spirituals were around much longer than those views proposed by liberal theological thought. God as immanent being is articulated in Benjamin Mays's summary of the content of several spirituals. Mays noticed in them that "God is near and there is a feeling of dependence upon Him."[25] Proctor's faith exhibited his belief in a God who lives in relationship and partners with humanity to bring about a moral order in the world.

Proctor believed in a God who has many roles and functions. In the introduction to his sermon "Thinking about God as Father," Proctor listed several ways in which the Bible describes God. He stated that the Bible speaks of God as creator, deliverer (e.g., Moses in Egypt and Daniel in the lion's den), comforter, father, and shepherd in the Psalms and gospels. Proctor claimed that persons give God these labels because these titles denote the ways in which they experience God.[26]

### *A World of Purpose: God as Creator*

At the foundation of Proctor's thoughts about God was God's creative purpose. Proctor affirmed that God created this world. God, Proctor contended, gave this world a purpose. God made this world and made it for a reason. And this world is the best one available to humanity. God is not hiding from humanity another world that is better than this one. Proctor remarked, "At the very beginning of my belief system stands the faith proposition that this world, planet earth, is the best one God could make for the purposes that God sought to accomplish."[27]

God not only made the world but its inhabitants as well. The idea of purpose made sense to Proctor, because God makes sense. The God of creation is an involved God who has good intentions for the world. God designed the world with a purpose in mind. This world is the one made for human beings, and it is equipped with what human beings need to live out God's purpose for it.

At the heart of Proctor's belief in God was the modernist theologian's concern for science, reason, and rationality. These tools were his resources for validating his experience(s) with God. His experiences with God were the bases for determining the truth of his beliefs. He highlighted this fact in his sermon "Trusting the Voice That Comes from Within":

> I would put this cognitive, rational test up front. I would not end with it. I would never say that all of my experience as a preacher has to be restricted to what is cognitive and what is rational. But, my soul, I would start with it because God is intelligent. God does not sponsor ignorance. It ought not to be self-contradictory. After all, God made logic. God made mathematics. He made chemistry and pharmacology, and music, and algebra, and medicine, and geology and astronomy. Now, would he tell me something that violates all of these things that he has already established in his world?[28]

For Proctor, God established (created) the world's laws and abides by them. God's law-abiding nature is a demonstration of God's intelligence, the manifestation of reason in the physical order of the world. One finds an example of the way in which Proctor reasoned through his understanding of God's law-abiding ways in that same sermon. Proctor spoke of a woman who asked him why God did not save the astronauts on the Challenger space shuttle in 1986:

> Some lady asked me the other day, who's been in church a long time, "Dr. Proctor, why would God let that capsule to explode and kill

> those seven people?" I said, well suppose God shut down all of the laws of energy, and heat, and flight, and gravity to save their lives when somebody did something careless or somebody did something unknowingly. Suppose God shut down all of the laws of physics, then, the hospitals would be out of equipment to heal the people all over the world. Airplanes would fall out of the sky all over the world. Three thousand flights taking off from airports all over America; have you any idea what you are asking God to do, to turn off the switch to save seven people while five billion more are depending on the regularity and constancy of His universe? God knows what He is doing.[29]

Proctor leaned on science and logic to filter his experiences of God. Proctor's theology is not deist by any means. God did not just lay down the laws of the world and leave it to run. Proctor's belief in the immanence and transcendence of God spoke to this concern.

### *An Immanent and Transcendent God*

When defining the immanence of God, Daniel S. Robinson states, "The consistent and ethical fundamental will of God pervades the world as a living force and . . . determines and guarantees a meaning and purpose for the development of the world."[30] This way of understanding the world is teleological in orientation. It differs from a cosmological approach that argues that the world is the effect of God as the First or Prime Cause. The tension between such views is a part of the debate that pits God's immanence against God's transcendence. Proctor sided with the teleological outlook. In his 1987 publication *Preaching about Crises in the Community*, Proctor wrote, "This is the good news—that God is more than a physical and chemical process, more than an ancient tribal deity, more than the answer to a metaphysical riddle, the resolution of a syllogism, or the first cause and prime mover of the universe. The good news is that God is infinite in wisdom, love and power. Besides being the monitor of the physical world, God is the guardian of the moral world. God is not distant and removed, but near and involved."[31] Proctor believed that God maintains a balance of activity on behalf of creation to collaborate with it and give it moral guidance.

Early seeds of this thinking are evident in a column Proctor wrote in 1947. He used similar language and posited, "God is the trustee of all righteousness and goodness. He is the monitor of the moral world."[32] The moral will of God "pervades" the world in such a way as to give guidance to the purpose that God seeks to accomplish. God is near. Proctor argued this point further in another column: "We do not feel that history is entirely in the hands of men. We believe explicitly that God regards the world enough to point the way to concord and harmony."[33] Before proceeding, clearly, the liberal theological tradition does not have a monopoly on this type of thinking. Proctor stated in an interview that black folks believe in the Providence of God. His view of Providence is such that God is at work in the world through persons who yield to the moral will of God. Incidentally, the same type of theology is echoed in the thought of Martin Luther King Jr. In his sermon "The Death of Evil upon the Seashore," King made his case for a God whose moral influence infuses the earth: "Above all, we must be reminded anew that God is at work in his universe. He is not outside the world looking on with a sort of cold indifference. Here on all the roads of life, he is striving in our striving. Like an ever-loving Father, he is working through history for the salvation of his children."[34] For Proctor too, the God who made the world out of nothing is at work in the world today.

To be sure, an understanding of God as immanent has a practical role in Proctor's thought. In his book *"How Shall They Hear?,"* Proctor identifies the need to preach about God's presence and activity in the world as a fundamental tenet in the sermon. Proctor believed that it is important to show that God is powerful and present in the affairs of humankind. Preaching is partially an act of bringing God's presence near to the listeners. Another way in which this happens is through prayer. Proctor stated in a sermon on that topic that prayer is a way in which persons stay connected to God. Birthed in the faith of the God of the spirituals, Proctor noted that prayer is simply one of the "traditional" aspects of his belief in God.

Proctor's belief system presupposed the transcendence of God. James Evans defined this transcendence as the freedom of God. For Proctor, God is not limited by time and space. God is everywhere; God is eternal. God's transcendence and immanence are expressed, for Proctor, in God's gift of freedom to human beings. Human beings reflect God's image in this manner. Practically, the transcendence of God is evident in several aspects of Christian belief. Proctor held that in worshiping God, the place is not nearly as important as the manner in which one worships. (God is not confined to a certain space.) Proctor felt that understanding God's presence in the world in this manner helps persons face the troubles that exist in it. For Proctor, a faith in God's presence and activity in the world is a "haven from the tempests of life."[35]

### *God as Personal Spirit: Partner in the Moral Success of the World*

Proctor embraced the idea of a righteous, just God who collaborates with human beings. Even if Proctor had not attended seminary and graduate school in the age of the social gospel and Boston Personalism, he would have known a God who works on behalf of the marginalized persons in society. Even before James Cone's groundbreaking work on black theology, Proctor's spiritual ancestry (African American Christianity) was such that he knew about a God of love who cares about black folk. Proctor's social and religious contexts were the incubators for his religious-ethical consciousness. Proctor was familiar with language that placed God on the side of marginalized humanity.

The social gospel assisted Proctor in revising his thoughts and language of a moral God who seeks the best for society. Through his mentors, Ellison and McKinney, Proctor received exposure to social gospel thinking as early as his undergraduate experience. Proctor also celebrated the influence of religious intellectuals such as Fosdick, Reinhold Niebuhr, Walter Rauschenbusch, and Elton Trueblood.[36] Biblically, Proctor identified with teachings of the eighth-century prophets and Jesus. Proctor sprinkled in the theme of the God of justice in most of his sermons. To be sure, the obstacle for the prophets and for Jesus was the ethical-spiritual decline of their communities. Proctor believed this to be the case with modern society as well. Proctor appropriated the themes of the Bible and held that God works with humankind to improve the world.

Two basic concerns about God in the face of an evil world are evident in Proctor's thought. He defined evil as "that condition that falls short of the good, that opposes the good, or that defies, threatens, jeopardizes, or defeats the good."[37] Proctor could not deny the presence of evil, for it is the "unfulfillment of the good that human beings desire." The first concern that Proctor identified was evil as enigma. He argued that human beings cannot explain the full extent of what takes place in the physical order (e.g., hurricanes, tornadoes, earthquakes). A second concern for Proctor was the freedom that God gives every human being. That freedom includes a proclivity for havoc. However, God did not intend for human beings to use this freedom in that manner. Proctor noted in a 1948 column that persons capitalize on evil: "Evil is organized today. Sin is rarely isolated, but rather it is commercialized and exploited. There is hardly any sin at all on which books have not been written, for which materials are not sold to make them practicable. . . . Men have become rich off the weaknesses of their brothers and sin is entrenched all the more deeply because of this widespread approval and monetary gain."[38]

The second idea represents the way Proctor explained racism. He viewed racism as an abuse of human freedom and power. It was an issue he experienced his whole life, firsthand and through watching events in society. Human beings contest God's will, but God's moral force pervades the world. For Proctor, God is not coercive; God is persuasive. God allows persons to assent to the will of God. The issue of a just and righteous God is born out of this notion of freedom. God did God's part, but humankind chooses not to comply with God's moral intentions for it. For in God's purpose for this world and humankind, God gives human beings help in fulfilling the purpose.[39] Placing Satan in a rivalry with God, then, is immature. Proctor acknowledged that Satan was considered a source of evil in ancient Jewish and Christian thought. Proctor claimed, however, that God does not have a competitor. The "devil" is a social construction that explains the places where good is absent in the world. While God is not the author of evil, God has purposes that human beings are too limited to perceive.

William R. Jones may come closest, in contemporary scholarship on African American theological thought, to framing a category that fits Proctor's theism: "humanocentric theism." Jones argues that humanocentric theism exalts the status of human beings. This theism promotes human freedom as a product of God's will for humanity. God grants codetermining power to human beings in order to accomplish God's will on earth. Human choice and responsibility are elevated while God's status of omnipotent being is revised. For example, God places the limits on God's participation in human affairs, thereby encouraging human freedom. God either can intervene directly or chooses not to do so. The alternative is a God that is powerless to intervene. The former is the case in humanocentric theism. God does become active in human affairs through persuasion. Proctor believed that God moves persons persuasively. Persons embrace God's will because they come to believe it is true—not because they have been forced to believe.[40]

While humanocentric theism places the bulk of responsibility on human beings, Proctor would not go so far. In his sermon "Beauty for Ashes,"[41] Proctor compared today's situation with the prophet Isaiah's world. Proctor noted the high incarceration rates of African American males and the poverty in which many children live as problems that should make concerned persons weep. Proctor preached that God will provide beauty for ashes, but humanity must do its part. The relationship is reciprocal: if you will, then God will. On many occasions, Proctor proclaimed that God would give persons the power to overcome the problems in their realities. When referring to racism in America,

Proctor listed countless persons who found that extra something on the inside (faith) to persevere. It is a power from God.

Proctor was consistent in his thinking on the matter of God's assistance. An example of this is in one of Proctor's notable sermon illustrations. Proctor wanted to help fix the eyes of a young man in rural North Carolina. He made a phone call to a professor of Christian ethics at Duke University, Waldo Beach, to help him find an ophthalmologist who would repair the boy's eyes free of charge. First, Proctor had to convince the mother that fixing the boy's eyes met God's approval. She felt that God had made him that way for a reason. Proctor countered that God had created the ophthalmologist for a reason. Beach secured the surgeons who performed the surgery, and the boy became another one of Proctor's biographical sermon examples of how God works with human beings for the good of humanity. Proctor preached, "Now I know that the world still has its problems. I couldn't feed every hungry child in India. I couldn't solve the problems of women's rights. I couldn't solve the civil rights problem. But God will take you as God took me, and focus you on something, and then test you and see what you're going to do with it."[42]

The highest example of this partnership between humankind and God is Jesus. The love of God, justice of God, and reality of God are on display in Jesus. In numerous sermons and reflections, Proctor maintained this thought. In his sermon "How Much Faith Is Enough," Proctor stated, "God is a just and righteous God. God has put order in His creation. God has shown His love for all humankind in sending Jesus in the world."[43] Proctor's God of creation became personal in the form of Jesus. The Trinitarian aspect of Proctor's thought becomes evident when moving toward an understanding of his thinking about Jesus. It is important, therefore, to continue the conversation by focusing on Jesus as a person of history.

## Jesus the Christ: The Historical-Ethical Revelation of God

Proctor understood Jesus to be the revelation of God, walking in flesh on the earth. To be sure, Proctor derived his understanding of an identity of Jesus from the biblical texts. Proctor found a way to harmonize the Jesus of orthodox Baptist beliefs with the Jesus of liberal theology. He reinterpreted those faith statements, aiming to awaken the moral consciousness of his congregation. He remained in the Abyssinian pulpit for seventeen years because he could translate well that synthesis of faith and ethics. Proctor believed that Jesus saves. The issue was how Jesus does it. Proctor merged the reality of a historical Jesus with the ethical purpose and function Jesus had as teacher of an enlightened way, the way of salvation.

Proctor emphasized a Jesus of history. In this capacity, Jesus was the revelation of God. Jesus showed humankind who God is and what God is to us. In his concern for a Jesus of history, Proctor looked to Jesus' example and teachings. Proctor reinterpreted issues like the divinity and mission of Jesus in light of Jesus' example and teachings. Jesus is *very* human in this model. In fact, Proctor did not have time for a Christ that inhabits unknown spiritual dimensions. The Hampton Minister's Conference lectures that Proctor presented in the late 1980s and early 1990s prove this point. Proctor felt that Christian ethics begins with the teachings and actions of Jesus. All aspects of the Christian life, Proctor contended, ought to fall in line with the life and teachings of Jesus.[44]

Proctor believed that Jesus was the "inexhaustible love" of God on display for human kind to see. Proctor maintained that one had not understood Jesus' divinity if one had not acknowledged the humanness of Jesus. For Proctor, Jesus was the revelation of God who came in flesh. In one sermon delivered to the Abyssinian congregation, he proclaimed:

> When the great architect of heaven set the plans for the universe and charted the boundaries of the seven continents and the seven seas, and when he drafted the anatomy of male and female and mixed the chemistry of life-giving blood and set the laws of physical and natural order and tuned the voice of the Lark and gave shape and speed to the Jaguar—when God gave rhythm to the tides of the mighty oceans and spattered his shining stars across the blackened sky, when he breathed into man a living soul, his wonderful word was with him. And in the fullness of time this Word became flesh and dwelt among us.[45]

The "Word" becoming flesh is a central concern for Proctor. He believed that Jesus' life was just as important as Jesus' death and resurrection. To an extent, this is a departure from Christian orthodoxy, especially Baptist beliefs. Proctor said that the church's leader (Christ) is not a "mysterious creature of the mind" but a "real person who set the pace for civilization." Proctor celebrated the social ethics of the biblical Jesus.

### *Jesus the Human Being*

The Bible provides enough information, in Proctor's view, for a person to learn about Jesus. As a biblical critic by training, Proctor was skeptical about the Jesus material that made it into the Bible. Concerning this material, he writes, "We will never know for certain, but, thank God, we have enough to give us the portrait of the life we honor as the Son of God."[46] Proctor used much of the gospels' material in developing his concept of Jesus. Early in his career as a pastor, he did a study on the Gospel of Mark to sketch the life of Jesus for his audience. His Easter columns in the *Providence Chronicle* newspaper focus on questions about resurrection and the divinity of Jesus. During the latter stage of his career, he used his Christmas sermons to examine the relationship of Jesus with his father Joseph. The point of the articles and the sermons was to focus on Jesus' development as a human being. The biography of Jesus, Proctor believed, was worth examining for these notions of human growth and spiritual development.[47]

Much of what Proctor presented about Jesus in lectures and sermons he taught from the perspective of human growth and development. Proctor saw the gospels as biographical material that display how Jesus interacted with people. A part of that biography attests to the fact that Jesus was born and Jesus died. Between these two events, Proctor stressed in sermons and talks, was a Jesus who self-identified with the messianic witness of Isaiah 9 and 53 and other passages in the Scriptures. Proctor believed that Jesus heard the Scriptures refer to the coming Messiah and concluded that he was the one. In other words, Jesus discerned his mission and purpose in the world. One finds an example of this line of thought in several of Proctor's sermons. He mentioned in his sermon "Jesus and the City" that Jesus was treated like a celebrity, upon riding into the city on a donkey. But Jesus understood the significance of his mission and did not let such treatment sway his ego. He remembered the words of the prophets and asked for the donkey when riding into the city. He was trying to convey a message to the people, Proctor preached. Jesus would not give in to the crowd's requests for a revolt. He was authentic, and he understood his identity and purpose more as he grew and matured.[48]

Proctor argued that Jesus had the type of surroundings that nurtured his intellectual-spiritual development. Jesus kept a close eye on life and translated it into his teachings. His parables included everyday circumstances, because these circumstances were a part of his daily existence. In 1991, Proctor stated, "He was human and divine, and this human part of the master was developed right there in Nazareth from the date of his birth until he was 30 years old and came forth to do the work of the Messiah."[49] Proctor held that Jesus received much of the truth that he learned in his home. Jesus took to heart the lessons on Mary's knee and in Joseph's carpentry shop. Throughout his career, Proctor remained consistent on this point. In a 1948 column, he wrote something very similar: "So, the real years of preparation are spent in unpublished, unheralded, undescribed [sic] scenes in Nazareth at the carpenter's bench. But undoubtedly Jesus was practicing and developing in his own mind and heart the ways of thinking and acting that he would later proclaim to the world."[50] Jesus did not have a formal education as a scribe. He did not learn in the school of the Pharisees. Proctor concluded that Jesus gained a spiritual foundation from family devotions and watching human interactions closely. Jesus learned his place in the world from his family, his environment, as all human beings do.[51]

Proctor believed that Jesus as a human being and historical figure experienced life as all human beings experience it. From the manger on, Jesus faced the celebrations and struggles that come with being human. Proctor argued in one Lenten sermon that Jesus never tried to hide his humanity. In the moments leading to the cross, Proctor noted, Jesus showed the human side of his nature. He cried. Jesus was hungry, thirsty, and tired. Jesus encountered temptations. Proctor also preached that when Jesus came, he came as a child, not as an adult, imperial, military leader. God came and entered time in the form of a child. This meant that God intended for Jesus to be acquainted with humanity in all of its raw details. Sickness, hunger, thirst, and heartache were all his to know. To be humankind's savior, he had to experience what human beings experience. Proctor felt that Jesus must have had a hard life; people were always trying to snare him in matters of the law.[52] Related to this concern for Jesus' humanity was Proctor's belief in the resourcefulness of all human beings. This topic will receive more attention in the next chapter. Yet one may already see the trajectory in which this reasoning points: if Jesus can do it, so can every other human being. Jesus was flesh and blood, a free moral agent.

Jesus was a free person. Proctor argued that God did not make Jesus do what he did. In other words, Jesus' life was not determined for him. Jesus had to choose between the care of his family and the mission of God. God chose Jesus for the work that Jesus did. Yet Jesus did not have to accept God's path for his life. God did not force the job on Jesus. Proctor made the case for this in a sermon in 1987. He stated that many people believe that Jesus had no choice in the matter of being the Messiah. Proctor felt that persons could argue this point either way, depending on what Scripture passage(s) they used. He chose to look at passages like the scene in which Jesus asked that the cup pass from him as a sign of Jesus' choice to be the Messiah. Proctor believed that Jesus earned the authority of his messianic title. Jesus refused the temptations of the devil and exhibited the type of authenticity that God cherishes. God made Jesus the savior. Proctor declared, "God did not force this Messiahship on Him. God let Him meet Him halfway." The same strand of thinking is clear in Proctor's earlier reflections. As early as 1949, Proctor wrote, "So see this problem of Jesus in light of human experience. It was a bitter choice to make. But he had to select his course, the safe way his family wanted for him, or the hazardous way that brought him to Calvary."[53]

In 1948, Proctor wrestled with the question "Did He Have to Do It?" Proctor questioned whether Jesus had to die in order for God to save humanity. Proctor presented two theses. First, he argued that Jesus fought for the moral supremacy he commanded. Second, Proctor stated, the kind of life that Jesus led ends in crucifixion (martyrdom). The social gospel influence is evident in the way that Proctor supported this point. Proctor noted that Jesus was fighting "powerful 'lobbies' and big interests." In the same column, Proctor claimed that Jesus was not ignorant of the consequences of the life he led. Proctor believed that Jesus faced special-interest groups that preferred silencing Jesus over letting him continue his radical ministry. For Proctor, Jesus was smart enough to know that he was meddling in the affairs of such powerbrokers:

> Now Jesus must have known this. It is elementary, the first axiom of a social life. This is why I feel that he was going to this cross under the pressure of his own faith in God and love of Man. I think he could have avoided it had he been weak enough. . . . He did it because he was yet under the sway of God's high purpose. And I love him all the more because he might have turned back but he did not. He is my Saviour because he gave his life for me, not because it was taken from him over his protest. Hallelujah!![54]

Proctor was concerned about the functional faith of his parishioners, of Christians in general. He did not have to split the academic from the pastoral. He touted a "commonsense" faith. To be sure, the views stated in the preceding quotation were not "orthodox" in the black Baptist fellowship. Those views are the influence of exposure to the "progressive" thought of the age. He was refining his theology at an early stage and developing a Christology that strayed from the doctrines implicit in the faith of many Baptist believers.

Proctor saw in Jesus the perfect presentation of moral living. For in Jesus, Proctor saw the personality of God. The traits that bore this contention were evident in the life of Jesus. He was the paragon of ethical living. Proctor called him the "humble Galilean." In Jesus, Proctor maintained, one finds the moral guide. This guide taught and practiced the best of what is found in the moral philosophies of the ages. Proctor believed that Jesus demonstrated the moral obedience that God required of humanity: "Jesus demonstrated simplicity, trustworthiness, honesty, and truthfulness *as well as* compassion, tenderness, and love with initiative."[55] Jesus' humility was such that he submitted his goals and desires to God's will. The notion of authenticity, for Proctor, describes Jesus' approach toward God and humankind. Jesus understood his abilities, his potential, and he chose to let God use him for God's purposes. In yielding to the will of God, Jesus demonstrated his moral superiority.

When Proctor preached during a mission tour (for the Baptist World Alliance) in Russia, he made sure to emphasize the virtue of Jesus. In one sermon, Proctor recalled his interaction with the tour guide on this trip. She stated that she and her friends did not know much about Christianity and were unimpressed by what they did know. With that in mind, Proctor decided to preach the narratives about Jesus at the churches his mission group visited. Proctor wanted to persuade the tour guide of Christianity's credibility. At the end of the tour, Proctor asked her what she thought about the preaching she heard from the group. She told Proctor she thought Jesus was a marvelous person. Proctor the gospel preacher understood the importance of Jesus the Christ as a moral exemplar. This message was a primary thread in Proctor's thought. In an approach typical of the liberal theological education of his time, Proctor promoted the image of Jesus as a virtuous person.

Proctor held that Jesus' freedom helped him transcend his religious traditions. The ancient systems of Jewish thought did not limit Jesus' teachings and religious practices. Jesus was not wedded to old systems of Judaism. Proctor believed that Jesus understood the changing complexities of circumstances. Proctor stated in the column "Manger Religion" that Jesus grew into a "religious radical."[56] This radicalism was the product of an ethical monotheism. Jesus discerned what people needed—to repent. Proctor stated that this was the message John preached, and Jesus signed up for that movement when John baptized him. This Jesus was the model that Proctor pressed upon his listeners.

Proctor challenged ideas that painted an otherworldly view of Jesus. Proctor noted that Jesus had too much concern for the affairs of this life. Jesus was a problem solver for the men, women, and children who experienced the situations of this world. In seeing Jesus as a moral figure, Proctor found the comfort zone of his Christian faith. Proctor embraced a public Christ with a public mission, a public faith. Proctor appreciated who Jesus was as a person in history. The stories about Jesus' life vouched for his status as savior, in Proctor's perspective.[57]

### *Jesus the Christ of God*

The topic of Jesus as Christ did exist in Proctor's thought. One gathers that Proctor did not distinguish the historical figure from a mythical Christ of faith.

Proctor saw in Jesus a cure to the human problem of sin. That is, human beings alienate themselves from God. To solve this problem, Proctor argued, persons need a relationship with God. Christ accomplishes this objective. Proctor believed that Christ led the way for persons to live in relationship with God because of how he lived and what he taught. Proctor summarized the matter in a tract on the ordinances of the Baptist church. In a section of the tract on the importance of the Lord's Supper, he reflects the basic belief that he held about the salvation that Christ offers: "This fellowship about the table is distinctive because we have not gathered around an idea, not around a book, not at a certain level of moral attainment, but we have gathered to remember a person who shared our common humanity while at the same time pointed us to God."[58] He goes on to write that the one who "seemest human and divine" exemplified the love of God to marginalized persons.

Proctor argued that the main aspects of Jesus' saving ministry were his teachings and his example. Jesus communicated the identity of God through his life and teachings. Proctor's view of Jesus was social and ethical. Jesus as Christ was the personality of God incarnate. He was the example and ethical paradigm of what God expects from humanity. Proctor is in the tradition of mid-twentieth-century black religious intellectuals who embraced the importance of Jesus' humanity and his teachings for humanity. Consider John M. Ellison's words about Jesus:

> Jesus had that kind of insight into the meaning of humanity. He had that profound awareness of God and man's relationship to God, and God's high purposes for all men. He wanted that conviction with His disciples and all of His followers in any age. Deep in His heart He carried the vision of what humanity could be if only the vital relationship between man and God could be established. And He had the profound conviction that it could be done. Toward that glorious ideal and goal all of His life's work and teachings were aimed.[59]

Proctor argued that the goal of Jesus' teachings was relationship. Proctor noted, "His teachings were aimed at bringing men into sonship to God."[60] Jesus directed his teachings to all who listened, but he had a special concern for the "lowly and outcast."[61] In 1947, Proctor wrote that a theme of Jesus' message was that justice and peace should supersede "greed and conflict." Proctor believed in the social-ethical gospel depiction of Jesus. In *My Moral Odyssey*, Proctor testifies:

> Among the beliefs in my faith structure is the conviction that Jesus is uniquely given to us as the Bright and Morning Star, the Lily of the Valley, and the Rose of Sharon, the anointed One. This is not only because of the record but because of the self-authenticating nature of his teachings and his example. When we put to the test—to any test whatever—what he taught and how he lived it turns out that it is the only way for us to proceed in our personal lives or as a people, a society, or a nation without chaos and self-destruction. . . . Indeed, Jesus is the way, the truth, and the life. And to believe in something so abstract and amorphous as the eternal love of God for lepers, children who are epileptic, beggars, habitual sinners, and thieves to the extent that one would suffer death on a cross, transcends all of the cheap and convenient compromises by which we live and causes him to hold such a victory over this mortal corruption that he leads us all in triumph over death and the grave, marching off the edge of time into eternal life.[62]

Proctor refers to Jesus as the Master for many reasons. Proctor believed Jesus to be the one who lived life to its fullest by embracing God's design for his life. Jesus' teachings and example reflect his mastery of the ethical mandate of God. What Proctor stated on several occasions he maintained throughout his public career: Jesus' teachings are axiomatic.

At a pastor's conference in Ohio in 1989 (and at the Riverside Church in the same year), Proctor preached a sermon entitled "The First Coming of Christ." He argued that persons should value and focus on the contributions that Christ made in his first coming. He suggested that a notion of Jesus' ministry that focuses on heaven is escapism. Proctor preached that Jesus brought the world to a new attitude toward the poor and homeless. The work Jesus did gave dignity and renewal to harlots and sinners. Jesus' message and example made God real to the masses and challenged the dead religion of the time. Proctor remarked that Jesus took the old commandments and made a new religion out of them. For Proctor, Jesus brought the creator God of Genesis, the shepherd of the Psalms, and the King of Glory "nearer than breathing, closer than hands and feet."[63] Proctor followed these claims by reminding the group that Jesus did all of this and then said, "Greater works than these shall you do" (John 14:12).

The Christ that Proctor had in mind was not a mythical end-times character in the traditional sense. Jesus as Christ is historical. For Proctor, the "essence" of Jesus' life and teachings was service to others. Proctor saw Jesus as the person who presents the embodiment of the kingdom of God. Jesus' goal was to preach the kingdom of God and display the conduct that God requires of the humanity. Stating his beliefs about Jesus, Proctor remarked that Jesus used "much" of his brief ministry to proclaim this kingdom. Proctor contended that persons enter this kingdom by embracing the mind and example of Christ. In other words, Proctor saw Jesus' religion as one that focused on societal concerns—God would take care of heaven. For Proctor, Jesus was a prophet of love and compassion. At the Abyssinian Church, Proctor proclaimed:

> You know, my friends, this is my type of Christianity. I must tell you, I am much more at home talking about Jesus sitting down with Simon the leper than I am at home talking about heaven and all of these things. Heaven is going to take care of itself! (Isn't that right?) You don't have to deal with that; God does the bookkeeping about that. I don't need to be frightening and threatening you about what is going to happen to you when you die. I am much more at home telling you about how Jesus found Simon's house and sat down and had dinner with him.[64]

Proctor saw Jesus through this lens. Jesus was a social agent of change. Proctor interpreted the social change that Jesus brings in a broad manner. Jesus' teachings were instructive for human beings to relate to God; he did not teach merely for the sake of social reform. Proctor believed that Jesus' priority for humanity is holistic. As with most of the theology of the liberal era, Proctor's focus on a social Christ *seemed* to deny the spiritual side of Christianity. But Proctor saw spirituality in light of an ethical relationship. If one loved God, one expressed it in one's social relationships. Social interaction was, for Proctor, a reflection of the development of one's relationship with God.

The ultimate good for humanity, in Proctor's religious perspective, does not end in traditional ideas about Jesus' death. Proctor argued in several media that Jesus empowers human beings to live on a higher moral plane. His being, his life gives persons the possibility of human fulfillment. Christ points persons to a power beyond themselves. He connects them with the power of God. As the personality of God, Jesus as Christ knows the way to God and teaches it, lives it.

Proctor believed that God loved us enough to get into action on our behalf through Christ. "God wanted us to have something to go by, something to guide us, and gave God's own personality in human form; so that we would know which way to go and how to conduct the affairs of life," Proctor preached.[65] What persons saw in Jesus was the power to overcome the status quo of life. Proctor's messages to his congregation promoted this belief. He delivered to his members a Christ that affirmed their humanity, set their priorities in order, and gave them access to the "inexhaustible power" of a living God. A summary of his beliefs are reflected in a 1947 column. Proctor noticed that Pontius Pilate missed what others saw in Jesus: "He ought to have seen how many people there were who saw God in his countenance and found salvation in his being."[66]

Questions arise from Proctor's belief in this "mysterious" power that Christ gives his believers. What is this power? In what ways does it manifest itself? Proctor held that Christ offered the power to control one's passions, one's urges. Proctor did not deny the reality of sin. He understood that human beings have complex drives and "glandular urges" that influence the decisions that persons make. Yet Christ gives persons the power to rein in such desires. How then did Christ save the world? Proctor proclaimed a Jesus who saves by love. The greatest expression of that love was in the life he led. He loved so much that his life ended on a cross. The power of the cross, for Proctor, is in the life that Jesus led. One gleans from that power, by interpreting that life and death, how one can live a life that is pleasing to God.[67] Proctor contended that a new birth results from the power that Christ confers. A Christian believer reorients herself to embrace the consciousness that Christ makes available.[68]

Proctor did not lay claim to all of the traditional propositions of the Christian faith. It is clear that he did not believe in bodily resurrection. He described resurrection as something that is for the "here and now." He wrote that resurrection is a new life in the spirit that is eternal. The real life that one has in God is eternal, without flesh as its "cloak." For example, in a 1949 column, "Dead Jesus or Living Christ," Proctor stated that Jesus would have been merely an honorable man if not for the "fresh revelation of his spirit" that followed the Passion Week. In an earlier column, he wrote, "Had not the report of the risen Christ spread abroad, he would have been regarded as just another good prophet crucified."[69] Later in life, Proctor continued to be careful about how he described resurrection:

> He was indeed crucified. Other historians of the day testified to his crucifixion, but only the Christian sources speak of a physical resurrection, the post-resurrection appearances, and an ascension into space. All of this is a stumbling block to the twentieth-century mind that is given to scientific verification of facts, the empirical method, and unvarying, natural law. . . .
>
> The resurrection was recorded years after the event. The church had

> begun, and stories of Jesus' life circulated orally. Many were rejected by the church as ill-founded. Nevertheless, there was a resurrection. Christ's presence was known.[70]

Proctor further explained the stories of resurrection by describing the actions of the disciples to justify the proof of Christ's resurrection. Moving from the seminary into the pastorate, Proctor seemed to hold back on sharing the skepticism of his formal theological education. The later Proctor does not really touch upon the issue of resurrection in much of his writings and numerous sermons. He has one of those "twentieth-century minds" that looked to science for what it offered on many subjects—including Jesus. Jesus the Christ, therefore, is a historical figure whose ministry was social, ethical, and spiritual. Proctor revised the meaning of the latter category.

## The Holy Spirit and Moral Energy

Proctor finds himself squarely in the Baptist theological camp when referring to the Holy Spirit. Like most Baptists, Proctor did not say much, publicly, about the Holy Spirit. It is the least developed aspect of his writings and sermons, lacking detail and articulation. He did, nevertheless, see the Holy Spirit as the agent that transforms human consciousness for the moral life.

Proctor defined the Holy Spirit as that spirit which gives divine energy to do what is pleasing to God. Human beings partner with the Holy Spirit to do the work that God requires of them. Proctor stated that the generations and cultural norms would change, but the Holy Spirit gives persons guidance concerning ethical issues. The Spirit guides persons' moral direction. Persons who follow the Spirit walk in God's will, Proctor contended. He argued, "Morality based on obedience to the Holy Spirit cannot be any higher, provided it is the Holy Spirit that one is obeying. . . . Indeed *if* it is God's Holy Spirit and *if* it conforms to God's revelation in Jesus, no higher moral direction could be found."[71]

The issue of the Spirit for Proctor is functional. Proctor drew a line between the ritual practices of religion and its fullest expression in the Holy Spirit. Proctor did not concede the Spirit's actions to ecstatic or "Pentecostal" practices. Proctor did not minimize those practices, but he believed that the Spirit has another way of operating. The Spirit, for Proctor, is God's personality "invading" the soul of Christ. In his writings about Communion in the Baptist church, Proctor made this designation clearer: "The Holy Spirit is the New Testament term used for the nearness of God which men knew and felt especially after they had found God in Jesus. Strictly speaking, then, it is that person of the Trinity which is nothing more than God known in personal, intimate fellowship."[72]

The Holy Spirit for Proctor is both conscience and consciousness. The Spirit is the way in which one embodies the teachings and actions of Jesus. The Spirit makes persons aware of the personality that God desires of them. Proctor highlighted this point in his lecture at the 1989 Hampton University Ministers' Conference, entitled "Is Respectability Enough?" He stated that persons could have numerous kinds of spirits. He joked that he caught the spirit watching the Los Angeles Lakers play the Detroit Pistons on television, but it was not the Holy Spirit! The Holy Spirit leads persons to do moral, right actions.[73] Proctor did not connect the Spirit's work to a mechanical form of inspiration. He did not see the Spirit as that thing that made the biblical writers produce their texts. He decried the idea that God used the biblical authors in robotic fashion. The Spirit, he held, is revelation and inspiration in that it makes clear what God requires from persons. Persons choose to embrace this power. The Spirit moved in Christ and revealed the personality of God. The Spirit does the same work for persons in this age and ages to come.

## The Church as Advocate for Society

Proctor accepted a model of church and ministry that combines the social and the spiritual in Christianity. In the days of his first pastorate, Proctor detailed the task of the church as "spreading the gospel of peace and redemption throughout all the world."[74] The ministry of the church was twofold for Proctor. The church has its social aspect: taking care of the widows, orphans, the sick, and the poor. Proctor also understood the church to be the community that leads persons to the power that Christ bestows. Proctor noted that the church is the people among whom a belief in Christ as Lord is celebrated. The physical structure in which the people worship is a monument to that faith in Christ. Proctor's focus for church life was practical. As a pastor, he was concerned about paying light bills and bringing in persons for membership. And his activism for a Fair Employment Act in 1940s Providence, Rhode Island, displayed his sense of the political responsibility of the church. He served in governmental and ecclesial posts. He used his ministry to define the ideal of church-state relations. For Proctor, this country allows for the influence of people, religious or not, who commit to engaging in debate about the common good.

Proctor was a realist in his expectations for the church. He understood that the church consists of persons who inhabit two realms. While persons are engaged in the affairs of the church, they are also committed to political parties and labor unions. At a 1966 conference in Richmond, Virginia, Proctor questioned whether persons should blame the church for its lack of influence on society when persons spend merely one to two hours in worship to "reverse the remainder of the week."[75] He was cautious of placing the blame for societal problems on the church's inaction. He stated in the 1966 talk that a secular humanism was taking over. Yet he argued that persons in churches have many reasons for being in them. He reasoned that religious persons with social concerns can manifest them in the totality of their lives. In other words, religious persons can show themselves faithful in the different communities of their lives by practicing their beliefs in these communities.

The focus of his definition of church did not change later in his career. His critique of a universal church became more pointed as African Americans pushed for equality during the civil rights age. He challenged the post-segregation Black Church to do more for its constituents. The more he noticed the decline in the success of African Americans, the more he felt that African American churches misdirected their focus. Implied in his criticism of the Black Church was an indictment of its inward turn. He argued that the churches were spending too much time serving those who were already comfortable and integrated into American life:

> We do have churches that are creatively reaching out to save and to serve those most marginal in our communities, but from where I stand it appears that we need a meeting like this badly. We need to come together and ask ourselves what is going to happen to our people if we continue to spend our ministry on those who are already imbued with the mind of Christ, self-directed, who have already pledged to support education, who already vote, who already own their homes, who have Visa cards and Hondas, who give to the NAACP and the UNCF, who get their teeth repaired on time and who have a Blue Cross card in their wallets.[76]

Proctor wanted to see the church in action to correct some, if not all, of the problems in society. He saw the black preacher and the Black Church as the person and institution to accomplish the task. Proctor believed that the church could improve the conditions of the black community. He saw a large segment of the black community experiencing the dismay of social disorder. The black community was a focus of his ministry as an African American preacher and a focus of the church he led. He never changed his stance on the responsibility of the church. The 1966 talk showed that he did not want the church measured by the same standards as other agencies and institutions, but he still considered the church responsible for marginalized members of society. The church remained responsible for people's well-being, social and spiritual. With his view of the church being so socially oriented, the interaction between the church and the state in his thought were inevitable.

Proctor cautioned audiences that problems could come from the church being too involved with politics. In 1981, he addressed several church-state concerns in a talk on the matter. He believed that one of the great benefits of a democratic system of government is that the country has charter documents that screen any "enthusiastic messiahs." The American charter excludes the country and its leaders from favoring certain religions. These documents reflect a system of values and moral priorities. (Proctor said these values derive from the teachings of religion, mainly the teachings of the Old Testament.) Every person has one vote and freedom of speech. The country abides by a notion of freedom of the press. This allows religious institutions to spread their influence across the land as well as other persons or institutions.

Proctor clearly defined what he believed the role of the church to be in light of the presence of secular government. He stated, "The role of the church, therefore, is not static and passive; that's not the kind of separation that we are talking about. But it is dynamic and active. There is a synergistic activity [sic], relationship between church and state."[77] He was conscious of the fact that religious groups should work through the processes established by the founding documents. He argued, "It is a violation of both the letter and the spirit of the bill of rights for any sectarian interest or any combination of sectarian interests to attempt to circumvent or destroy the privileges, protections, immunities, and liberties of the constitution in order to impose a particular view on the country." Proctor said he was confused about the term "moral majority," referring to Jerry Falwell and his organization. He asked, "When has the majority been moral?" He held that religion must find its way through the courts and legal establishment to allow its influence to enter society. The church and the state, he claimed, should operate in a symbiotic relationship. They can work to accomplish the same goals.

Proctor also saw problems created by the relationship between church and state. He believed that even though persons cherish the notion of the separation of church and state, it has not had the type of success persons envisioned it to have. For example, several preachers become renowned for having breakfast at the White House. Such a relationship between clergy and government officials might force preachers not to question the immoral acts of government. Both church and state idolize the rich and the powerful, Proctor held. State and church, he argued, acquiesce to interests of money and power.

In practical terms, the lines between church and state have blurred. Another example of this was the way in which churches built schools to continue segregation, he claimed. These schools became private schools or academies to keep the government from integrating white children with black children in the public schools. Proctor disapproved of the fact that many private colleges built by churches were upholding segregation longer than the state colleges and universities. He maintained that the church should be the moral and spiritual remnant in the world set aside to redeem the state. He continued by noting that the church should be the conscience of the state, not its echo. Proctor was concerned that the church did not accept its role as something other, a morally transcendent community in a world of conflict. These words summarize that concern:

> If the state must be preoccupied with defense, then we should be preoccupied with peace. If the state is preoccupied with inflation, stock markets, interest rates, and money funds, we should be preoccupied with building up an awareness of a simpler life with less clutter and less thickful [sic] consumerism. If the state is preoccupied with more jails, we should be preoccupied with changing lives from within. If the state is busy giving tests to prove that some students can't learn, we should be busy seeing to it that they are taught and that they do learn. We should be the conscience of the state, not its echo, not its sycophant, not its honor guard.[78]

Proctor believed that the church can be in dialogue with the state. He contended that the church's influence can lead the state to implement person-oriented service programs. What Proctor meant by this is that a group of persons that understands what God expects from the church can influence the larger society. Proctor highlighted the gestures of the Theodore Adams of the First Baptist Church in Richmond. Adams provided a job for one of Proctor's brothers during a time in which race relations were unsteady. He also talked about the example of Sparks White Melton, the local Norfolk pastor who gave Proctor books and provided him with a scholarship to Crozer Seminary. In segregated Norfolk, Melton opened the doors of his predominantly white congregation to the Bank Street members when their building burned. Proctor saw these persons as signs in which "the church within the church" operated. That true church can live in the symbiotic relationship between the church and the state. The true church abides by the standards of God's kingdom, not the influence of the larger society. He cited the work with Crossroads Africa of Dr. James H. Robinson (1907–1972) from the Harlem Presbyterian Church. Proctor stated that Robinson's idea led to the formation of the Peace Corps. Proctor also cited Hull House in Chicago and its influence on the birth of the social work movement.

Proctor believed that individuals can cross between the two entities. He felt that it is proper for a Christian to take up jobs in which there is a need among state institutions. He cited his record of accomplishments as an example. His time at North Carolina A&T State University reflected this dynamic. He was president of a state school, fulfilled commitments in churches, and took leave to work on behalf of the U. S. government. The fact is that this symbiosis is an ever-present reality. Persons occupy both worlds, religious and secular. Religious persons do live in two realities. The same people, unregenerate or regenerate, make up the church and the state. Proctor said he was a citizen of the state and a citizen of God's kingdom, all at the same time.

A final consideration is the church's more obvious ministry, worship. Proctor did not restrict the church's ministry to social outreach and justice. He was a pastor who had the responsibility of leading his congregation in worship. From this experience came an appreciation for what takes place in the life of the church through worship. Proctor believed worship to be a primary way in which the church expresses itself. (Although conscious of racial differences in worship settings, Proctor struggled with defining "black worship.") He warned Abyssinian that church could become too much of a social club if its members did not take time in worship to reflect upon the faith that it shares in Jesus. Although he did not believe that the practices of the church have power in and of themselves, he believed that one's heart and soul must change to understand the value of the church's ministry. He expressed this sentiment in his memoir. He stated that he contended with a bunch of "street prophets" about Abyssinian's purchase of a $250,000 organ. The group told Proctor they could have used the money to buy food for persons in the streets. He reasoned with them that one meal could not match the value of the experience persons had in worship, listening to the beautiful music the organ played.[79]

## Liberalism and a Black Social Gospel Proponent

A few concerns arise from Proctor's commitment to liberal theology. He did not interrogate or advance beyond theological liberalism. Proctor was not a professional academic. Proctor was a public theologian/intellectual. He did not keep up with current scholarship in Christian theology. This is somewhat problematic based upon much of the white liberal tradition's silence on the fundamental issue that occupied Proctor's thought: racism. And he never called out liberal theology for its shortcomings on the issue. While liberal theologians including Rauschenbusch and Fosdick were critical of poverty and labor issues, their stances against racism in their writings and sermons amounted to lip service.[80] Proctor continued to celebrate, uncritically, their contributions to Christian thought. He was openly critical, however, of the language of black theology.

A second concern is the issue of method in biblical studies. Proctor leaned heavily upon the historical-critical methods. But he did not advance with the changing literature and scholarship in this area. He broadened his reading list beyond theology and religious studies post seminary. For example, in a 1991 lecture at the Hampton Ministers' Conference, Proctor referred the audience to a book published in 1938, *The Mission and Message of Jesus*.[81] He showed no real signs, late in his career, of keeping up with the literature in theology. But he could talk cogently about John Rawls's *Theory of Justice*. For one who accepted the principles of the liberal era of theology, Proctor had little context for entering conversations in late-twentieth-century Christian scholarship outside of his praxis and dusty bibliography. He could not, therefore, be an impartial critic of black theology and other contemporary theological developments. He was a public theologian whose interests were social and pastoral, not academic per se.

Samuel D. Proctor's theology is the consequence of his theological foundation. He was a black Baptist who matured in the Black Church and the liberal theological tradition. While his early theological experiences were formed by an Afro-Baptist context, he appropriated much of the conceptual framework and language of his theological education. He inherited the Baptist concerns for separation of church and state and the emphasis on the New Testament. His concern for the Afro-Baptist environment was evident throughout his career. The same applies to his appropriation of modernism and emphasis on the social gospel. Seeing himself as a bridge figure, he synthesized theology with his experiences and developed his own voice. The evidence is clearer in his response to the issue of race. For in matters of race, a "Christian" concern for humanity informed by the intellectual influences of his religious development come to the fore of Proctor's public faith.

## Notes

1. See chapter 1 for information about the development of Proctor's racial consciousness. Although intellectual turning points took place during his education at Virginia Union University, Crozer Theological Seminary, and Boston University School of Theology, he received his

foundational lessons on religion and race early in his life. The Black Church experience nurtured him, and he embraced his role as a "race man." He fought, moreover, for African Americans to have the same opportunities that America promised all of its citizens. As an evangelical black preacher who preached the gospel, he was well received at African American congregations all over America. As a preacher, Proctor had the ability to communicate in the environment that produced him and was able to employ the fruits of his formal education in this setting. To be sure, Proctor received numerous honors and spoke in several academic institutions that had large white populations. His popularity among persons of all races is a testament to his understanding of people. He attended reputable institutions and was able to speak fluently and freely among the "elite" and the "ordinary."

2. Proctor received some of his earliest exposure to social gospel language from persons like mentors John Malcus Ellison and Richard McKinney. Ellison's theological concerns were social and his activism in line with this as well. Ellison's numerous publications address problems in the world. A well-read theologian in his own right, Ellison was a primary filter for Proctor's thoughts on theology and society. Their relationship was very close for years, as Proctor worked for President Ellison as a college student and became his colleague after returning from graduate school. McKinney was instrumental in Proctor's vocational path.Concerning the Boston school of Personalism, Proctor may have acquired some of the language and theological constructs while attending the school. I do not think, however, that he intentionally tried to master Personalism as a theological system. Proctor was not that type of theologian. It is more likely that he gravitated to some of the concepts and ideas because Personalism was a part of the theological landscape in liberal seminaries and graduate schools. He rarely quoted his sources in his writings, so it is hard to credit the Boston University School of Theology for much more than his degree. In his biographical writings, he talked more about his year at Yale than he did about Boston.

3. For an overview of Baptist beliefs, see William H. Brackney, ed., *Baptist Life and Thought, 1600–1980* (Valley Forge, PA: Judson, 1983); Bill J. Leonard, *Baptists in America* (New York: Columbia University Press, 2005); Bill J. Leonard, *Baptist Ways: A History* (Valley Forge, PA: Judson, 2003).For works that deal with the topic of Afro- or African American Baptist history, experience, and beliefs, see Walter F. Pitts, *Old Ship of Zion: The Afro-Baptist Ritual in the African Diaspora* (New York: Oxford University Press, 1993); Mechal Sobel, *Trabelin' On: The Slave Journey to an Afro-Baptist Faith* (Princeton: Princeton University Press, 1988); Leroy Fitts, *A History of Black Baptists* (Nashville: Broadman, 1985); Peter J. Paris, *The Social Justice Teachings of the Black Churches* (Philadelphia: Fortress Press, 1985); James D. Tyms, *The Rise of Religious Education Among Negro Baptist* (New York: Exposition, 1965).More work may be necessary on the topic of black Baptist beliefs. Anthony Pinn does this in a much broader way by describing the beliefs of the "Black Church" in his book *The Black Church in the Post–Civil Rights Era* (Maryknoll, NY: Orbis, 2002). Others have examined African American beliefs and practices as expressed in the denominational statements of the established conventions. That was the case in Peter Paris's study. James D. Tyms researched the educational material that circulated among the African American Baptist churches from the late nineteenth century to the mid-twentieth century. Tyms traced the development of religious education among African American Baptists. By analyzing the literature used for Christian education among African Americans, Tyms identified ways in which the materials helped African American Baptists forge their identity. Another source may be the biographies of black Baptists. It is here that some persons make mention of and value the Easter speeches and Christmas plays of their Sunday church school experience.

4. Leonard, *Baptists in America*, 64.

5. Pinn, *The Black Church in the Post–Civil Rights Era*, 44.One can see this critical approach to the Bible at work in statements like those of Howard Thurman's grandmother. She did not want Thurman to read from Paul's epistles. Slave owners used the epistles to sanction slavery as a Christian institution. See also Howard Thurman, *Jesus and the Disinherited* (Nashville: Abingdon, 1949; Boston: Beacon, 1976, 1996); James H. Cone, *A Black Theology of Liberation* (Philadelphia: Lippincott, 1970).

6. See Tyms, *The Rise of Religious Education among Negro Baptists.* Tyms has a whole section that analyzes the content in black Baptist Sunday school material from 1896 to 1961.I contend that Baptist theology can be somewhat light when dealing with issues of pneumatology. Of course, the same may be the case for many Protestant denominations that are not "Pentecostal" in orientation.

7. Virginia Union was a Baptist college. It was a college sponsored by black and white Baptists. Therefore, one could argue that he did not really leave the Baptist tradition by going to Virginia Union. Crozer found itself in the liberal theological tradition. It had a reputation for being a liberal school. Although it was Baptist, it was far from the traditional Baptist Sunday school.

8. Samuel D. Proctor, "What Makes Holy Ground?," sermon presented at Union Theological Seminary, Richmond, 1986, UTS-PSCE, audiotape. See also, Samuel D. Proctor, "Evil: The Unfulfillment of the Good," in *Facing Evil*, ed. Paul Woodruff and Harry A. Wilmer (LaSalle, IL: Open Court, 1988), 212.

9. While some authors distinguish between what is a liberal theologian and what is a modernist theologian, I contend that much of the issue resides in self-identification. Many modernists and liberal theologians approached their work with similar views. Moreover, much of the literature on liberal and modernist theologians lists the same figures. I will use these terms interchangeably, understanding that there are subtypes and characteristics specific to the two groups. The idea of self-identification in this epoch of liberal theology is important. See Charles Harvey Arnold, "The Terminology of American Religious Liberalism, 1876–1939," *American Journal of Theology and Philosophy* 1, no. 2 (1980): 45–59. For studies on liberal theology and its age, see Sydney Ahlstrom, *A Religious History of the American People* (New Haven: Yale University Press, 1972); Lloyd J. Averill, *American Theology in the Liberal Tradition* (Philadelphia: Westminster, 1967); William Dean, *American Religious Empiricism* (New York: State University of New York, 1986); Gary Dorrien, *The Making of American Liberal Theology*, 3 vols. (Louisville, KY: Westminster John Knox, 2003); Kenneth Cauthen, *The Impact of American Religious Liberalism* (New York: Harper & Row, 1962); Frank Hugh Foster, *The Modern Movement in American Theology: Sketches in the History of American Protestant Thought from the Civil War to the World War* (1939; repr., Freeport, NY: Books for Libraries, 1969); William Hutchinson, *The Modernist Impulse in American Protestantism* (Oxford: Oxford University Press, 1976); Kathryn Lofton, "The Methodology of the Modernists: Process in American Protestantism," *Church History* 75, no. 2 (2006): 374–402; and, Henry P. Van Dusen, *The Vindication of Liberal Theology* (New York: Charles Scribner's Sons, 1963).

10. Van Dusen, *The Vindication of Liberal Theology*, 27; Hutchinson, *The Modernist Impulse in American Protestantism*, 2.

11. Dorrien, *The Making of American Liberal Theology*, 1.

12. Van Dusen, *The Vindication of Liberal Theology*, 27.

13. Daniel S. Robinson, *The God of the Liberal Christian: A Study of Social Theology and the New Theism*, (New York: D. Appleton and Company, 1926), 2–3.

14. Fosdick, *The Modern Use of the Bible*, 155; Van Dusen, *The Vindication of Liberal Theology*, 34.

15. Charles A. Briggs, "Orthodoxy," in *American Protestant Thought in the Liberal Era*, ed. William R. Hutchinson (Lanham, MD: University Press of America, 1968), 31.

16. Dorrien, *The Making of American Liberal Theology*, 1.

17. Lofton, "The Methodology of the Modernists," 394.

18. Samuel DeWitt Proctor, "New Testament Interpretation within the Northern Baptist Convention" (Ph.D. diss., Boston University School of Theology, 1950), 11.Biblical scholars have failed to account for such figures as Proctor and even King when describing African Americans and the Bible. They have done well to create and chronicle some of the generalizations of an African American hermeneutic, but they have missed the influence of the theological seminaries in the early to mid-twentieth century on visible high-profile persons like Proctor. Proctor was not

like most contemporary African American biblical scholars, who have focused on retrieving the African presence in the Bible to affirm African American Christianity. He was concerned about the Bible as a standard for social claims, but he had a race-neutral eye toward the Bible. The racial situation was pressing to the extent that he could use the Bible to express the ethical concerns that racism in America posed. The Bible revealed the great liberator, Jesus.For more information on African Americans and the Bible, see Allan Dwight Callahan, *The Talking Book: African Americans and the Bible* (New Haven, CT: Yale University Press, 2006); Vincent L. Winbush, *The Bible and African Americans: A Brief History* (Minneapolis: Fortress Press, 2003); Michael Joseph Brown, *Blackening of the Bible: The Aims of African American Biblical Scholarship* (Harrisburg, PA: Trinity Press International, 2004).

19. Proctor, "New Testament Interpretation," 202, 205.

20. Samuel D. Proctor, *"How Shall They Hear?" Effective Preaching for Vital Faith* (Valley Forge, PA: Judson Press, 1992), 50–51. See also Samuel D. Proctor, *Preaching about Crises in the Community* (Louisville, KY: Westminster John Knox, 1987), 43.

21. L. Susan Bond, *Contemporary African American Preaching: Diversity in Theory and Style* (St. Louis: Chalice, 2003), 37–38. While I acknowledge its place as a foundational text for Proctor, I believe that the Bible is more of a starting point for Proctor; it is not alone at the center. This is evident in his advice on sermon preparation. He believed that preachers could find a theme from which to preach based upon the crises in the community and then match it with a text. What he saw in the Bible was an account of human struggles with "instinctive behaviors" and a moral paradigm for defeating those behaviors. Another problem with such a claim is that she seems to have built this argument based upon one of his writings (*Preaching about Crises in the Community*) and without historical investigation. Proctor was open to sources outside of the Bible for theological discernment.

22. Samuel D. Proctor, *The Certain Sound of the Trumpet: Crafting a Sermon of Authority* (Valley Forge, PA: Judson, 1994), 70.

23. Samuel D. Proctor, "Unfinished Business," sermon presented at Abyssinian Baptist Church, New York, 1987, audiotape.

24. Proctor, *The Certain Sound of the Trumpet*, 45; Proctor, *"How Shall They Hear?,"* 49–51; and Samuel DeWitt Proctor, *Samuel DeWitt Proctor: My Moral Odyssey* (Valley Forge, PA: Judson, 1989), 103.

25. Benjamin E. Mays, *The Negro's God: As Reflected in His Literature* (Boston: Chapman & Grimes, 1938; repr., New York: Negro Universities Press, 1969), 21.

26. Samuel D. Proctor, "Thinking about God as Father," sermon presented at Abyssinian Baptist Church, New York, 1993, audiotape.

27. Proctor, *My Moral Odyssey*, 97.

28. Samuel D. Proctor, "Trusting the Voice That Comes from Within," sermon presented at the Union Theological Seminary, Richmond, 1986, audiotape.

29. Ibid.

30. Robinson, *The God of the Liberal Christian*, 144.

31. Proctor, *Preaching about Crises*, 13. See also,

32. Samuel DeWitt Proctor, "Psalm 51:1," L&S, *Providence Chronicle*, November 8, 1947.

33. Samuel DeWitt Proctor, "Christianity and World Unity," L&S, *Providence Chronicle*, March 15, 1947.

34. Martin Luther King Jr., *Strength to Love* (Philadelphia: Fortress Press, 1981), 84. For a survey of Proctor's thoughts on Providence, see Adam L. Bond, "The Right Person, Place, and Time: Samuel DeWitt Proctor on the Life and Ministry of Martin Luther King Jr.," *American Baptist Quarterly* 25, no. 3 (2006): 273–90.It is important to see that Proctor, like King, is a product of a theological-intellectual tradition and a cultural-spiritual theological tradition. His views are shaped primarily in two theological traditions.

35. James Evans, *We Have Been Believers: An African American Systematic Theology* (Minneapolis: Fortress Press, 1992), 68; Samuel D. Proctor, *"How Shall They Hear?,"* 22, 28; and Proctor, "What Do We Want to Get Out of Our Worship of God?," sermon presented at Abyssinian Baptist Church, New York, 1987, audiotape.

36. Proctor, "Evil: The Unfulfillment of the Good," 211.Proctor may not have consciously attended to the fact that he rarely cited the influence of Ellison and other black preachers on his theological development. A connection does exist, however. Consider a quote from Ellison to understand some of the similarities in their (Proctor's and Ellison's) thought. Ellison wrote, "We are God's children and co-workers with Him in bringing the blind to see, the lame to walk; and in setting at liberty those in bondage, whatever the nature of that bondage." See John Malcus Ellison, *Tensions and Destiny* (Richmond, VA: John Knox, 1953), 40.

37. Proctor, "Evil: The Unfulfillment of the Good," 211.

38. Samuel DeWitt Proctor, "Organized Good," L&S, *Providence Chronicle*, April 10, 1948.

39. Proctor, *My Moral Odyssey*, 97–98.

40. William R. Jones, *Is God a White Racist: A Preamble to Black Theology* (Garden City, NY: Anchor, 1973; repr., Boston: Beacon, 1998), 187–89.While Jones's theological category more than adequately describes Proctor's thought, it will not explain his Christology. I argue in chapter 4 that Proctor's theology *is* heavily human-focused. I believe, however, that Proctor's thought is a type of theism that is Christocentric in orientation and anthropocentric in practice—a Christocentric anthropology. By this I mean that his anthropology is focused on Christ as example for humanity. In other words, the emphasis is on Jesus as savior, teacher, and paradigm for human living. This differs from the way I describe Proctor's Christology (anthropocentric Christology). Proctor's view of Christ is very human oriented. Proctor does not demonstrate the humanism that Jones depicts, in that Proctor's belief identifies fellowship with God (in Christ) as the telos idea of human fulfillment.

41. I came across two versions of this sermon. The latter version has the same content with illustrations that correspond to that time. See Samuel D. Proctor, "Beauty for Ashes," sermon presented at the Massanetta Springs Bible Conference, Harrisonburg, VA, 1977 (Richmond, VA: UTS-PSCE, 1977), audiotape; and Samuel D. Proctor, "Beauty for Ashes," sermon presented at Trinity United Church of Christ, Chicago, 1993, audiotape.

42. Samuel D. Proctor, "Everybody Is God's Somebody," in *Sermons from the Black Pulpit*, ed. Samuel D. Proctor and William D. Watley (Valley Forge, PA: Judson, 1984), 22.

43. Samuel D. Proctor, "How Much Faith Is Enough?," sermon presented at Abyssinian Baptist Church, New York, August 1987, audiotape.

44. One can find a probable source for understanding Proctor's theological development in *The Papers of Martin Luther King, Jr.*, vol. 1, ed. Clayborne Carson et. al. (Berkeley: University of California Press, 1994). King completed several essays assigned to him by George W. Davis, Professor of Systematic Theology at Crozer Theological Seminary. The required two-semester course had as its assignments summaries on the works of William Newton Clarke, William Adams Brown, and other theologians in the liberal theological tradition. By reading King's essays for the course, I noticed that he developed a liberal approach to his Christology. In other words, King began to see Jesus' divinity in the way that Jesus approached God morally and spiritually. King showed earlier traces of a literal acceptance of the biblical account. This acceptance seemed to dissipate with each assignment that King completed. Davis's course touched upon the major topics in theology (e.g., God, Jesus, humanity, church, etc.). Since Davis arrived at Crozer in 1938, it is likely that Proctor (Crozer class of '45) went through the same required course with similar assignments.Just as Proctor said, he was a product of the social gospel theology. I argue that the social gospel theology has a most notable influence on his religious language. But the fact that Proctor remained grounded in the Black Church speaks to his religious-intellectual home. To be sure, Proctor was influenced by those persons at Virginia Union who received their liberal theological education at reputable institutions (Ellison at Oberlin, McKinney at Yale Divinity and at Bank Street, D. C. Rice from Union Theological Seminary). Therefore, seminary and graduate

school were probably not the first places where he heard social gospel ideas. The fact that he spent three years in Crozer, plus several more in Yale and Boston combined, provide evidence for understanding the appropriation of the social gospel language that he acquired. In turn, the social gospel theology gave Proctor a "sophisticated" language for his thought. Though it is not clear how much of this affinity toward social action and outreach was present in his earlier thought, social gospel theology resonated with him in his ministry. Proctor was equipped to translate his interpretation of Jesus into something parishioners could hear and read. His weekly newspaper column remained a fixture in the *Providence Chronicle* for nearly two years; Proctor was in Providence for about four years.

45. Samuel D. Proctor, *Sermons to the Abyssinians* (New York: ABC, 1977), 18.

46. Proctor, *My Moral Odyssey*, 105.

47. See Samuel D. Proctor, "Manger Religion," L&S, *Providence Chronicle*, December 27, 1947.

48. Samuel D. Proctor, "The Childhood of Jesus," sermon presented at Abyssinian Baptist Church, New York, 1992, audiotape; Samuel D. Proctor, "Thinking of God as Father," sermon presented at Abyssinian Baptist Church, 1993, audiotape; Samuel D. Proctor, "He Taught as One Having Authority," sermon presented at Abyssinian Baptist Church, New York, 1987, audiotape; Samuel D. Proctor, "Dimensions of Human Growth," sermon presented at Abyssinian Baptist Church, New York, 1987, audiotape; and Proctor, "Jesus and the City," sermon presented at Abyssinian Baptist Church, New York, 1987, audiotape.

49. Proctor, "He Taught as One Having Authority."

50. Samuel D. Proctor, "Carrying Christmas through the Year," L&S, *Providence Chronicle*, December 25, 1948.From my experience in the Baptist tradition, many of its members believe that since Jesus is God, he did not need a formal education in the law—he knew everything. For more on the idea that Jesus is omniscient, see n. 50.

51. Proctor, "He Taught as One Having Authority"; and Proctor, "Carrying Christmas through the Year."From my experience in the Baptist tradition, it is almost de facto belief among many of its members that Jesus was omniscient. Believers come to this conclusion using a Trinitarian logic. The logic follows that Jesus is God, and because of that, Jesus knew everything. If the same views I have observed held true in Proctor's life, his belief differed from a "theology of the pew."

52. Samuel D. Proctor, "The Cross that We Bear," sermon presented at Abyssinian Baptist Church, New York, 1987, audiotape; and Proctor, "Dimensions of Human Growth." See also Harry Emerson Fosdick, *The Manhood of the Master* (New York: Association Press, 1913).

53. Proctor, "He Taught as One Having Authority." See also Samuel DeWitt Proctor, "Family of God," L&S, *Providence Chronicle*, February 19, 1949.

54. Samuel D. Proctor, "Did He Have to Do It?" L&S, *Providence Chronicle*, March 20, 1948. See also Samuel D. Proctor, "Humility," sermon presented at UTS-PSCE, Richmond, 1976, audiotape.

55. Proctor, *Preaching about Crises*, 41.

56. Proctor, "Manger Religion."

57. Proctor, "Humility." See also Proctor, *Sermons from the Black Pulpit*, 10; Samuel D. Proctor, "Manger Religion"; and Samuel DeWitt Proctor, "The Aim of Jesus' Teachings," L&S, *Providence Chronicle*, October 9, 1948.

58. Samuel DeWitt Proctor, *The Christian Ordinances in Baptist Churches* (Richmond, VA: self-published, n.d.), 22–23. See also Samuel D. Proctor, "The Ministry of Reconciliation," L&S, *Providence Chronicle*, October 2, 1948.

59. Ellison, *Tensions and Destiny*, 30.

60. Proctor, "The Aim of Jesus' Teachings."

61. See Samuel DeWitt Proctor, "The Jesus Program," L&S, *Providence Chronicle*, February 4, 1949.

62. Proctor, *My Moral Odyssey*, 106.

63. Samuel D. Proctor, "The First Coming of Christ," sermon presented at the 1989 Ohio Pastors Convocation (Nashville, United Methodist Publishing House, 1989), audiotape.

64. Samuel D. Proctor, "Jesus and Simon of Bethany," sermon presented at Abyssinian Baptist Church, New York, 1987, audiotape.It is not a stretch to believe that the social gospel resonated with African American religious intellectuals in the early to mid-twentieth century. Proctor was not the only African American theologian who bought into the social gospel theology. A look at Howard Thurman's *Jesus and the Disinherited* (1949) exhibits a similar social outlook. Thurman (1900–1981), much older than Proctor, labeled African Americans members of the "least and left behind." To be sure, Thurman felt the social gospel influence as a student at Rochester Theological Seminary. Although Walter Rauschenbusch passed before Thurman entered the seminary, the social gospel influence is evident in Thurman's publication. Thurman, like Proctor, concentrated on the historical Jesus. However, Thurman drew his argument from a racial and social awareness of Jesus' personhood. Thurman highlighted the fact that Jesus was a Jew, and as a Jew, Jesus experienced the oppression of a marginalized people. Proctor does not talk about Jesus as a "poor Jew." Proctor refers to Jesus within the context of his mission to a poor and marginalized people—not as one who is poor and marginalized.Proctor was aware of issues of race, but Jesus was not a racial figure to him. For Proctor, the gospel dealt with matters of race inasmuch as it dealt with issues of personhood. The racial component of Proctor's thought is contextual. He saw the suffering of African Americans clearly because he was African American, growing up in the segregated south. The gospel responds best to the circumstances of blacks in America because, for Proctor, African Americans were oppressed for so long. I say more about race in chapter 4. See also Dennis C. Dickerson, "African American Religious Intellectuals and the Theological Foundations of the Civil Rights Movement, 1930–1955," *Church History* 74, no. 2 (2005): 217–35. Dickerson's article traces the theological contributions of persons who had a direct influence upon Martin Luther King Jr. He also presents ideas from Richard I. McKinney, one of Samuel DeWitt Proctor's mentors.

65. Samuel D. Proctor, "The Cosmic Dimension of Christmas," sermon presented at Abyssinian Baptist Church, New York, 1992, audiotape.

66. Samuel D. Proctor, "On Being Neutral," L&S, *Providence Chronicle*, March 29, 1947.

67. Samuel D. Proctor, "The Coping Capacity that Christ Provides," sermon presented at Abyssinian Baptist Church, New York, 1993, audiotape; and Samuel D. Proctor, "Abiding in the Light," L&S, *Providence Chronicle*, December 6, 1947.Interpreting Proctor's thought is not easy in the sense that some dots are only tacitly connected. He does not employ the traditional labels and dogmas of Christianity. One must feel for what he believed based upon what he says and/or implies about Jesus.

68. Samuel D. Proctor, "The Life of the Inner Man," L&S, *Providence Chronicle*, April 5, 1947. In this piece, Proctor wrote, "Easter should strengthen our faith in the life of the inner man, for it was Christ who made the life of the inner man possible. He confers the second birth—the spiritual birth—upon us which is the real birth of the inner man. The Risen Lord must find access to your life and create within you a right mind, actuate in you this second birth, confer upon you the eternal life of the inner man, or Easter is for you a mere, colossal fashion show."

69. Samuel D. Proctor, "Dead Jesus or Living Christ," L&S, *Providence Chronicle*, April 16, 1949; and, Samuel D. Proctor, "The Magnetic Christ," L&S, *Providence Chronicle*, April 19, 1947.

70. Proctor, *My Moral Odyssey*, 125.

71. Samuel DeWitt Proctor, "The Holy Spirit," L&S, *Providence Chronicle*, August 16, 1947. See also Samuel D. Proctor, *Fruits of the Spirit*, lecture presented at the 1990 Hampton University Ministers Conference, June 1990 (Hampton, VA: Hampton University, 1990); and Proctor, *My Moral Odyssey*, 84.

72. Proctor, *The Christian Ordinances in Baptist Churches*, 14.

73. Samuel D. Proctor, "Respectability Enough?," lecture presented at the 1989 Hampton University Ministers Conference, Hampton, VA, June 1989 (Hampton, VA: Hampton University, 1989), audiotape.

74. Samuel DeWitt Proctor, "Stewardship," L&S, *Providence Chronicle*, March 6, 1948. See also Samuel DeWitt Proctor, "Church Building," L&S, *Providence Chronicle*, May 15, 1948.

75. Samuel D. Proctor, "People, Religion, and a Changing Virginia," speech presented at the Conference on People, Religion and a Changing Virginia, Richmond, VA, November 29, 1966 (UTS-PSCE).

76. Samuel D. Proctor, "The Black Church and the Crises in the Black Community," *Chicago Theological Seminary Register* 80 (1990): 5–10.

77. Samuel D. Proctor, "Church-State Consultation," lecture presented in Richmond, VA, 1981 (Richmond: UTS-PSCE, 1981), audiotape.

78. Ibid. See also Samuel D. Proctor, "What the Law Cannot Do," lecture presented at the 1990 Hampton Ministers Conference, June 1990 (Hampton, VA: Hampton University, 1990), audiotape. Ideas from "Church-State Consultation" became a part of "What the Law Cannot Do." In the latter lecture, Proctor combined a "stump" sermon that he preached in various settings with ideas about the relationship between the church and state.

79. Samuel D. Proctor, "The Change that Contact with Christ Can Bring," sermon presented at Abyssinian Baptist Church, New York, 1987, audiotape. See also Samuel D. Proctor, *The Substance of Things Hoped For: A Memoir of African American Faith* (New York: G. P. Putnam's Sons, 1995), 166–68, for story about the 0,000 organ.

80. See Gary Dorrien, *The Making of American Liberal Theology: Idealism, Realism, and Modernity, 1900–1950* (Louisville, KY: Westminster John Knox, 2003), 431. Dorrien writes, "On the whole Fosdick's ministry aided the cause of desegregation and racial progress, but not nearly as much as it could have, and always with a whiff of white supremacy."

81. Samuel D. Proctor, "He Taught as One Having Authority," lecture presented at the Hampton Ministers' Conference, Hampton, VA, June 1991 (Hampton, VA: Hampton University, 1991). See also H. D. A. Major, Thomas Walter Manson, and C. J. Wright, *The Mission and Message of Jesus: An Exposition of the Gospels in Light of Modern Research* (New York: E. P. Dutton and Co., 1938).

# 4

# Everybody Is God's Somebody

## *A Defense of Black Humanity*

Proctor's public faith had at its foundation a concern for black humanity. His numerous sermons and publications reflect a belief in the worth of persons, especially, but not limited to, African Americans. Race remained a constant in his religious reflections. His own experience as an African American included Jim Crow, the civil rights movement, and the introduction of affirmative action. The relationship between race and religion in the United States, moreover, is obvious. As Dwight Hopkins notes, one cannot speak of theological anthropology in America without race entering into the conversation.[1] In his public presentations, Proctor argued for the equality of African American existence. He grounded his beliefs about humanity in the claim of God's parenthood and humanity's kinship and equality. He preached this message: "Everybody is God's somebody." This idea represents his complex response to racism and its consequences in American public life. As Proctor saw it, a "spurious anthropology" plagued the United States. He fought the racist practices that stemmed from that anthropology with a public faith that reflected a dominant theme among many black Christians in this country.

The basis of Proctor's claim was simple: all human beings are the children of God. This basic tenet of Christianity was foundational in the liberal theology of his age, but it also had meaning among African American Christians dating back to the eighteenth century. Proctor was an integrationist who fought for equality in America. He was an activist who fought against racism with the power of persuasion. He believed that racism was at the root of many of the problems that adversely affected African Americans. He wanted to increase the opportunities that would create greater prospects for children of all races to achieve educational success and for persons who were in poverty to achieve a reasonable standard of living. He wanted to eradicate racism. He argued that it is an antecedent to many of the problems in society. His claim for equality was a call for a moral regeneration among persons who opposed racial uplift among African Americans. His fight for equality also displayed advocacy of a black middle-class ethic of self-help by way of thrift, piety, education, and political participation. This is indicative of a longstanding tradition of African American Christianity that concerns itself with social ethics and the problem of racism in American life.[2]

## Proctor on African American Life: The Negation and Promise of Humanity

To be sure, Proctor was well aware of the problems of race in American society. The focus of several of his sermons and talks was racism and its concomitant issues. He saw racism's connection to poverty, crime, and many other social concerns. For him, the problem was an American one. He did not see racism as merely a black concern or white concern. All Americans should understand the consequences of racism in American life. In a 1985 sermon entitled "Jesus Christ, Prince of Peace," he proclaimed:

> We are still fighting the Civil War in so many places. We've not yet settled down and decided that blacks are free; that they are human; that they don't bite; that they don't go around all the time thinking of something violent to do; they do learn when they are taught; they can think; they can be responsible. Everyday we are being nagged over and over again by this issue rising up to haunt us. It is practically impossible for us to spend the day thinking about things that everyone else would want to think about without having to pause at some time during the day and reckon with this strife that follows us on the basis of race in this country. We need to see this whole issue reconciled and the nation become one in freedom; and one in purpose; and one in fairness; one in justice; one in opportunity; one in the well-being of all her people.[3]

A life in segregated Norfolk, Virginia, observing the racial codes of the South displayed clearly for Proctor the problems of American society. It is fair to say that he saw racism as a primary cause of the moral crisis in the United States. At the root of racism was the devaluation of black personhood.

The racial problem in the United States concerned Proctor much more after his missionary tours in Europe and Asia. In 1954, Proctor reported his impressions of the world after returning from his missionary tour of 1953. He was a Baptist envoy along with several American Baptists who worked with local leaders in places such as India to turn over control of Baptist schools to the indigenous groups in those countries. During the trip, he reported that several residents questioned him about the nature of his relationship as a black person with the colonizers of the world. He was pressed to consider who he was as an American and as a citizen of the world. In one account, he recalled, "The bottom line was that I saw how many dark-skinned people lived in the world and that they all had been colonized by Europeans. This gave me an authentic identity with Third World people and their struggles for clean water, nutrition, food, health care, safe housing, basic education, and hope for a brighter future."[4] The report that Proctor submitted to the *National Baptist Voice* represents one of the earliest *written* statements that we have in which he presents his thoughts on matters of race. Prompted by J. Pious Barbour, editor of the *Voice*, to recall his travels, Proctor shared stories about the way in which white missionaries raised questions about the ability of African Americans to proselytize persons in foreign countries. The sentiment affected the mood of the native residents, prompting them to look askance at Proctor until conversing with him.

Proctor discerned the legacy of colonialism during that trip and realized the far-reaching influence of white supremacy. He saw, moreover, the extent to which European Americans, especially white Christians, were viewed with distrust in several locales. He stated, "One night I 'had it out' with 'leftist' students in Jamshedpur, India. They scolded me for being an American and a black person. They thought I should have fled my country or shot myself." Proctor's response says much about his faith in America: "I explained that despite the injustices, I had accepted America as the place most likely to mature into a free, pluralistic society with individual liberties, a government by the consent of the governed, and an economy that could provide equal employment opportunities, housing, and education."[5] The trip alerted him to the urgency of the problems in the United States. He described the results of his travels by stating that his conscience underwent a "real metamorphosis."

Proctor witnessed an era of movements and changes in American society that kept him hopeful throughout his life. Yet he stated in one of his autobiographical accounts that he was awakened to the fact that integration was taking place "altogether too slow."[6] He believed that both whites and blacks in the United States were too comfortable with the state of race relations during the 1950s. That racism existed was not a question for Proctor. He was well aware of the existence of racism in the United States. He traced the effects of racism back to the origins of black-white relations at the founding of the American colonies. He wrote that racism "pervaded American culture since

1619." He argued that it arrived with the first slaves at Jamestown, Virginia. When whites realized that Africans could hold up under North American weather and diet, they made racial slavery an institution. He continued, "So today's black minority condition is traceable to this incipient condition."[7]

Proctor saw in racial slavery the foundation of prejudice in American society. That prejudice contributed to the problems of black America was a given. The net result of it, he contended, was a "crisis in self-concept" among African Americans. In his memoir, he stated that some African Americans "grow to hate their identity," paralyzing any useful way of addressing the problems that those persons face. He observed, "An African American needs a healthy ego to shadowbox all day in a world not designed for her or his occupancy."[8]

Proctor believed that racism reached into most, if not all, aspects of American culture. He noted that Caucasian persons maintained most systems of power in the United States. In the "religious right," he saw a threat to the rights of African Americans due to the fundamentalists' collusion with the state. Technology largely was limited to whites and was lacking in access to minority populations. Wealth remained in the hands of an elite few. To be sure, he took issue with white backlash over programs such as affirmative action and the work of the Office of Economic Opportunity. He argued that many of the attacks against integration were made on specious grounds: "Whites who argue today that integration should not be forced and that groups should fall naturally into their own homogeneity freely and without interference have short memories. They have forgotten how segregation was invented and forced."[9] The late 1960s also proved to Proctor that African Americans who were vocal about gaining access to equal opportunity in the United States were treated poorly. As an integrationist, Proctor concerned himself with racism and the welfare of the nation. He was determined to see the nation live up to its pluralistic identity while embracing its national destiny and purpose. Within this framework, he contended, African Americans have historically represented the nation's great dilemma.

### *Black History and Identity: A Dialectical Interpretation*

History provided for Proctor a template by which he could assess the problems in America. Being ever mindful of the inevitable tensions that stem from monumental change, he was well aware of the shortcomings that still existed. Proctor interpreted history in terms of the triumphs and travails of African Americans. This view of history may be a product of the influence of German philosopher Georg Wilhelm Friedrich Hegel. Proctor had acquainted himself with the fundamentals of Hegel's dialectical philosophy in the seminary and in graduate school. Proctor saw in life and history the constant interaction between opposing forces. Nowhere may this strand of thought be more apparent than in his book *The Young Negro in America*. In it, he charted out the existence of African Americans.

Proctor labeled the period immediately following the Emancipation Proclamation (1865–c. 1890) "disintegration."[10] Disintegration referred to the physical separation that took place among Caucasians and African Americans. He considered slavery a type of integration. In slavery, blacks and whites in the south shared an existence, however unequal. Although African Americans lived in slavery, "they were involved in every aspect of the lives of whites." In the Emancipation, many African Americans were not prepared to enter the larger society. As a result, numerous African Americans returned to farms, working in "a modified form of slavery."[11] In disintegration, African Americans had freedmen schools and semiautonomous circumstances for their "cultivation." But not all African Americans were able to take advantage of these educational and social benefits. Most lacked the skills and resources to advance in society. In Proctor's words, it was "a time of great disintegration."

The second stage (1890–1935) was "alienation," referring to the violence against African Americans and the invention of segregation.[12] Proctor contended that the Hayes-Tilden presidential election of 1876, the dismissal of the Civil Rights Bill of 1883, and the Plessy v. Ferguson decision of 1896 brought about this era. Proctor saw in this stage the malicious intent of whites to reclaim the south. Lynchings, mob violence, and racial hatred became a normal part of black existence in the United States.

Proctor labeled a third and overlapping stage "imitation" or "acculturation" (1890–c. 1905). He stated that blacks built their own institutions and communities that emulated white society: "Negroes were establishing a replica of the white world when they were compelled to create their own society. Completely and unquestionably ousted from the white world, they went about building an entire society alongside that of their white neighbors. It was a copy of the white world in every detail—fraternities, cotillions, literary societies, and stores that sold "plain and fancy" groceries. They even learned how to elect delegates to send to conventions in England with expenses paid!"[13] He called this practice a rehearsal for the "eventual reintegration" into mainstream society. African Americans were trying to prove their humanity to the larger culture. Proctor alluded to the great debate between Booker T. Washington (1856–1915) and W. E. B. Du Bois (1868–1963), two African American leaders who had different ideas and programs for the elevation of the race, as an expression of the period of gradual acculturation for African Americans.[14]

The remarkable work of the National Association for the Advancement of Colored People (NAACP) on the local and national levels created the stage Proctor called "litigation" (1935–1954). For him, the heroes of this era were persons such as Thurgood Marshall (1908–1993) and Charles Houston (1895–1950). These men fought against racial segregation in courtrooms all across the country. Proctor remembered well the NAACP case for equal salary brought before the courts by his high school science teacher around 1938. The "39 successive victories" won by these African American lawyers paved the way for the monumental decision in the 1954 case *Brown v. Board of Education of Topeka*. Proctor saw the court decisions and the persons who fought for them as heralds of an integrated society.[15]

The final stage Proctor listed is "reintegration" (1955–c. present).[16] African Americans, he believed, had come "full cycle." They were moving back into full participation in society. The civil rights movement made African American integration a legislative reality. He challenged African Americans to have the courage to move into the "center of society" and embrace the equality that the law promised. Proctor described this stage as incomplete. Although Proctor saw that many blacks had taken advantage of the gains that had been made during the previous five decades, he knew that more work was needed. During the last years of his life, he questioned policy decisions made by the first President Bush that adversely affected African Americans. For example, the issue of school vouchers reminded Proctor of the way in which white Protestants established private schools to keep from sending their children to integrated public schools.[17]

Proctor went after "Christian academies" that functioned to keep white children from mixing with black children. But what did integration mean for Proctor? It meant the full participation of blacks in every aspect of America. He envisioned a society in which that reality became the norm. He dedicated himself to preparing African Americans for that day. He saw the need for a full-fledged social change before integration could be a reality. Early in his career, he believed that eradicating poverty and providing a good education for African Americans presented the best hope for achieving integration. Integration represented the ideal for Proctor. He remained cognizant, moreover, of the enemies of racial progress. With every major step taken on behalf of African Americans, Proctor could see the desire of right-wing conservatives to erase such gains.

Proctor wanted African Americans to move beyond living into stereotypes and embrace a self-understanding of blackness that would allow them to move freely among whites. In this way, Proctor might have been not only an integrationist but an accommodationist as well. This notion of accommodation was his belief that blacks had to compromise on some aspects of their cultural behaviors. He sought compromise by way of the visual presentation of African Americans. He was concerned that whites would misinterpret "pro-black" hairstyles (afros) and clothing (dashikis) of the 1960s. At the same time, he wanted white persons to see black militancy and a focus on black identity as a logical outgrowth of the social circumstances in the United States. In a 1969 article, he was both an apologist and mediator. He argued, "Let the catharsis take place. Let the chants and the slogans continue. Let the new styles in dress and medallions do for these youngsters what guitars, long hair and short skirts do for others."[18] He believed that black militancy was an opportunity to direct the energy of black youth into education and job training. The affirmations of blackness by militant youth represented an opportunity to fulfill the promise of American pluralism. Proctor observed:

> Racism, then, which once fell before the legal and scientific pressures is revived on pragmatic grounds. The blacks don't want integration! Then the logic has gone full cycle: blacks rejected; blacks become difficult; whites retreat; blacks further rejected. That is the simplest form of the argument. The more highly developed logic goes this way: the blacks are forced into cultural insularity; while insulated, they are treated unequally. This insularity and unequal treatment breed a sub-culture. The sub-culture is so repulsive [to whites] that further insularity is encouraged. Then the young blacks add to the logic by averring that this is what they want, a world independent of "whitey."[19]

With this type of philosophical approach to matters of race, he navigated a fine line between integration and accommodation.

Proctor represented the precarious standing of a black leader whose approach to social uplift modeled a black "bourgeois" approach. As an integrationist, he advocated for opportunity, using his academic and government offices as well as his pulpit to shed light on the conditions that blocked paths to true integration and progress for African Americans. He sounds more accommodating when he recommends on more than one occasion that African Americans should shed portions of black "soul culture" in order to mesh in a pluralistic society. (His answer implies that blacks will scare whites with this "soul culture.") This type of ambivalence or double consciousness is evident in several articles and speeches. For example, in a 1969 article on the African American contribution to the American experiment, Proctor heralded the ethos of black life and its offering to the United States. He noted that African Americans provided the labor to build the American empire, simple creature comforts, music and other artistic forms, and a style of oration that combines "moral exhortation and political protest." He stated that this sermonic contribution became a novel form of American literature that "appealed to the authority of religion and to the implicit ideal of political democracy." (He embraced this style as a preacher and educator.) Yet he concluded the article with an interesting challenge:

> Let the black man saturate himself in his own background. Let him hear from his past and learn who he is. Let him search out the African roots of the American black community. Let him overcome his alienation and his identity crisis. Then let us say to him, "All right, it's time now for all the Americans to bring their own peculiar gifts to the enrichment of the whole society. Go on and be yourself. But remember that part of yourself lies in the fact that this is *your* country. Come now and help to make it great."[20]

Proctor would probably consider this a cultural synthesis. He could accept racial pride to the extent that it did not interfere with American pluralism. He was not a racial chauvinist, but he believed that African Americans could help redeem the soul of America.

Black messianism, or a belief in the salvific nature of black existence, was not far from Proctor's thought. He would not go as far, however, as others would in describing the African American contribution to the American experience. Lewis Baldwin details how Martin Luther King Jr. saw in black people a group that would redeem the world (morally and spiritually). Baldwin writes, "For all their shortcomings, many of them born of oppression, King considered black people generally more humane than their white oppressors."[21] Refuting arguments that attribute racial chauvinism to King, Baldwin contends that King saw African Americans as vessels that would liberate America as a "spiritualizing and humanizing force."

Proctor would acknowledge that African Americans have made longstanding contributions to society. He would also argue that African Americans have qualities from which a larger culture of persons could learn. For example, he was quoted in a 1967 *Chicago Defender* article stating that the years of oppression had found African Americans turning to peaceful methods for a solution to the race crisis. In that same article, he reportedly said that blacks have displayed more than enough courage by remaining dedicated to the United States throughout the terrible ordeal they have experienced.[22] A primary reason for blacks' peaceful approach to American racism, Proctor believed, has been the influence of Christianity. In later years, he wrote, "One reason why black people have clung so tenaciously to Jesus, despite the apostasy and failure of Christians in acknowledging our human kinship and despite Christians' exploitation of one another through slavery, colonialism, and rank racism, is that blacks have found in Jesus the authentic, transcendent God incarnate, above and beyond race and clan and class. In truth we are one human family."[23] Nevertheless, Proctor did not allow his theological idealism to obstruct his view of reality. He understood that human beings would not change without some struggle. Proctor saw at different stages of his life that the collective moral will of the country did not unite on the issue of integration and racial harmony. He stated in a 1987 Christmas sermon that Americans have the brains to do it but not the heart for it.[24] One will find more examples of this type of narrative in Proctor's sermons. To be sure, if anyone was qualified to identify racism, it was he.

Proctor spent the majority of his life arguing for an integrated, prejudice-free society that affirms persons of all races. Although he saw a great deal of progress on the matter, he was able to see the issues that remained at hand. Proctor lived long enough to witness several changes, but it is obvious from his sermon illustrations and writings that he was still combating racism during the twilight of his life. He fought for a racial progress that was real, validated by moral and legislative support. He celebrated legal victories but considered them hollow without the type of moral consensus and goodwill that is necessary for love to exist. Proctor saw integration as a step toward the kingdom's ethic of inclusiveness.[25] He embraced a belief in the personhood of all human beings.

## "What the Law Cannot Do"

Two sermons that bear similar names and themes display Proctor's move to a religious vision for the United States and its racial dilemma. In 1988, Proctor preached a sermon entitled "Some Things that the Law Cannot Do" at the Union Theological Seminary in Richmond, Virginia, proclaiming that laws and federal mandates alone could not bring the United States to its ideological ideal—equality for all Americans. Two years later, Proctor presented a similar talk entitled "What the Law Cannot Do," which he presented again at the predominantly African American Hampton University Ministers Conference in 1990.[26] In both messages, the core thesis was the same: it takes more than legalism to change a person's heart. These sermons exhibit an important aspect of Proctor's Christian understanding of humanity. They suggest the grounds for a moral society. In asking whether laws are enough to bring about an orderly society that looks upon all human beings as equals, Proctor implies the failure of the American political system to uplift marginalized minority persons and communities. For him, legislation and government-enforced sanctions have been inadequate approaches to bringing about the type of moral changes that the United States needed to defeat racism; only Christ-centered ethics can accomplish the feat.

In matters of ethics and morals, Proctor stated that the law was too weak to bring about the type of moral and spiritual standing that Jesus required. The law was a "measuring stick" for morality. But Proctor maintained that morality could not work with an external measure as its guide. He remarked that the law was "authority from above and not empowering from within."[27] The law could represent a weak moral consensus that did not reflect the feelings and desires of a people who practiced it. In one instance, Proctor proclaimed:

> Let's face it, the capacity of the law is limited. The law can compel conformity to certain overt patterns of behavior. It is helpless to deal in the area of motives, and loyalties, and ideas, and affections, and personal priorities. This is the real stuff of life. And here, legalism is ineffective; it can neither engender love, nor can it hinder love. It cannot emancipate the mind or set free the life of ideas. You can't pass a law, making folk think. You can't pass a law, making folk love each other. The law can place no limit on human thought or imagination. It cannot create an artist nor can it stifle the creativity sealed in the soul of a painter, a poet, a sculptor, a playwright, a singer, a dancer, or a mountain climber.[28]

He was intimately aware of the weakness of the law and its flawed status in America based upon his background. He lived in a segregated society that sought to deny his humanity by denying the rights due him as a citizen. He also saw how fragile a moral consensus could be during the 1960s and 1970s, when Richard Nixon began to reverse the "gains" that had taken place during the Kennedy and Johnson administrations. Proctor came to see the political climate in light of this moral consensus. Yet he saw the American political system as the best one available. With that in mind, he discerned how important it was that Christians understood their role in it. Concerning the morality of the age, Proctor preached that America needed Christ's spirit to bring about change that the law cannot transact. He went on to say, "We need to hear from God's prophets again that justice should roll down like waters and righteousness like a mighty stream."[29]

This turn to the power of Christ and Christ's agents reflect Proctor's upbringing. Specifically, Proctor turned to preachers as the primary agents of this moral outpouring of Christ's spirit throughout the land. I will say more about this in the next chapter. Yet it is important to note that Proctor believed that American Christians should know of their responsibility to their country and their Christ. He claimed, "And especially as church men and women in a free and a democratic republic, we ought to know the relationship between what happens in the society and what the kingdom of God ought to be like."[30] Proctor argued that the moral consensus of the nation changes because things change. Persons and institutions may lag behind with this change. He contended that the law must be responsive to the rising moral and spiritual discernment of the people of God. Christians (preachers) bore the responsibility of raising the moral and spiritual consciousness of the country.

Proctor desired a world in which every person grew up valuing herself. He commented, "And there is no law that can make people feel like they are somebody. All of this must come from within."[31] The law did not eradicate the world of racism and the problems that racism created. The law had not done away with poverty. The law, moreover, could not teach people to value the worth of others. Proctor believed that the most important issues flowed from the heart, and the law could not dictate such matters. What was necessary for this job was a committed band of Christians who would make plain the ethics of Christ. Proctor noted that America is open to conversation about what it should be and that the political system yields room for critical changes. The nation, the world, could change through the moral and spiritual suasion of the church. Proctor argued that such a prophetic witness could find no freer expression than in a democratic republic—the United States.

## Humanity and a Black Public Faith Response to Racism

A fundamental starting point for talking about Christian notions of humanity from an African American perspective is the issue of racism in the United States. Historically, theologians, ethicists, preachers, and activists such as Frederick Douglass (c. 1818–1895), Francis J. Grimké (1850–1937), Ida B. Wells (1862–1931), Benjamin E. Mays (1894–1984), and Howard Thurman

(1900–1981), not to mention a host of other religious women and men, have expressed their theological understanding of humanity by way of responding to racism in America. These preachers and a host of others made an effort to defend black humanity. African American Christian ministers and theologians spoke the language of Christianity and steeped their arguments for equality in the biblical texts and the founding documents of the United States. Proctor situated himself in this black Christian tradition, with its biblical affirmations that God is parent of all and that all humanity shares kinship. This black Christian tradition—a tradition that predated American liberal theology, as Peter Paris demonstrates in his book *The Social Teaching of the Black Churches*—maintained a nonracist posture toward whites and loyalty to the principles of the nation. It was the conflict between theory and practice on matters of race in American society that necessitated a distinct Christian response born out of the experience of African Americans.

Paris argues that black Christians constructed their theological opposition against white racism in a distinct fashion. In his work, Paris identifies two traditions that make up American Christianity. He labels one tradition "Western." This tradition has been guided by a principle of "societal exclusion" based upon race. The second tradition is the black Christian tradition. For Paris, the black Christian tradition spurred the development of the black churches in America. Contrary to the Western tradition of racism, the black Christian tradition is one of racial self-respect. It lacks the racist element of the Western tradition. Historically, it found expression in the independent Black Church movement. Its primary principle, which embodies this nonracist position, is that God's parenthood and humanity's kinship denote equality. Equality was the logical offspring of the biblically based conception of humanity. This principle became the conventional response of the black churches to racism. Paris explains that the black churches sought to mediate the biblical principle with "the racial situation in every period of history."[32] He goes on to state that this mediation has always been the mission of black churches to America. Although the religious responses to racism have varied throughout the years, the black Christian tradition has remained steadfast in its belief in that principle.

Examples of persons in this tradition include Proctor's elders and contemporaries. Benjamin Mays, a product of the black Christian tradition and the black Baptist family, embraced the prophetic principle. He wrote, "From the standpoint of the Christian faith, man has a common creator-father, God. From the point of view of science, man has a common ancestry. It is implicit in the Christian faith that all men are brothers, sons of one creator-father. Science proves that by blood all men are brothers."[33] Even persons who were influenced by the ideas and rhetoric of black liberation theology sounded a similar chord. Consider J. Deotis Roberts: "In interpreting man in Christian theological perspective, the black theologian has to bring a meaning of self-respect to people who can no longer accept themselves. According to the Christian faith, we are all God's children, and as Creator and Redeemer of life God accepts us even though, according to our self-estimate or the estimate of others, we are unacceptable."[34]

The black Christian tradition directly responded to the contradiction in much of white American Christianity. One cannot examine Proctor's religious outlook on humanity and society without understanding that which it addresses directly: racism in America. Proctor inherited the black Christian tradition growing up in the black Protestant mainstream, and it did influence him.

## On the Recognition of Personhood

The solution to the problem of racism for Proctor begins with the recognition and worth of all persons. Personhood for him is the inherent dignity that God assigns to every human being. Within Proctor's definition of personhood is his portrayal of the Christian principle of *imago Dei*. Proctor recalled, "I had to affirm this personhood that had been conferred upon me. I was not a statistic, a digit, a shell, a cube, a bundle of tangled instincts and drives; but a thinking, reflecting, remembering, reacting, feeling, analyzing, choosing human being, a unique creation of a loving, eternal, holy God."[35] It follows that Proctor embraced the belief that God had endowed humanity with these attributes. Proctor claimed that human beings are the highest order of creation and demonstrate this in their relationships with each other and with God. The recognition of personhood opens one to a world of potential. One needs guidance, though, to make use of the information that comes with one's personhood: "Personhood is a dynamic concept. One does not make this discovery and then consider that it is a permanent given. The discovery that one is more than a package of chemicals is an important human achievement that requires nurture and sustenance."[36]

Proctor said that he concluded at an early age that he was the only one of him. This was, in a sense, the way he affirmed his own personhood. He learned that God did not have any other Samuel D. Proctors inhabiting the earth. Proctor's home environment reinforced these early religious concepts. He noted on several occasions that he was a child of the Great Depression. The fact that he and his family did not have much money did not deter his parents from giving him the type of Christian nurture to reinforce his personhood. The Proctor family created an environment that nurtured his sense of self. He observed, "The kind of parenting that we had as children not only encouraged one to recognize what I have called personhood—a sense of self, a sense of worth, a feeling of approval from within—but it also meant an early induction into the life of the mind."[37]

For Proctor, moral and intellectual development proceeds from this affirmation of personhood. One becomes aware of one's humanity and builds upon this fact with the mental capacity to learn new ideas. Those early days in the Norfolk school system not only brought with them basic academic lessons. Proctor learned about his humanity. His teachers, moreover, taught him and his classmates about the importance of black identity through African American history. He stated that his teachers injected the curriculum with lessons on the contributions of African Americans to history, science, and literature. He learned about prominent African Americans, sang spirituals, and read black poetry. He received this in the Norfolk *colored* public schools. He reflected, "All of this pointed us toward self-approval and a stronger posture for facing this society and working for a better day for ourselves and all the oppressed people of the world."[38] Proctor was proud of these lessons. He stated on several occasions that his family and his teachers had prepared him for the racist world in which he lived. He could not avoid the messages that white persons put in place to diminish or erase his sense of self. But it was intact and well equipped to fight conflicting messages. African American history was a source of his understanding of personhood. He learned of his importance from hearing the story of notable African Americans. The healthy racial pride he learned at home and in school had in it a challenge to make the world better.

This education in "blackness" was not a type of racial chauvinism. But it did have class implications. Proctor learned that African Americans could identify with the more accomplished members of the race. Several prominent black Americans in history provided examples for others to follow. Persons such as W. E. B. Du Bois, Harriet Tubman, Booker T. Washington, and others exemplified the greatness of the race. Proctor bought into the argument that persons should judge the race by its best members. He did not mean, however, athletes and movie stars. They could not remove stereotypes that blacks faced, for they could be "rationalized away and accounted for."[39] In this matter, Du Bois probably influenced Proctor with a belief in creating an educated class of African Americans who fought on behalf of marginalized African Americans.

The same type of self-affirming reinforcement took place at Virginia Union University, Proctor maintained. He believed that Virginia Union was a haven for blacks during the time he attended the school. While noting its shortcomings in resources, he believed he had received what he needed from the school:

> We did not have all we needed of anything. But we had people committed to the notion that I was *somebody*, born "a little lower than the angels and crowned with glory and honor."After a while I began to understand that you could call me any name you wanted to, make me sit anywhere you pleased, put up any sign—I had already been possessed of a new selfhood, a sense of personal worth.
>
> So I transcended the dusty, narrow streets of Huntersville, and with the help of my teachers on that campus on Lombardy Street I had acquired a long view of history, a deep understanding of human nature, and the highest aspiration for my own life.[40]

The lessons he received at home and in school encouraged Proctor to "work for a better day" for all persons—especially oppressed persons. He saw this demonstrated in the lives of notable African Americans and in the lives of persons in his community (i.e., home, church, school, and college). His moral-spiritual formation called for him to recognize his personhood and then make a turn to see the personhood in others.

Proctor's Christian beliefs about humanity reflect his concern for the discovery of human purpose. Proctor wrote, "God made persons to become very special beings, created for interpersonal relations quite different from the way mice, rabbits, and frogs mate and reproduce."[41] Proctor held that God had created humanity in such a "special" way that reflects human beings' intimate connection with God. God had something special in mind when God made humanity. Proctor did not learn a selective approach in determining which persons deserve equal treatment and recognition. Social barriers that included race, class, and wealth were not indicators of God's understanding of human value for the Proctor family. Proctor noted, "Next, our early moral rearing and the assurance of our own personhood enable us to recognize personhood in others, to respect their worth and dignity and to honor the human potential in them. Incidentally, this is the basis of fairness, democracy, family stability, interracial justice, and world peace!"[42] For him, valuing the personhood of others is the basis of an ideal society. The basis of democracy is the equality of all persons. He saw this in the Declaration of Independence and in the Bill of Rights. He believed that "Western civilization has been outstanding" in lifting up the person and focusing on individual flourishing.[43]

Proctor's moral rearing raised his awareness of the disparities in social outcomes. An example of this point is the story of "Crazy Ida." Proctor spoke of a woman named Ida who lived in the Huntersville community of Norfolk, Virginia, during his childhood years. She was a social outcast whose appearance and behavior made her the object of ridicule in that community. Proctor recalled that the children in the neighborhood would call her Crazy Ida, and she would chase after them when they did. He remembered that he had wanted to call her by that name but had not had enough nerve to do it. A day came when he was alone near the house and saw her walking down the street. He thought no one was near to hear him, so he yelled, "Crazy Ida!" at her and ran in the other direction. His mother heard him from the kitchen window and ordered him to come in and explain his actions. At that point, she told him how Ida had experienced a series of events that had led to her mental and social condition. Proctor said the impression his mother's explanation and concern for Ida left on him lasted for over fifty years of his life.[44] One can attribute his understanding of personhood to lessons like the one he learned when caught teasing Ida. To be sure, Proctor learned and believed that everybody is God's child.

Proctor held that equality extends to all persons, regardless of social status. He understood that societal conditions have created some of the economic disadvantages we find in the world. Yet he believed that there are practical solutions to the inequalities that exist. Proctor reasoned that personhood benefits from having the physical necessities of life. He observed that the poor could be better off in society with better educational preparation. During his time in the Lyndon B. Johnson administration, Proctor's work for the Office of Economic Opportunity was dedicated to the fight against poverty. As a member of the agency, Proctor was instrumental in procuring government funds to provide scholarships to low-income students. This, for him, reflected the Judeo-Christian ethics that informed the nation's values.

The biblical witness presents the message and paradigm that Proctor seized for his public faith. He knew that the Bible proclaims the equality of all humanity. He preached a sermon that highlighted his understanding of personhood, entitled "Everybody Is God's Somebody." Using a passage (Acts 17:26), Proctor stated, "Paul served notice. . . . He came there to tell them that *the whole human race was one*, that one God had made all people, and *that in Christ God was bringing this whole human family to a knowledge of himself*. In other words, in Christ everybody is God's somebody."[45] The Bible, for Proctor, proclaims the fundamental truth of human equality: God made of one blood all nations. Proctor believed that this was a prominent feature in Christ's life and teachings. Christ showed God's love to everyone. Christ treated everyone as a child of God. Through his teachings, he gave humanity the power to become the children of God. The teachings and example of Jesus parallel the democratic principle of the United States, Proctor held. He stated, "His [Jesus'] view of the worth of persons is the cornerstone of modern democracies."[46] Jesus' ethics pervade notions of humanity, in theory.

The reality of human relations in the United States was such that Proctor constructed a public theology to battle "spurious anthropologies." It is necessary, then, to understand the purpose of a sermon such as "Everybody Is God's Somebody," because it exhibits Proctor's concern for the effects of racism in America. In a 1969 article in the journal *Liberal Education*, he wrote:

> The logical and moral conclusion that should follow from our national heritage of the Judeo-Christian ethic, the Constitution and 350 years of national, bi-racial experience is that the black and white community in America—in the South—should by now effectuate a just and compatible rapprochement. At this point in history, only the most spurious anthropology, the most anarchistic social philosophy or the most eccentric racial chauvinism could lead to any other conclusion. Our destinies, social, cultural, economic and political, are inexorably bound together on this patch of real estate unless we pursue an irrational, illegal and immoral course that would lead to an intransigent estrangement between our people.[47]

Proctor contested racist notions of personhood on the basis of science as well as faith. He drew from scientific evidence to advance his claims, using the empirical discoveries that science revealed. He found support on many levels from the fields of science, psychology, and sociology. He argued, "But in further witness of what Christ teaches, there is the obvious physical kinship—that all men are made of one blood. The great contribution of the black medical expert Dr. Charles Drew was his proof to the world that except for blood types—types that *all* races have in common—human blood is the same."[48] From there, Proctor argued that human similarities are numerous. Behavioral sciences were a tool with which he could integrate his Christian beliefs to interpret life. He preached, "We are all children of the same Father. We have the same needs and drives and urges, the same hungers and the same cravings."[49] In some instances, he noted that psychology and counseling support much of what Jesus said. Proctor also believed that all humans display their kinship in their desire to know God. Human beings want a relationship with God. Proctor held that most persons, if not all, seek some spiritual direction from a transcendent being.

Proctor's argument for human equality—the worth of African American personhood—stands firmly on his belief in a God of justice. Proctor maintained that if God made all nations of one blood, then every human being is of equal worth in God's sight. Proctor appealed to God's fairness and justice. Proctor could proclaim that God does not judge on the basis of the outer person but the inner. God does not use the same categories of judgment that human beings use. God determines worth in a different manner. Proctor maintained that the justice of God is much more equitable than the Darwinism that permeated American culture. Proctor stood firmly against the notion of "survival of the fittest." He objected to the belief that each person gets what she or he deserves. Rather, Proctor held that some persons come into this life with deficits that they cannot control. They should not be punished because of them. To be sure, he contended, persons with deficits deserve more help in order to be in an equitable position with others.

Proctor was realistic enough to recognize that there are conditions in life that hinder human development, as he understood it. He maintained, moreover, that these conditions lead others to overlook the potential of persons whose life circumstances are not as favorable as those of other persons. The exposure he received to the problems of poverty taught him that some persons struggle in their development because of their income. He also related directly the issues of poverty with those of education. He observed that poor persons were punished by their lack of education. He contended that poverty held African Americans back in several ways. Dealing with the consequences of poverty was a major focus of his time in the government. He continued his work on the matter with the Children's Defense Fund. He teamed with Marian Wright Edelman to address the issue of children without health care. Poverty was not just a theoretical issue for him. He realized that it had dire effects on numerous persons'—especially African Americans'—understanding of self.

His position on poverty came from his time working closely with the Office of Economic Opportunity. In his book *The Young Negro in America*, he maintained that poor persons are more likely to live in dirtier, crime-ridden neighborhoods. He argued that poorer persons' options for leisure may create "problem personalities" that lead to criminal activity. He believed that the overcrowding in slum neighborhoods is not conducive for social uplift. He even felt that many of the religious leaders in poorer urban areas carried on suspicious activity. He listed several explanations for the problems: politicians sell out the poor residents in poor communities; several persons in poor environments are not healthy influences on children; persons in poverty may go long periods without health care; and a person in poverty receives no respect from authorities—including those in the justice system—because of her or his address. To the contrary, most persons with higher incomes go to well-funded schools with better reputations.[50] Lack of adequate funding for schools in poorer neighborhoods continued to be a major problem in America.

The lack of educational opportunity became the most problematic aspect of poverty for Proctor. He concluded, "It was all new to one who had been reared to regard education as essential as breathing. I found out in Head Start, Job Corps, and Community Action programs that the poor were basically and primarily poorly educated. It meant that education took on a new significance for me, and I saw being inducted into the world of thought as *the* critical experience of living."[51] I will say more in the next two chapters about Proctor's ideas of education and its role in the social uplift of African Americans and humanity in general. For many black leaders (religious and nonreligious), churches, and institutions, education has been an integral part of black salvation in America. Proctor believed in the salvific role of education. For in education, persons were able to cultivate their potential and harness their freedom.

## On the Margin of Freedom

Proctor understood that freedom, a God-given freedom, relates to the notion of personhood as a fundamental component of humanity's inherent dignity. To understand the importance of the concept of freedom in Samuel D. Proctor's thought, it is important to examine the use of freedom in the theological traditions from which he received his formation. Freedom has always been an important idea in the African American Christian experience. Freedom was the goal of black persons from slavery through the civil rights movement. Baptists cherish freedom in such practices as the autonomy of the local church in matters of congregational authority, freedom of religion (separation of church and state), and soul freedom. The last freedom refers to the right of the believer to commune with God without mediation from clergy. A helpful summary of the liberal theological stance on freedom comes from American religious historian Sydney Ahlstrom.[52] He stated that liberals emphasized human freedom and the "natural capacity" of human beings to live a moral life. Sin, for liberal theologians, comes from human error or one being underprivileged. One could fix this by following the example of Jesus, receiving a moral education, and/or the social reform of institutions. Proctor, as a black Christian shaped in the liberal theological tradition, merged these understandings of freedom, seeing human moral development as a counteracting force against America's major sin of racism.

Proctor saw freedom as a primary topic of human moral development. By freedom, he meant the power of choice that God gave all human beings. Proctor argued that human beings are not predetermined automatons. Persons have the power through choice to decide their own course in life.[53] The freedom that Proctor described is not comprehensive in the sense that it covers all aspects of life. Acknowledging the role of social conditioning, he noted that several influences contribute to a person's choice(s). Family background, societal conditioning, and education account for a large area of our behavior. But human beings do have freedom in many aspects of their lives. He observed, "Freedom includes freedom to fail, freedom to choose to quit, freedom to be turned around, and freedom to look for the resources to remain steadfast."[54] He found numerous illustrations of this idea in his own life. For example, while southern society at that time would have frowned upon the generosity of the Reverend Sparks Melton (the local white pastor in Norfolk who gave Proctor a seminary scholarship), he used his freedom to aid Proctor's journey into seminary. For Proctor, the freedom of humanity is a basic aspect of personhood a fundamental reflection of the *imago Dei.*

Several traits characterize Proctor's notions about the use of freedom. First, freedom can be expansive and grow with use. The more one uses one's freedom, the more it expands. By this idea, he meant that the use of one's freedom can lead a person to develop her or his potential. Practically, persons can grow their freedom by enlarging the number of persons with whom they associate. Making choices to learn more about other lives, cultures, and languages broadens a person's world. In doing that, one makes bigger one's margin of freedom. Proctor stated that his few months in Nigeria during his Peace Corps tenure helped him learn more about the world. He first had to make the choice to go.

A second quality of the use of freedom is that, if directed properly, it can enable a person to work toward an ultimate goal. Proctor described it well when detailing his call to ministry. He felt many other influences pulling him away from the work of the church. In the midst of his time in college, he enjoyed being in a fraternity and playing in a jazz band. But the hazing incident in which he was involved challenged him to reconsider the choices he had made. It was at that time that Proctor used his freedom to choose the work of the church. The choice to decide one's course, he believed, is the "most crucial" use of human freedom. This, in some instances, establishes a trajectory of where one ends up in life. A person's sense of purpose derives from her sense of worth. Discovering that sense of worth and the freedom that comes with it gives birth to such purpose. Proctor wrote, "Concerning our freedom, perhaps the most crucial use of freedom is the long reach into our future that we make when we commit our lives to a life's work, such as teaching, preaching, medicine, military service, or the performing arts—to a career calling for a heavy investment of preparation and a long risk. In 1940 I made the commitment to the work of the church, and when I returned to college, I was serious about it."[55] Proctor's mind allowed him to explain the core motivation of this decision in the language of the "call" to ministry. Stated in a different way, this was his theology of vocation.

Human freedom, however, has its negative aspects. Sin, for Proctor, is related directly to freedom. He was very careful to identify the sources of sin as "drives" and "glandular urges" that manifest themselves in selfish behaviors. Concerning this matter, he wrote, "We have all been beset with drives and necessities of the flesh. Every human. We all have an element of vanity and pride, too, that comes with every self—every age." Proctor defined sin in one instance as a person's refusal to give up their known advantages for the sake of others. He argued that one cause of evil in the world is human freedom. He held that humanity "must continue to examine human proclivities and propensities to learn the better uses of human freedom." In one edition of the "Letter and the Spirit" (Proctor's *Providence Chronicle* column), he stated that one must acknowledge one's guilt to God as a precondition for relating to God.[56] This guilt resides in the human family. Proctor observed that sin is "a condition" that can influence a community, race, or nation.

Proctor saw sin as a communal condition. When one person is affected by it, the whole community is affected by it. Early in his career, he stated, "Sin is a community thing." He went on to say, "If you do not get out and try to check it, it will affect us all. Away with this idea of individual salvation alone! We are learning things now. We need social salvation, too. Everybody pulling together."[57] Proctor's statement "We are learning things now" may suggest the influence of his education. He realized that persons can act morally and still contribute to the immorality of society through omission. In his sermon "The Rich Young Ruler," he noted that moral persons can help maintain a sinful society through ambivalence, apathy, and/or by failing to serve others. The gospel narrative of the rich ruler demonstrates how persons who are moral (by legal standards) do not always measure up to the ethics of Jesus. This signifies Proctor's distinction between the Christian ethics and forms of morals that pass for respectability in "polite" societies. Is one driven by external standards (laws) alone or by an internal motivation (the spirit of Christ)? Within the context of

Christian freedom, Proctor saw that the law of sin and death binds persons. The spirit of life in Christ counters it and gives persons real freedom.[58]

Proctor's sermons aimed at persuading persons to choose Christ as their guide in life. Proctor saw freedom's highest expression in the life and teachings of Christ. In his sermon "Personhood in a Computer Age," Proctor argued that a person should choose her or his direction in life. He used the analogy of a computer receiving a program. A programmer puts into a computer what is necessary for it to function properly. A person receives the programming but has the power to veto what is morally incompatible with Jesus' ethic of love. He argued that the Apostle Paul's words in 2 Corinthians 5:13–14a are an example of one choosing one's programming for life. Paul chose Jesus as his guide, and Proctor deemed that Jesus is the finest standard of moral living. Amidst the various commitments that persons have in life, Proctor believed, Christ should be the ethical guide for human beings.

The proper use of human freedom, for Proctor, is to allow a spiritual ideal to capture it. He wrote, "Most of all, it is a freedom to take all of life's gifts and place them under the constraint of a spiritual ideal, and for Christians that ideal is the constraint of Christ."[59] This is how Proctor envisioned human redemption; human beings make a choice to accept the life and teachings of Jesus. This thread in his thought exhibited itself in his early statements. In 1948 (probably the earliest published statements of this notion), Proctor noted that human beings are similar to animals until we are "captured by the eternal love of God." This is how one moves from a state of sin to becoming an occupant of God's kingdom. God brings about the change that makes one fit to live in the kingdom of God.[60]

Morally, Proctor held that giving Christ the reins of one's life is in keeping with the democratic doctrines of America. Proctor saw in Jesus the focus on the human person. This was what Proctor saw in Western civilization—a focus on the person, his or her liberties and rights. The point of comparison for him was the way that one functions in a free society. He appealed to Christian ethics in order to suggest that Christ's teachings are relevant in such matters. Proctor noted that Christian ethics describe an experience with God through Christ that gives the believers freedom. Proctor sometimes quoted Augustine during sermons that expressed this idea. Proctor reminded his audiences that Augustine said, "Love God and do what you please." For Proctor, this statement says much about one's moral commitment and social activity. Proctor believed that persons have to have a commitment to society (national and global). He expected even more from Christians. Christians are citizens of the world and of God's kingdom. Yet he realized the obstacles that persons must navigate in life.

Proctor often described the fragile balance between being an earthly citizen and being a citizen of God's kingdom. To explain this "Augustinian" concept, he used as an illustration his instructions to his sons during their time in Richmond, Virginia. He stated in a sermon that he had to remind his boys that Lombardy Street in Richmond was both a local street and U.S. Highway 1. He stated that the mail carrier and other local citizens would recognize his children and look for them while passing on the street. Visitors traveling on Highway 1 might not be as careful as they "zoomed" past on their way to some other destination. He used this narrative to highlight the tension that comes with being a citizen with dual alliance. But this dual citizenship is not mutually exclusive. He maintained that one can be both:

> I am Sam Proctor, Baptist. I am also Sam Proctor . . . citizen of the USA with a passport, a birth certificate, and a tax bill. Now, if as Sam Proctor, Baptist, I am nothing, what makes me suddenly become something with a Social Security card? But, if as Sam Proctor, Baptist, I have sought the Lord while he may be found, and called upon him when he is near; if I have beheld the beauty of the Lord and enquired in his Temple; if I have tried to keep his Commandments and done justly, loved mercy, and walked humbly with him, I am then not only Sam Proctor, Baptist: I am Sam Proctor, worthy citizen as well.[61]

Proctor discerned that citizens of God's kingdom can function and prosper as citizens in America. In Christ, the balance of these citizenships is maintained. Proctor drew a distinction between true human freedom and acts that follow societal definitions of what is "respectable." The conscience can filter between Christ and culture. Within the larger body of Proctor's thought, the *right* use of one's freedom is the imitation of Christ. Proctor stated, "The person whose conscience is equipped to imitate Christ finds that this imitation is not so much a philosophy or calculated code of conduct as it is a relationship, a loyalty to a Person whose life has a magnetism to it. Following him is joy and fulfillment as well as a logically and empirically sound moral approach to life."[62]

## Passing from Death to Life

The moral character given over to the constraint (imitation) of Christ is, for Proctor, a transcendent pathway to immortality. This is Proctor's distinctive interpretation of immortality. He believed that immortality begins in this life. It is for Proctor a quality of life and not a temporal setting. In this sense, he saw time as an extension of eternity. The source of this altruism is the Christian notion of love. He understood Christ's example as the willingness to create value in a person's life. For Proctor, immortality is a consequence of the Christian moral life; it is a state of being that transcends the limits of temporal reality, a true fellowship with God.

Biblically, the basis for Proctor's view of eternal life came from John's first epistle: "We know that we have passed from death to life because we love one another" (1 John 3:14). Proctor said that this scripture gave him the impression that eternal life is not something that just happens after death; it happens right now. He argued from this verse that persons can pass from death to life without physical death. A person is both a physical life and a spiritual life. Yet a person can be healthy physically and dead spiritually. Proctor characterized regeneration, the initial step in the process of salvation in Christian theology, as the moment in which one moves beyond selfishness toward love. He would not side with persons who believed that the new birth of regeneration is for heaven alone. In other words, Proctor did not find worth in a salvation that merely places a person in heaven upon death. In 1948, he contested a bodily resurrection in his weekly column. He was adamant about a resurrection experience that begins with life on earth. Years later, he would echo this sentiment by stating that immortality begins now. One has already passed from death to life based on the quality of one's life. If the inner life is refined, morally and spiritually, one knows no distinction between time and eternity. This proleptic sense of life mirrors the teachings of Jesus that the kingdom of God is at hand.[63]

The moral teachings of Christ, Proctor argued, require a change in the inner person—a second birth (John 3). It is important to remember that Proctor translated Christianity into a religion of ethical living. Those persons who follow the mind of Christ are transformed. They are renewed within by the power of God's Spirit. The inner person is made new, born again, and that person is called upon to act morally in life. Concerning this moral growth, Proctor wrote, "The very height of moral growth is this transcendent quality of life, beyond legalism, custom, instinct, habit, or mutual reciprocal behavior. It is intrinsic human goodness, already passed from death into life. And this goodness is its own reward; it leads to communion with God."[64]

The quality of the life, the legacy it leaves behind is what makes it immortality. Proctor maintained that God made human beings for immortality. Human beings are equipped with soul and mind. Humanity, Proctor claimed, has "far more significance" than any other creature on earth. Moreover, there are degrees of immortality. There are accomplishments and successes that live on for ages. There are persons and/or groups who build institutions or create novelty in history. A person's legacy may span numerous generations. Proctor referred to his grandmother in this light. He observed, "My grandmother graduated from college in 1882, and her descendants with college degrees number over one hundred—and still counting every May! That is immortality."[65] Proctor addressed this idea of a person's legacy in his sermon "What It Means to Believe in Eternal Life." He argued that the quality of a person's life is the standard for understanding immortality in light of one's legacy. Proctor included in his examples Adam Clayton Powell Jr. and Martin Luther King Jr. When Powell passed away, persons came from all over to talk about how much good he did during his life. And although King's popularity had waned when he was killed in Memphis, persons reflected upon all of his accomplishments after he died. Proctor stated that the public had a better picture of his life after he was gone. Powell Jr. and King Jr. lived with a moral quality that left a mark on history. That is immortality.

Proctor acknowledged that Christianity has an otherworldly side to it. He noted that Jesus talked about a life after this one; specifically, Jesus referred to a judgment upon those who show compassion and those who do not. Proctor recalled two parables that display eternal judgment: the story of Lazarus and Dives and the judge who separates the sheep from the goats. Another example of this is the Sermon on the Mount, in which Jesus says, "Great is the reward of those in heaven" (Matt. 5:12).

While Proctor could state with conviction that Christianity has an otherworldly component, he also believed that Jesus spent as much time—even more time—teaching about human relations on earth. Proctor declared, "But very often when Jesus talked about eternal life, or everlasting life, he was talking about a life that began, not at death, but about a certain quality of life, an aspect of life, a dimension of life that begins right here and right now."[66] Proctor noted that his "type" of Christianity manifests itself in service to persons in need. He said that Jesus' stay in the house of Simon the leper during the Passion Week exemplified the essence of Christianity. Jesus loved, assuming the initiative to find/create value in the lives of others.[67] Mortality and immortality intersect at that point—love.

Holding this understanding of immortality together is Proctor's affirmation of God's love, justice, and order. Altruism becomes the aspect of life that is transcendent. For Proctor, these concepts merge at the topic of immortality. He appealed to God's love and argued that a God of love would not play such a harsh trick by letting life end with the grave. He believed that in the life that is to come, God would take care of persons who were burdened by genetic flaws and undeserved conditions. The God of justice, Proctor held, balances out the scales for persons who compete against the inequities of society. God is aware of the imbalances and injustices in the world, Proctor wrote. He believed that a just God sees all that takes place on this earth. Yet this justice is not exempt from mercy. Proctor looked to Jesus as the example of God's mercy.

Proctor recalled one of his student days at Virginia Union in which he attended a session of the undergraduate ministers' lyceum. The lyceum was a gathering for the young student preachers on the campus. They preached and conducted business meetings similar to the ones carried on by professional (employed) ministers. In this story, Proctor highlighted the fact that many of the young men would come in trying to look like big preachers. He noted that the preachers would arrogantly critique the sermon of the presenter for the day. This worried Proctor, because on one occasion, a young man who was a "spastic" was called upon to deliver the sermon for the evening. Proctor remembered that this young man was not able to present messages the way the others did, due to his disabilities. He also stated that the young man did not have a suit to wear. When the preacher walked up to the pulpit, he started singing, "All oer those wide extended plains shines one eternal day." Proctor said it looked like he was looking to another place. The song continued, "I am bound for the promised land." Proctor said that, despite his condition, the young man had already passed from death to life. Clearly, Proctor described his thoughts on immortality well in 1948: "We pass from death unto life, the resurrection is a real experience for us here and now, but so few people experience it. It is a new life in the spirit which is eternal. Death is no more than a shedding of this cloak of flesh and that life once born in us will live for all eternity."[68]

## A Product of His Time

Samuel D. Proctor proclaimed the inherent equality of all persons as children of God. His Christian beliefs about humanity responded to the American environment of racism and argued for a new political, religious, and social reality for African Americans. As exclusive as the previous statement may sound, it portrays his upbringing and the religious ethos that shaped it. In addition, the statement suggests an acute awareness of the tensions between "black" and "white" Christianity in the United States and the political-cultural-religious battle that laid claim on the soul of America. Proctor sought to defend the equality of African Americans by contesting the "original sin" of the American experience—racism, with its faulty understanding of black humanity—with a biblical claim about humanity that was forged in a black Christian experience.

He also shaped that defense in the historical narratives of the black American experience and his own biography.

Proctor stood within the black Christian tradition. His ideas about humanity fit the "biblical anthropology" of the black Christian tradition. God is parent of humanity, and human beings are siblings.[69] One notices that Proctor rarely, if ever, uses the phrase *imago Dei* when referring to human beings. The more fitting descriptor for Proctor is familial language: children of God. In God's parenthood of humanity, all human beings have inherent worth. With this principle as the primary starting point for human uplift, Proctor took his stance. He believed that every person should begin life by knowing her or his intrinsic worth in the eyes of God. This was especially important for Proctor's ministry to young African Americans. As a professor, college president, government emissary, and preacher, he demonstrated his love for young persons. He concluded that many black young persons were not receiving this fundamental message of the Bible. He felt that it was important that they hear, as early as possible, that they have value and are equal to *all* persons. This he gained from examining his childhood. For in learning about God's parenthood and the equality that comes with being a child of God, persons will know that their existence is valuable. Proctor preached, "*This is the main lesson* that we must get across to many black youth today. Before we do anything else, we must convince them that no matter how the society perceives them or treats them, they are God's precious children. We must convince them that they are loved with an infinite love and that when Jesus went to his cross, it was for the oppressed and forgotten people of the *whole* world."[70]

One can understand the focus of his preaching in light of his notions about racism in the United States. Proctor argued that racism produced a crisis of self-esteem or self-confidence among certain groups of people. If the "net result" of racial prejudice is the crisis of self-concept among African Americans, it is important that persons understand that *everybody is God's somebody*. It just so happens that his religious claim is the fundamental basis for his public faith. He is pragmatic, so his message cuts across many aspects of life. Proctor argued that self-esteem affects the choices that persons make. These choices determine how persons participate in society. He wanted responsible citizens.[71]

Proctor attacked racism on religious grounds. He presupposed the truth of the biblical claim that God created all nations of one blood. Proctor would verify this claim with scientific evidence later in his career. He dedicated a whole chapter to "Racism" in his memoirs, showing ostensibly the role it occupied in his thought. However, in making Christianity a religion of morals, did he place too much faith in humanity's desire to respond—as Christ would—to racism? But his optimism may be valuable. Proctor had a long view of history that appreciated the gains that African Americans had made over time. He saw those gains as God's work through Christ in the hearts and minds of the American people.

Proctor is a member of Cornel West's "Humanist tradition" of response to racism. In his book *Prophesy Deliverance!*, West describes four traditions of response: the exceptionalist, assimilationalist, marginalist, and humanist traditions. The exceptionalist makes ontological and sociological claims about the superiority of African Americans. The assimilationalist makes ontological and sociological claims about the inferiority of African Americans. The marginalist claims that African American culture is restrictive and "emphasizes the suppression of individuality, eccentricity, and nonconformity within Afro-American culture."[72] The final category, the humanist tradition, views African Americans as human beings with as many positive and negative qualities as any other racial/ethnic group. West writes that the humanist tradition accepts black culture for what it is. He states that black culture is, "the expression of an oppressed human community imposing its distinctive form of order on an existential chaos, explaining its political predicament, preserving its self-respect, and projecting its own special hopes for the future."[73] West argues that several literary artists and musicians from the Harlem Renaissance fit into this category. But the political viewpoint of the humanist tradition fits Proctor's agenda as well. Persons in the humanist tradition see in electoral politics the opportunity for social change, and they embrace pragmatic methods to transform society. West notes, "The humanist response to the challenges of self-image and self-determination is this: a promotion of an individuality strengthened by an honest encounter with the Afro-American past and the expansion of democratic control over the major institutions that regulate the lives in America and abroad."[74] Proctor would agree with most of what this tradition embraces. His political, academic, and ecclesial commitments demonstrate this assertion.

Like much of liberal theology and its social gospel emphasis, Proctor had no real interest in focusing on sin. He concerned himself with the development of moral persons and their potential to follow the example of Jesus. Proctor seemed to believe that one can move out of sin with education. Racism and capitalism reflect the selfish nature that defines sin for Proctor. And he believed he was fighting off social Darwinism's influence on the United States. He argued that the example of Christ can change people. Education, moral education can teach persons about the effects of their actions; the world, then, will be a better place. He was optimistic about that plan for social transformation. His own narrative may have presented him with the grounds for such optimism. Yet his story did not describe the totality of black experience.

It is interesting to note that Proctor struggled for gender equality in ministry late in the game. He was a product of his time in that regard. Few, if any, of his early sermons or other writings expresses this concern for gender equity in the pulpit. He said little about women and their role in the church until it became a "pressing" issue among black Baptists and other black Protestants. The more visible issue on the table during his life was that of racism in America. Racial equality dominated his agenda for the larger part of his career. To his credit, he ordained a woman minister at the Abyssinian Church during his tenure as pastor. Toward the end of his career, he made strong statements against gender discrimination in the ministry at black preaching conferences and at churches.[75]

He was invested in other projects for the majority of his public ministry. He was engaged in projects for children and young adults most of his life. As a college professor and president, he worked with a young population and enjoyed his opportunities to nurture young persons. He joined with Marian Edelman Wright to promote the work of the Children's Defense Fund. In addition, he spent a sizable portion of his career occupied with academic and global issues.

What is clear is that his notions of humanity did not change. His understanding of what makes for effective social change shifted around the 1970s. He was wary about the power of government to change America. Political solutions that addressed economics and education remained possibilities for Proctor, but the church in general and black preachers specifically became the target of his desire for racial uplift. The fifth chapter shows that, once Proctor was firmly situated again in the pulpit, he began to move away from political solutions alone for the African American community. He found his hope in educating an elite group of preachers who would make justice and the ethics of Christ the focal point of preaching and ministry.

## Notes

1. Dwight N. Hopkins, *Being Human: Race, Selves, Culture* (Minneapolis: Fortress Press, 2005), 118. Hopkins writes, "In the United States an obsession with race is deeply embedded in the concept of a human being. The 1607 Jamestown, Virginia, and 1620 Pilgrim, Massachusetts, arrivals of white Christians from Europe created a ranking in which human beings were placed on a racial scale in the so-called New World. This racial hierarchy inspired the Christian genocide of and land removal from American Indians, and the Christian enslavement of millions of Africans and African Americans in North America. These movements were marked by their color-coded

aesthetics and power. Consequently, every single American, as well as those who visit the United States, receives a racial status within the anthropological hierarchy. And in the historical definition of the God-human interaction, race seeps in and out of the doctrine of theological anthropology."

2. Richard W. Wills Sr., "Civil Rights and the Idea of *Imago Dei*: A Theological Reconsideration of Martin Luther King Jr." (Ph.D. diss., University of Virginia, 2005). He states a similar thesis for the public witness of Martin Luther King Jr. Wills also argues that King's concern for humanity and the pursuit of justice are informed by his religious beliefs about humanity. Wills claims that King was able to synthesize the positions of figures in Christian history, the Black Church, and voices from his formal theological education to establish his own ideas. Proctor and King are very similar when one considers their backgrounds and their views. Where they differ may be in their activism. King was a very vocal proponent of nonviolent protest. In addition, he led the demonstrations and marches that grew out of the notion.

3. Samuel D. Proctor, "Jesus Christ, Prince of Peace," sermon presented at Abyssinian Baptist Church, New York, 1985, audiotape.

4. Samuel D. Proctor, "Dean Proctor, Virginia, University, Reports on Trip to India," *National Baptist Voice* 26, no. 10 (1954): 1, 13. I make this distinction "earliest *written* statements" because Proctor gave speeches at rallies during the Fair Employment Act movement in Providence, Rhode Island. At this time, there is no access to any written material that he produced during that time. He spoke on the radio and at a mass meeting to promote the cause, but these documents (if written) have not surfaced. In the weekly column for the *Providence Chronicle*, he said little to nothing about the racial problems in America.Proctor stated early in the 1954 article, "My discussion will be limited to the angle of a Negro, representing a foreign mission Board which has not succeeded in integrating Negroes into its work. I kept my eyes wide open and my ears to the ground for such overtones as only a Negro reared in the South and trained in Northern schools is capable of hearing."

5. Samuel D. Proctor, *My Moral Odyssey* (Valley Forge, PA: Judson, 1989), 89. I believe this first trip sensitized Proctor to the global experience of white supremacy.

6. Ibid.

7. Samuel D. Proctor, "Equity from a Racial/Ethnic Perspective," ERIC Document Research and Development Series No. 214J, National Center for Research in Vocational Education, 1981 ED215166, 4–5.

8. See Samuel D. Proctor, *The Substance of Things Hoped For: A Memoir of African-American Faith* (New York: G. P. Putnam's Sons), 189.

9. Proctor, *The Young Negro in America, 1960–1980* (New York: Association Press, 1966), 132.

10. He stated that this period covered the first twenty-five years after the Emancipation Proclamation.

11. Proctor, *The Young Negro in America*, 153.

12. Proctor cited these five stages in a later publication. See Samuel D. Proctor, "King: What Progress Since the Dream?," in Reflections of the Dream, 1975–1994: Twenty Years Celebrating the Life of Dr. Martin Luther King, Jr. at the Massachusetts Institute of Technology, ed. Clarence G. Williams (Cambridge, MA: MIT Press, 1996), 100–101. He listed the second period as acculturation (previously known as imitation).

13. See Proctor, *The Young Negro in America*, 153.

14. Proctor, "King: What Progress Since the Dream?," 103. Proctor writes, "Both men were trying to prepare black people to obtain a substantial and a continuing participatory role in this society."

15. Proctor, *The Young Negro in America*, 154.

16. Proctor does not clearly date an end of this period. It would be interesting to know how he would interpret the racial climate of the contemporary United States.

17. Proctor, "King: What Progress Since the Dream?," 104; and Proctor, "What the Law Cannot Do," lecture presented at the Hampton University Minister's Conference, Hampton, VA, 1990 (Hampton, VA: Hampton University, 1990), audiotape.

18. Samuel D. Proctor, "The College and the Urban Community," *Liberal Education* 55 (March 1969): 80–81.

19. Ibid., 83.

20. Samuel D. Proctor, "The Black Contribution to the American Experience," *National Elementary Principal* 49 (September 1969): 20–22.

21. Lewis V. Baldwin, *There Is a Balm in Gilead: The Cultural Roots of Martin Luther King, Jr.* (Minneapolis: Fortress Press, 1991), 237.

22. "Some Soul Culture Must Go if Integration Wins," *Chicago Defender*, January 14, 1967, 33.

23. Samuel D. Proctor, "Everybody Is God's Somebody," in *Sermons from the Black Pulpit*, ed. Samuel D. Proctor and William D. Watley (Valley Forge, PA: Judson, 1984), 28.

24. Samuel D. Proctor, "Jesus: The Prince of Peace," sermon presented at Abyssinian Baptist Church, New York, December 20, 1987, audiotape.

25. Proctor, *My Moral Odyssey*, 111.

26. Samuel D. Proctor, "Some Things that the Law Cannot Do," sermon presented at the Union Theological Seminary–Presbyterian School of Christian Education, Richmond, VA, 1988, videotape; and Samuel D. Proctor, "What the Law Cannot Do." Proctor used several verses in Romans 7 and 8 for this sermon in its various forms.

27. Proctor, "Some Things that the Law Cannot Do."

28. Proctor, "What the Law Cannot Do."

29. Proctor, "Some Things that the Law Cannot Do."

30. See also Samuel D. Proctor, "Deep Calleth unto Deep," sermon presented at Abyssinian Baptist Church, New York, 1995, audiotape. Proctor stated in this sermon that a spiritual revival must come from people who understand the worth of others. Later, Proctor said, "We've got something to tell the whole world about how you can rise up out of that kind of heap of humanity where people say the nastiest and ugliest things about you; all about your genetic inferiority and all of that and go and climb the heights."

31. Proctor, "What the Law Cannot Do."

32. Peter J. Paris, *The Social Teaching of the Black Churches* (Philadelphia: Fortress Press, 1985), 17.

33. Benjamin E. Mays, *Seeking to Be Christian in Race Relations*, rev. ed. (New York: Friendship, 1964), 21. Mays is well known for his tenure as the president of Morehouse College. He was a mentor to Martin Luther King Jr. and was respected for his work with the YMCA. Mays was a graduate of the University of Chicago, where he earned a Ph.D. in religion.

34. J. Deotis Roberts, *Black Political Theology* (Louisville, KY: Westminster John Knox, 1974; 2005), 91.

35. Proctor, *My Moral Odyssey*, 20.

36. Ibid., 23.

37. Ibid., 36. In the autobiography of his moral development (*My Moral Odyssey*), Proctor borrowed theories from three social development scholars—Jean Piaget, Lawrence Kohlberg, and James Gustafson. It is not my intent to determine how closely Proctor followed their categories.For more on this idea of personhood and the role of parents, see Samuel D. Proctor, "The Four Daughters of Philip, the Deacon," in *Women: To Preach or Not to Preach*, ed. Ella Pearson Mitchell (Valley Forge, PA: Judson, 1991). Proctor wrote, "All of us are created, framed and detailed by the hand of God with our own personalities, our own DNA-genetic equipment, and with our own selective environment. We are bound to be different, and nothing like the love of sensitive parents can recognize and celebrate our unique personhood." Proctor argued in this sermon (on Acts 21:8) that Philip and his wife impressed upon their daughters the notion of their personhood in the sight of God. This idea was what allowed the daughters to believe that God had

called them to their respective ministries. Proctor went further and stated that what Philip and his wife did for their daughters is what persons should now do to "save" the world.

38. Proctor, *My Moral Odyssey*, 44.

39. Samuel D. Proctor, "The Black Church and the Crises in the Black Community," *Chicago Theological Seminary Register* 80 (1990): 8.

40. Samuel D. Proctor, "A Mind Is a Terrible Thing to Waste," *Phi Delta Kappan* 60, no. 3 (November 1978): 202.

41. Proctor, *My Moral Odyssey*, 54.

42. Ibid., 56.

43. Samuel D. Proctor, "Personhood in the Computer Age," sermon presented at Union Theological Seminary–Presbyterian School of Christian Education, Richmond, VA, 1988, audiotape.

44. Samuel D. Proctor, "The Bottom Line," in *Sermons from the Black Pulpit*, 94-95.

45. Samuel D. Proctor, "Everybody Is God's Somebody," in Proctor and Watley, *Sermons from the Black Pulpit*, 26.

46. Ibid., 27.

47. Samuel Proctor, "The College and the Urban Community: Racial Insularity and National Purpose," *Liberal Education* 55, no. 1 (March 1969): 78.

48. Proctor, "Everybody Is God's Somebody," 27.

49. Ibid., 28.

50. Samuel D. Proctor, *The Young Negro in America* (New York: Associated Press, 1966), 109–11; and Samuel D. Proctor, "Margin of Freedom," audiotape of sermon presented at Union Theological Seminary–Presbyterian School of Christian Education, Richmond, VA, 1980.

51. Proctor, *My Moral Odyssey*, 135.

52. Sydney Ahlstrom, *A Religious History of the American People* (New Haven, CT: Yale University Press, 1972), 779.

53. Proctor, *My Moral Odyssey*, 100.

54. Ibid., 60.

55. Proctor, *My Moral Odyssey*, 60. See also Proctor, "The Margin of Freedom."

56. Samuel D. Proctor, "Positive Faith," L&S, *Providence Chronicle*, February 28, 1948. See also Samuel D. Proctor, "Evil: The Unfulfillment of the Good," in *Facing Evil: Light at the Core of Darkness*, ed. Paul Woodruff and Harry A. Wilmer (LaSalle, IL: Open Court, 1988), 209–26; and Samuel D. Proctor, "How Evil Are We," L&S, *Providence Chronicle*, May 29, 1948.

57. Samuel D. Proctor, "Consequences of Sin," L&S, *Providence Chronicle*, August 21, 1948. See also Samuel D. Proctor, "Christian Liberation," L&S, *Providence Chronicle*, August 28, 1948.

58. See Samuel D. Proctor, "The Rich Young Ruler," sermon presented at Union Theological Seminary, Richmond, VA, 1980, audiotape.As with other areas of his theology, Proctor remained steadfast in his view of sin. The early conversations on this topic and its relationship with Christian freedom prefigure his later thought. The sermons "Some Things that the Law Cannot Do" and "What the Law Cannot Do" seem to be the summary of this thought.

59. Samuel D. Proctor, "The Gospel in the Computer Age," sermon presented at Union Theological Seminary, Richmond, VA, 1988, audiotape.

60. See also Samuel D. Proctor, "The Resurrection in Your Life," L&S, *Providence Chronicle*, March 27, 1948.It is important to understand that Proctor viewed the kingdom of God as a moral-spiritual realm—a utopian community where personhood is celebrated and the reign of God (morally and spiritually) flourishes. Christianity was primarily a moral religion for Proctor.See also Proctor, *My Moral Odyssey*, 103–4, 106. Proctor's Christianity focused on the ethical life of the person. To accept Jesus' life and teachings means that one is in touch with God's design for human living. Proctor wrote, "I believe that those who believe in this unique divinity of Christ and whose loyalty to his life and teachings as central are brought thereby closer to God and within the orbit of God's healing power. It is the answer to tension, fitful insecure living, obsessive self-

aggrandizement, and indolent, unproductive living. The fact is that such belief does confer the power to become."

61. Samuel D. Proctor, "The Black Community and the New Religious Right," *Foundations* 25 (1982): 186.

62. Proctor, *My Moral Odyssey*, 84.

63. Samuel D. Proctor, "The Resurrection in Your Life," L&S, *Providence Chronicle*, March 27, 1948; and Proctor, *My Moral Odyssey*, 117–19. Proctor was concerned about the way in which persons described heaven and hell and how these locations were used to frighten people.

64. Proctor, *My Moral Odyssey*, 119.

65. Ibid., 122–23.

66. Samuel D. Proctor, "What It Means to Believe in Eternal Life," sermon presented at Abyssinian Baptist Church, New York, September 1987, audiotape. See also Samuel D. Proctor, "Easter Sunday," sermon presented at Abyssinian Baptist Church, New York, April 1987, audiotape; and Proctor, *My Moral Odyssey*, 122.

67. Samuel D. Proctor, "Simon of Bethany," sermon delivered at Abyssinian Baptist Church, New York, April 1987, audiotape.

68. Proctor, "The Resurrection in Your Life."

69. Paris, *The Social Teaching of the Black Churches*, 10.

70. Proctor, "Everybody Is God's Somebody," 30. The parenthood of God is the consistent premise from which Proctor preached and served. Several sermons affirmed God's parenthood. One Christmas sermon, for example, stated that one message of Christmas is that God made all of humanity precious: "I think the most important thing for people to know . . . the first thing you need to do is to wake up and find out that you are God's child, you're something precious." See Samuel D. Proctor, "The Cosmic Dimension of Christmas," sermon presented at Abyssinian Baptist Church, New York, December 1992, audiotape.

71. Proctor, "Equity from a Racial/Ethnic Perspective," 5.

72. Cornel West, *Prophesy Deliverance! An Afro-American Revolutionary Christianity* (1982; repr., Louisville, KY: Westminster John Knox, 2002), 70–71.West does not expressly state whether the claims made by each tradition have a theological foundation. For example, he states that these claims are "ontological" and "sociological." One is led to believe that claims made on theological grounds make up one of the two categories or that it is not a factor in the claims made by persons in this response tradition. Ontology may draft theology into its purview, but theology requires its own category inasmuch as persons have defined their existence through a religious/Christian hermeneutic.

73. Ibid., 85.

74. Ibid., 90.

75. The 1990 and 1991 Hampton University Minister's Conference became a platform for him to use his statesmanship on the issue of women in ministry. He scolded the "brothers" for their sexism.

# 5

# Preparing Public Theologians

## *Black Preachers and Racial Uplift*

Samuel D. Proctor moved into retirement in 1989 with a desire to enhance the work of Christian ministry in America. He wanted to pass along the knowledge he had accumulated over his long and fruitful career. The instruction he sought to provide for up-and-coming church leaders brought together his public, practical, and pastoral theologies. He especially wanted to convey his understanding of preaching and the role that preachers should play in society. During the latter part of his career, he returned to and/or expanded his understanding of the importance of the preacher in the public sphere. This understanding entailed the desire to develop a literate clergy that could address the problems in society. In this light, his stints in numerous seminaries, publications on preaching, and sermons and lectures all provide a basis for arguing this idea.

Proctor wanted to produce public theologians, black public theologians specifically, who would discern the ills of the American environment and proclaim a truth that would resolve the problems in the black community and in the world. Proctor spent the last years of his career teaching at seminaries, preaching at churches across the nation, and giving lectures at black and white preaching functions and religious conventions. This chapter analyzes his motives and purpose for committing himself as a resource for black public faith. I examine the content of his presentations during his "retirement" ministry. His focus on the sermon was the medium by which the preacher would transmit the content of a public theology that proclaimed, "Everybody is God's somebody." For Proctor, the preacher is the person positioned best to address many of the problems caused by racism in the United States. The sermon, moreover, is the religious vehicle of moral suasion.

Before continuing, I must define the terms I am applying to Proctor's ministry. His pastoral theology reflected upon the role of the pastor-preacher in creating and implementing policies and procedures in the local church setting. He defined the vocation of the pastor. In a broad sense, he provided counsel for pastors in various communities and institutions through his lectures and writings. He was a pastor's pastor. Proctor was a model similar to the Apostle Paul's mentoring presence for evangelists in the early church. Many of Proctor's writings were "pastoral epistles." He focused on practical theology. He was intent upon interpreting and explaining the significance of the tools used in the course of pastoral ministry. For example, preaching and church administration are disciplines within the practical theology curriculum. Proctor's texts on preaching fall into this category. He became an instructor in the art of preaching (homiletics) during those final years.

A public theology also was at work throughout his career, so a final theological term to consider is *public theology*. Public theology is the way in which a theologian represents a theological perspective in the public sphere in order to converse with and/or influence public-policy considerations. According to Victor Anderson, one arrives upon an "adequate" public theology when it distinguishes the freeing power of life lived in community.[1] As a public theologian, Proctor argued for the value of all humanity. Taking this conversation into the public square, he wrote and preached to influence public policy. He called upon the sacred texts of Christianity and his own experiences in a struggle for civil-human rights. Robert Michael Franklin's words seem a tailored description for Proctor's ministry. Franklin writes that public theologians enter public conversations with a "profound sense of humility." They also respect the "sacredness of people and traditions."[2] During his "retirement," Proctor channeled his public theology into a focused educational curriculum for clergy serving African American churches and communities. He attempted to raise awareness of the social crises in the United States. The Bible's witness etched, in Proctor's mind, the need for ethical changes in society. He dedicated the last portion of his life to preachers with these notions as his foci.

As an aside, there is a lack of studies on the sermon as a source of public theology or, for that matter, theology in general. The sermon is the primary product of the Christian pulpit, and it is the focus of ministry for many religious leaders. The influence of preachers on religious persons is immeasurable but obvious. Black preaching infused much of the protest and demonstrations during slavery and the civil rights movement. Even contemporary preachers such as the Reverends Al Sharpton and Jesse Jackson move crowds with passionate oratory steeped in the black preaching traditions. The sermon's role in colonial American life was influential in articulating some of the major themes that led to the American Revolution.[3] Preaching has remained an important part of American religious life, and this may especially be the case in African American religious communities.

The preacher and sermon are important actors in the American religious experience. Recent works by E. Brooks Holifield and Larry Witham on American preachers and sermons display evidence of this fact. The notion of a "pulpit theology" led William B. Lawrence to state that preaching and the preachers who do it have a profound impact on American life. Several persons in evangelical Protestant communities would agree with this claim. The preacher and her or his sermon occupy a lofty place in the lives of many devout Christians. The opportunity to hear "the word" on Sunday morning tops the list of inveterate practices in most Protestant communities.[4] Proctor understood the importance of the sermon. He wanted to enhance the preacher's craft for greater works. Improving sermon preparation habits, providing sermon models, and suggesting content for the sermon were his ways of approaching that task.

After a hiatus from teaching theology, Proctor returned to formal theological education and focused on developing preachers. The final stage of Proctor's career saw an expansion of his belief in preachers as primary social agents in a reform effort of American society. Proctor as preacher helped convey his public faith, his public theology. He intended to mark church leaders with his perspective and approach to preaching. Proctor was a product of a type of black preaching tradition, so it is important to situate him within this experience.

## A Context for Understanding the Black Preaching of Proctor's Time

Few will doubt that the content of the sermon in the African American Christian experience has had periods in which it differs from the content of sermons from white ministers.[5] Several reasons may lead to this conclusion. There has been a disproportionate balance of social power in the white American Christian tradition. To counter this imbalance, black preachers' sermons aimed to empower the marginalized and left-out persons in society—black people. While this may not have been the case for all black preachers, an overwhelming number of them preached a social gospel long before Walter Rauschenbusch made it popular. The issues in African American life have always been complex because of the issue of race in America. The black church and its preacher were willing, therefore, to provide the sanctuary and balm for its constituents. Black Churches attempted to defend and equip persons who were beaten, figuratively and literally, by whites in society. Simply put, black preaching has differed from much of white preaching. The content, in many instances, has reflected the unique struggle of black existence in America and the diversity of that existence.

Black preaching traditions have produced many a preacher who embodied the tenets of the Christian faith and ideals of racial uplift. More than a few black preachers focused on conversion and the salvation of the soul and/or the salvation of the black race from white oppression. Many attempted to accomplish both. The black preacher was in some instances the only person free enough to provide the type of commentary that was necessary to address the ills of society. The black preacher saw truth telling as a part of the job description. Even among illiterate preachers, the gospel found in the Bible took aim at slavery and segregation. It is from this understanding of the religious and social meaning of the "black" sermon that we are able to label such a thing as black preaching.

Homileticians and historians have produced numerous books on the topic, and most come to the same conclusions about black preaching: what makes preaching "black preaching" is the content of the sermon in the African American Christian tradition. For the most part, one can find the generalized characteristics of musicality, emotionalism, and vivid imagery in other preaching traditions. But the experience of being black in America provides a substance that is matchless in other preaching cultures. It is also Christian preaching. Black preachers have "taken a text" from the biblical pages for centuries. The Bible has remained the text of choice for black preaching, and Jesus has remained the focal point of the sermon. It is rare that a congregation will affirm a black preacher if the Bible is not a, or *the*, primary source for the sermon.

Black preaching has maintained a prominent place in the Black Church and black community, and the black preacher has remained a celebrated figure in the African American Christian experience, as Charles V. Hamilton affirms: "The black preacher has been called upon by politicians, parishioners, peacemakers and all others. He has been a natural leader in the black community."[6] Hamilton continues by stating that black preachers have a "perpetual constituency" in the congregation. The black preacher, historically, remains a revered figure for that constituency. The numerous roles that she or he assumes in the community also provide a platform for this person's status. Historically, the black preacher has been a prominent leader in the structures of African American life. The importance of religion and the status of the preacher have gone together in the United States.

While the ministries of black preachers in America became more public during slavery, few of these preachers received education and recognition from religious denominations and institutions in that era. Racist practices produced segregated worship spaces within congregations and condescending attitudes toward black Christians. While this was mainly the case in the South, the northern part of the country did not foster a spirit of total cooperation and fellowship. Richard Allen, before becoming the first presiding bishop of the African Methodist Episcopal denomination, was escorted from the sanctuary of an established white congregation in Philadelphia in the late eighteenth century. The formation of the "Black Church" out of what Albert J. Raboteau calls the "Invisible Institution" becomes evident during the following century. Communities of African American Christians sought alternatives to the Christian practices of their Caucasian counterparts. The black preacher became the de facto leader of these Christian churches.

In answering how the black preacher learned to preach, Henry H. Mitchell maintains that apprenticeships and self-education made up most of the curriculum for early African American preachers. The segregated environment did not promote the formal education of the black minister, but it did make him (primarily) the authority in the community. Hamilton argues that the black minister benefited from segregation in the United States. With the church as a major institution in the black community, the preacher had been the "unrivaled" leader.[7] For the most part, that remained the case when black preachers did receive admittance into colleges and seminaries in the United States.

In the post–Civil War South, two types of black preachers developed: a charismatic but formally uneducated preacher and the emergence of the college-educated preacher who benefited from the construction of black colleges and theological academies established by northern missionaries. Understanding the two traditions of black preaching is necessary for the sake of placing Proctor into a black preaching context. These missionaries had in mind the desire to educate African Americans and turn out theologically literate pastors. It is not a coincidence that several major "race women" and "race men" sharpened their intellect in the halls of historically black educational institutions. Even today, several historically black colleges maintain seminaries and/or religion departments. In black colleges and seminaries, great men and women preachers from the past and present received the critical equipment needed to engage the world. Not all black preachers were able to take advantage of the opportunity to study in formal settings. Similar to the struggles between New and Old Lights in colonial America and the age of frontier revivalism, tension existed about preparation for ministry. A formally educated group of black preachers coexisted with a class of black preachers who had not matriculated in the nation's colleges or seminaries. By the twentieth century, those two primary forms of black preaching continued to dominate the platforms in black communities.

To be sure, differences in content and style among black preachers are, in some cases, the direct result of theological education—apprenticeships or formal classrooms. Two simple yet telling traditions in black preaching stem from the notion of ministerial preparation. An "educated" and "Spirit-led" partition is implied by these categories. Though most black preachers do what preaching scholars or homiletics professors call "black preaching," one finds obvious differences in subtle areas such as style, audience appeal, and emotive-cognitive emphases in a sermon's development. Preachers in the different traditions emphasize different aspects of the sermon. These distinctions are not fixed or rigid. Contemporary preachers such as Dr. Charles Adams of Harvard University Divinity School and the Hartford Memorial Baptist Church in Detroit combine formal education and folk/revival preaching to produce sermons that exhibit the synthesis of heart and head, black "folk" culture and "white" academic theological education. Such a mixture results in labels like the one given to Adams: the "Harvard Whooper."[8] The combination of formal education and folk/revival preaching is seen in current practitioners like Ralph D. West of the Brook Hollow Baptist Church in Houston, Texas; Johnny Ray Youngblood of the Saint Paul's Baptist Church in Brooklyn, New York; Bishop Vashti McKenzie of the African Methodist Episcopal Church; and Gina Stewart in Memphis, Tennessee.

These categories are more complex than the labels suggest, but there is a history behind current practices. Most black Methodist and Baptist churches are ancestors of the revival experiences of the Great Awakenings in American history. Yet two traditions allow for generic descriptions that cover fundamental trends in the history of black preaching.

### *Folk/Revival Tradition of Black Preaching*

The first black preaching group comes from a folk/revivalist tradition. Some suggest that this style of preaching is a continuation of African religious practices in the Diaspora. If not that, it at least depicts the musicality and imagination of work songs from the fields of slave labor. This tradition emphasizes the charismatic styles of revival preaching championed during the First and Second Great Awakenings. I will not attribute this tradition to one person or one group of people in America. The dominant trend has been to situate revivalism around white preachers such as Jonathan Edwards, George Whitefield, and Charles Finney (and later, Billy Graham). In the process of holding up these men, there is a fundamental neglect of the African American evangelical tradition and its primary role in the revivalist culture. Consider American Christianity in the twentieth and twenty-first centuries. The Azusa Street Revival (1906) and the prominence of T. D. Jakes are visible representations of the revival spirit. The black revivalist tradition might have been at its apex in the twentieth century with notable Holiness preachers William Seymour (1870–1922), Charles Harrison Mason (1866–1961), and Charles Price Jones (1865–1949) carrying on itinerant preaching ministries across the country. Several revivalist preachers in the twentieth century made the "folk," "country," or "chanted" sermon mainstream, as some of them recorded and sold records or had national radio broadcasts.[9] Albert J. Raboteau writes about the folk sermon, "It is 'country' since its development took place primarily in the prayer meetings and revivals of the rural South. But it has long since spread West and North to the cities, where radio, television, and records extend the preachers' voices beyond the churches into cars and homes of their flocks. This preaching style is 'folk' art because it is a creation of popular rather than elite culture and because it is an oral rather than literary form."[10] The folk art form distinguished itself in electronic media during the 1920s forward.

The commercialization of a type of folksy African American preaching delivery became popular in the mid- to late twentieth century as well. Baptist preachers C. L. Franklin (1915–1984), W. Leo Daniels, and Jasper Williams Jr. (1943–) broadened the scope of revival preaching by producing vinyl recordings with Jewel/Paula Records during the 1960s and '70s. Unfortunately, black revivalists have not received much attention in conversations about revivalism in the United States. The national success of the evangelist Billy Sunday might have seen its appeal rivaled in the successful radio, recording, and revival ministries of Clarence LaVaughn Franklin, the noted black Baptist minister of the New Bethel Baptist Church in Detroit. Franklin and others placed folk preaching in record stores and on broadcast radio across the country.[11]

The musical preaching, chanted sermon, or "whooping" done by Franklin and others provided the environment for emotive call-and-response encounters that ended in the "frenzy" referred to by W. E. B. Du Bois. These "singing preachers" translated well into radio and vinyl recordings. While few black preachers reached commercial success, preaching at annual denominational conventions and conferences, and invitations to preach on "the revival circuit" also signified the appeal of such preaching and preachers. One might be amazed at the amount of time contemporary black revival preachers spend on the road. Numerous invitations may keep a revivalist out of a daily pastoral charge for most of the year. (Most preachers do three-day to weeklong revivals and return home for Sunday-morning worship with their home parish or congregation.) The popularity of this tradition as an expression of American revivalism is missing in scholarly literature.

Revivalism remains a significant part of the African American Christian experience. Numerous churches schedule set seasons for well-known evangelists to "set the church on fire." The charismatic, and well-televised, ministries of T. D. Jakes, Juanita Bynum, and Eddie Long are cultural feats that remind one of tent meeting revivals staged in a multimillion-dollar facility. The legacy and spirit of African culture and the revivals of the Great Awakenings on the North American continent live on in the African American religious experience.

Folk/revival preaching is not without its opposition. Charges that folk preaching is anti-intellectual have persisted but do not express the complexities of its content and delivery. The craft of folk preaching is rhetorically innovative. The revival preacher's knowledge of the Bible, discernment of the audience, timed repetition of words and phrases, and use of cadence-laced oratory come with study. Tidy distinctions like educated and uneducated are more pejorative than accurate descriptors. Some persons use the label "Jacklegs" or "Jacks" to describe the education level of certain preachers in this tradition. This, however, is problematic. As seen in the examples of this chapter, preachers in this tradition have varied characteristics. Several formally educated and self-educated preachers employ the chant in their sermon delivery. Grounds exist for revising the anti-intellectual designation as a general description for this tradition of preaching.

Being anti-formal theological education is not the same as anti-intellectual. Folk preaching has had an implicit or environmental educational system. Preaching in this tradition does require a learning curve. As noted by Mitchell, apprenticeships have been a part of the spiritual nurture of black preachers. The revival preacher learns a good deal of his craft through emulating the pastor or revival preacher with whom he studies. Memorization and careful practice allow for the polishing of the skill set, or God-given gifts, involved in delivering the chanted sermon. It is, I believe, Raboteau's designation of the chanted sermon being an oral form—not literary—that assists one in distinguishing the traditions to a certain extent. Preachers in the revival tradition, often known more for their delivery than their content, their sound, not their argument, thrive in energetic call-and-response settings. Raboteau even argues that the delivery of the chanted sermon determines the success of the preacher in this tradition. The word *performed* is the emphasis. "In this case, more than in most, style is content," Raboteau maintains.[12] Delivery has also been at the heart of an implicit debate between black preachers.

Some black revival preachers believe that the Holy Spirit dictates the words the preacher should say to the people. To an extent, the preacher is the harp on which the Spirit plays. All of the sounds are distinctly that of the instrument, but the musician plays the right strings. "Spirit-led" preachers, then, sometimes discredit the "manuscript preacher" for her or his lack of faith in the Spirit's work. But this tradition leans on its tried-and-true history in black church settings. One can usually identify the structure of the chanted sermon, with its move from diminuendo to crescendo. By no means does this discredit the development or sincerity of the folk preacher. Revival preachers are nurtured in an environment that produces its own educational system. There is an informal seminary, of sorts, that perpetuates the chanted sermon and its popularity. The second tradition opts for a different route.

### *College Chapel/Lecture Preaching*

The second major tradition in black preaching has been that of the college/seminary-educated clergy. The label *chapel/lecture preaching* signifies a general understanding of these preachers' educational background and style of delivery. Their delivery reminds persons of a classroom lecture. These preachers have had access to the college, seminary, and university settings. The black college and university chapel circuit of the twentieth century was unique in that it required a certain level of preparation from its preachers. It may not surprise observers of the black experience that folk preachers were not extended many invitations to preach in the college settings. The desire to maintain a "civilized" or "intellectual" environment probably upheld this partition among black preachers. Most preachers invited to the chapels during Proctor's time were alumni of the colleges or well-known formally educated preachers. In Proctor's circle of contemporaries, well-known black preachers Martin Luther King Jr., Benjamin Mays, Howard Thurman, John Malcus Ellison, Vernon Johns, and Mordecai W. Johnson frequented various black colleges and universities during "Religious Emphasis Week" and on other occasions.[13] An important part of the black college experience, Religious Emphasis Week provided opportunities for the student bodies to hear from exemplars of the Christian faith and the black race. Many of these preachers were influential in notable black academic institutions.

For the most part, the chapel/lecture preachers received recognition in black newspapers, published extensively, and carried on conversations in print media. In the nineteenth century, such predecessors to chapel preachers as Henry Highland Garnet (1815–1882), David Walker (c. 1785–1830), and Frederick Douglass (c. 1818–1895) all used print to converse about issues of utmost importance. People heard their ideas from the pulpits and read them in pamphlets. The legacy continued in the twentieth century. (Mays, Ellison, Thurman, King, and Proctor wrote several books.)

Writing has been a major contribution of the lecture preachers' legacies. Their commentaries on social issues, preaching and pastoral ministry, and biographical writings provide a black cultural perspective on theology and society. Mays wrote editorials for the *Pittsburgh Courier* and books on major topics. Proctor wrote "pastoral epistles" for the *Providence Chronicle* and produced several articles and books on theology. Martin Luther King Jr. wrote a series of religious advice columns for *Jet* magazine and numerous books of sermons and social commentary. Thurman was among this group with several publications and listening rooms of materials such as sermons and meditations in locations on both coasts. Ellison's sermons appeared in several publications on preaching, and he published books with reputable denominational presses. Two of his books consist of meditative sermons on issues of life. His engaging style appealed to psychology, theology, and sociology to answer the riddles of life. As previously mentioned, he published a preaching manual (a how-to book). This manual covered numerous topics related to preaching and emphasized the sermon's value as a literary form.

Print media were not the only access preachers in this tradition had to African American religious publics. Yet the reach of their ideas seemed to either begin in or extended to print. These men were preachers, orators, and scholars. They had an unrelenting dedication to the Christian church and its African American constituents.

Lecture preachers were influential outside of academic environments. Many of them appeared at major denominational events. They were called upon to "lecture" or preach at religious conventions, among black and white groups. And, as was the case with Proctor, Ellison, and King, they received respect from leaders within black denominations. King's father was good friends with Joseph Harrison (J. H.) Jackson (1900–1990), former president of the National Baptist Convention, USA, and King Jr. had a collegial relationship with Jackson until he and others supported Gardner Taylor for the presidency of the convention. Ellison and Proctor maintained amicable ties with Jackson, and letters between the three support this claim. All of the aforementioned chapel preachers were at some point in their ministries local church pastors. Disconnecting an understanding of social concern from the church's life was not an option for these preachers. These scholar-theologians were preachers. They were going to preach.

Seeing the sermon in the context of literature, many black preachers in the chapel/lecture tradition are known as manuscript preachers who focus on using a preaching method. Yet labeling the preachers in this manner is too general for this tradition. For example, Gardner Taylor, the pastor emeritus of the Concord Baptist Church in Brooklyn, New York, memorizes his manuscripts and preaches without notes. Proctor used a manuscript and read it. In many cases, methods and content became the focus of the lecture preachers' sermon development. A contrast is evident in Raboteau's description of the folk preacher and my analysis of the lecture preacher. The chanted sermon usually results in the emotive celebration of the preacher and the congregants. To be sure, many lecture preachers are not without emotive moments in the sermon. The lecture preacher is not a robot. But as John Malcus Ellison argued, quality of sound is not the preacher's intent when delivering the sermon. The content of the sermon should trigger these moments. He declared:

> The men who help people understand eternal verities and God's presence in human experience must do so soberly. They wisely avoid undue dramatics and refrain from sensational, spur-of-the-moment pronouncements that have no basis in fact. At best, such things make only momentary impressions which do not strengthen Christian faith. Careful preparation through writing helps the preacher consciously refrain from the spontaneous sensationalism that is prevalent in many worship services. When the preacher is intellectually serious and evinces warmth of personality, a sense of the nearness and reality of God's presence seems to fill the atmosphere. . . .
>
> Worshipers then know that in religious services, God is central. That is the end of all worship. That is the supreme purpose of all preaching and of all preparation for preaching. The sensational dramatist in the pulpit destroys the sense of worship because he makes himself central instead of God.[14]

Revival preaching, or a certain kind of revival preaching, concerned Ellison. Proctor could not help but be influenced by persons whose ideas about preaching were similar to Ellison's ideas.

J. Pius Barbour, the former editor of the *National Baptist Voice*, strikes a most apparent case for Proctor's place in the "educated" preaching tradition. Barbour wrote Proctor in 1951, requesting that Proctor write an article for the *Voice* on "My First Trip to the National Convention." The problem he wanted Proctor to address is at the heart of a tension that still exists among black preachers:

> In this article I want you to do a hatchet job on the educated preacher who has not learned the art of controlling the Masses. The Jacks control them with Voice. What is our technique? Therein lies our trouble. And believe me the trouble of the White World. Hitler and Stalin know how to control the Masses. The Press, Radio etc. get them [sic]. Is the Church licked? Now take the Ball. No sense in Ph.D's standing around at the mercy of Jacks. WE NEED A TECHNIQUE. What is it? I am preaching like Hell.[15]

Barbour's description notes his concern for black preachers in the lecture tradition. Proctor grew up in a preaching environment that affirmed the lecture-preaching model. These attitudes date back to notions of education and theological preparation espoused by his parents and the members of the Bank Street Baptist Church in Norfolk, Virginia. They sealed Proctor's preaching fate.

Further study should take place on this tension in black preaching. This facile divide may be at the heart of black clergy responses to issues of race in the United States, reveal approaches for African American uplift, and show similarities or differences in pulpit theology (the sermon's theological emphases). Henry Mitchell and others speak of it in their brief histories, but more work is necessary. Proctor is a child of the black preaching experience in America, and this brief history explains a model he embraced. Authors such as Charles V. Hamilton, Henry H. Mitchell, James H. Harris, and Cleophas J. LaRue have done well to locate their definitions of black preaching in the content of the experience. As fluid as the characteristics just mentioned are in such a discussion, experience makes black preaching black. The range of education received by black preachers is from no education to terminal degrees. The theology of sermons in black churches includes emphasis on the eschatological to the social-political. Black preachers have been on the front line of insurrectionary, abolitionist, and civil rights movements. Black preachers have been congressional representatives and city council members, and a couple of them have run for the presidency. Yet a historical study that charts the development and divergences in style, attitudes, influence, and theology in black preaching is an intriguing prospect. The history reveals a source of Proctor's preaching.

To be sure, Proctor is a product of the second tradition. Developing in the lecture/chapel preaching experience allowed him access later into "white" venues at which one would rarely, if ever, see a revival preacher speak. The commencement addresses that Proctor gave at predominantly white colleges and universities are too numerous to count. He maintained a schedule of delivering speeches/sermons at colleges and universities from the 1960s until his death in 1997. He was nurtured for the preaching ministry as a race man who represented "the best" of African Americans in speech, dress, and education.

## The Product of "Educated" Preaching

The black preaching tradition laid claim on Proctor before he knew it. At work in Proctor were a black Baptist heritage and a liberal theological education. Several persons had a hand in guiding Proctor the preacher. From the earliest voices he heard from the Bank Street Baptist Church pulpit to the congregations he served, he had help developing his theology of preaching. By this, I mean that practical theology, for Proctor, was not an academic course alone. Lessons in the seminary classroom could not produce the whole of Proctor's preaching intelligence. His understanding of preaching was tested and proven over the course of its interaction with instructors, colleagues, and congregants. His biography revealed the intellectual sources that shaped Proctor the public theologian. Some of the same persons and places shaped Proctor the preacher. Identifying some of those links to his preaching reveals various themes that lasted the majority of his public career.

A notion of an educated clergy laid the path for Proctor's early view of the black preacher. After experiencing his call to ministry, he was able to test his ideas of preaching and ministry on several persons. Lewis V. Baldwin explains a similar situation in which Martin Luther King Jr. forged an understanding of black preaching. Baldwin argues that King's father and his father's contemporaries had an immense influence on the younger King. Benjamin Mays, Howard Thurman, and William Holmes Borders all were a part of the younger King's upbringing. Proctor's childhood lacked the presence of such preaching luminaries. But the influence of the Reverend D. C. Rice at Bank Street is evident in Proctor's call story. (Rice matriculated at Union Theological Seminary in New York.) Proctor also flourished by interacting with John Malcus Ellison and Richard V. McKinney as an undergraduate at Virginia

Union University. Proctor's "apprenticeship" came during those early adult years.

Conversations between John Malcus Ellison and Proctor about preaching are evident. In *They Who Preach*, Ellison cites Proctor's preaching method (a Hegelian dialectic model) and refers to its usefulness in constructing the preacher's message. Ellison was important to Proctor for so many reasons. He was a paradigm of the "consummate professional" for Proctor. Ellison exemplified the pastor/scholar's role for the church and academy. Ellison modeled what it meant to be a churchman with academic credentials. He served Baptist congregations and became the president of Virginia Union. Ellison never stopped working on behalf of the church. He continued to conduct his research on topics related to the preacher's role in society. Perusing the Virginia Union archives turned up outlines of book-length studies on ministry penned by Ellison. He put his work in writing. He encouraged Proctor to do the same.

Proctor attempted to follow Ellison's literary example when he joined the faculty at Virginia Union. Between 1951 and 1955, Proctor wrote several letters to different publishers, requesting a review of his materials, beginning with his dissertation. He wanted his work to be published by the American Baptists' publishing house, believing that the dissertation could curtail the conflict between theological modernism and fundamentalism. He wrote a tract on the ordinances of the Baptist church as an instruction manual for the churches. He attempted to have it published by a large press before allowing the local Baptist convention in Virginia to print it.[16] Yet Ellison's main influence on Proctor may have come in his belief that a preaching manual was needed for the black preacher. Ellison's audience would have been predominantly African American, though his preaching books may have had a larger audience. Ellison was recognized among African American clergy members in the "lecture" tradition. Proctor listened to Ellison on this topic, and that helped set a standard for his ministry. Proctor could move on from Virginia Union as an undergraduate to attend Crozer Seminary with an image of an educated black preacher as a blueprint for his studies.

J. Pius Barbour at the Calvary Baptist Church in Chester, Pennsylvania, continued Proctor's education in preaching. Barbour's presence allowed Proctor to filter the education he received at Crozer Theological Seminary through the sieve of a Black Church perspective. The Crozer classroom of Gordon Poteat was a preaching laboratory for Proctor. It exposed him to the sermons and methods of renowned English preachers. Proctor refers to such preachers on occasion. But Proctor's second track of seminary education came from Barbour, whose influence might have settled Proctor on the use of a dialectical method of preaching. Barbour schooled Proctor and other black preachers after him on how to make his education work in black settings. Proctor described the process to Richard Lischer in the book *The Preacher King*. In editorial pieces and sermon samples for the *Voice*, Barbour displayed a structure that models a dialectical approach to preaching—antithesis, thesis, and synthesis—similar to the one employed by Proctor. Barbour's was a school of ministry and preaching that Crozer could not give Proctor.[17]

In addition, like many persons in America during the 1930s and '40s, Proctor tuned in to hear Harry Emerson Fosdick. Proctor credits Fosdick with helping him develop a model of sermon structure. Concerning this reference, it is clear that they were influenced by similar theological sources. One obvious source was a loose kind of structural adherence to a system of dialectics. The thesis, antithesis, and synthesis are present in Fosdick's and Proctor's sermons. They acquired this philosophical system from that age of theological education. Although Fosdick does not give much credit to Hegel when describing his "Project Method," the philosopher's system is a structure by which many persons in the liberal theological tradition preached.[18]

Similarities exist between Proctor and Fosdick. Fosdick wanted to address some problem that a person in the pew faced. He then moved to solve that problem in his sermon. Proctor offered the same perspective in his sermon method. He aimed at providing resources for the parishioner. This meant dealing with concrete problems and presenting pragmatic solutions. The Hegelian tension between the *is* and the *ought* weighed heavily in Fosdick's and Proctor's preaching. Some of Proctor's sermon transitions are fashioned after Fosdick, using phrases like "Come next and see." Proctor even used the phrase "My soul," borrowing from Fosdick's preaching vocabulary. Yet Proctor is far from being a clone. An important point to understand is that Proctor, like many preachers, appreciated Fosdick's pastoral-preaching model. The two men were products of a shared tradition—American liberal theology—with theological ancestors who saw the gospel from a social-ethical position. While Proctor gives Fosdick credit for his preaching model, he may be, however, more indebted to Barbour for the specifics of the dialectical method.

After years of travel and experiences in varied positions, Proctor began writing the ideas that informed his preaching. He was a national preacher whose words and counsel clergy members sought. He probably became aware of this national appeal and sought to channel it in constructive ways. Producing publications on preaching and ministry provided a platform for extending his vocational charge. The literary genre was a medium consistent with his background and preparation. In this way, he sought to develop public theologians. Through his writings, he could converse with preachers about the form and content of their preaching. He could shape their theologies of ministry. Proctor knew that his audience would be local church pastors or persons who aspired to be local church pastors.

## An Engaged Preacher, a Public Ministry

A key component of Proctor's theology of ministry was the preacher's academic preparation. Proctor defined the preacher as that person who is "called by God, set apart, and acknowledged by the church as God's special agent."[19] (The terms *preacher* and *pastor* are used here interchangeably.) The preacher is authorized to preach the message because God "enters history" and gives people the assignment to preach. The calling that God places on one's life is the basis for one's ministry. Yet, Proctor argued, preachers should avail themselves of theological education. Proctor is adamant about the minister's preparation in some form of educational environment, preferably the seminary setting. On different occasions, he lamented the perils of the uneducated ministry. He called it sad when a pastor "has only a shallow preparation and is unable to teach."[20] He asked rhetorically about the consequences of a community that is "the victim of an untrained pastor." He implied that the result may be a community that must deal with a preacher who is a burden or embarrassment. Proctor seems oblivious to the effectiveness of preachers who lack formal education. He saw education as the linchpin for the preaching ministry. The educated preacher receives the tools to engage the larger world and confront secular society. Proctor believed in a literate, formally educated clergy that could transmit the gospel message in the contemporary setting.

Proctor had a particular vision for the education of church pastors and preachers. Understanding the traditional curriculum in the theological seminary, Proctor argued that its educational goals should be more practical. He desired a curriculum that moved away from theory and abstract concepts: "It is a mistake, I believe, for preachers in training to focus more time and effort studying discursive, abstract, and analytical topics *about* Christianity than witnessing in detail the lives of those who followed Jesus in rare and creative *kingdom living*. It is also a mistake, I believe, for ministers in training to be exposed to many secondhand reports of discipleship at the expense of more hands-on practice in adventurous, selfless Christian and servant participation."[21] A concept-focused education would not accomplish what Proctor felt ministers for this age required.

Proctor took a more earthy approach to the topic of ministry. He served two congregations in his career and taught ministers in a seminary environment for a number of years as well. He wanted to mentor pastoral/practical theologians who would become public theologians—agents of change. At the heart of Proctor's thought was the idea that preachers should have a prophetic concern in their understanding of ministry. Yet his concern was holistic. He did not want a preacher to mount the pulpit forty Sundays in the year, talking about social issues on each of those Sundays. He did have a concern for caring for the church as a community and for the person as a child of God. Proctor understood that persons need counsel, and he cared for the soul. He understood that the sermon would reflect diverse concerns. His major issue, however, was for the preacher as a public theologian. He maintained that the preacher is uniquely positioned to comment on all of the "crises" that arise in the community. It is the vocational responsibility of the preacher. Proctor argued that the preacher may not see a burning bush or feel led to liberate "enslaved sisters and brothers" in a hostile country. "But we are called by the crises of our times to be aware of the needs of people in our communities," Proctor insisted.[22]

Proctor charged the preacher to see society's ills as content for the sermon. He argued that social concerns are nonexistent in some sermons. This was problematic for him. He held that the gospel of Christ is a response to the community's issues. Therefore, it is important that the preacher give meaning to the gospel for the contemporary setting. The preacher must be equipped to "transpose" the message of the gospel for the modern mind. The modern person does not live among sheep and goats, so preachers must give meaning to parables and environments that are foreign to their listeners. He stated, "Our first pulpit assignment is to make the congregation aware of the content, the body, the meaning of the gospel."[23]

Proctor understood that preachers have primary and secondary emphases in their sermons. With this in mind, he listed categories for the types of preachers who occupied the pulpits of his day. He provided these images of the work of the preacher's sermons: (1) the comfort dispenser; (2) the pedantic dilettante; (3) the social prophet; (4) the Bible repository; and (5) the faithful pastor. The comfort dispenser provides relief for the pains that persons suffer during the week. This preacher provides temporary pain relief for the bumps and bruises of life. The pedantic dilettante is the scholar who wants to be known for her or his displays of academic brilliance. This preacher prefers recognition for the sermon's intellectual content and presentation. Social prophets call out the failures of the institutional structures in society and the way in which they contribute to the decaying social order. A preacher who is a Bible repository seeks to be an expert on the content of the Bible; Scripture memorization and quotation are frequent signs of this person's approach to preaching. Incidentally, Proctor cautioned that he had seen many a Bible-quoting preacher who knew more about the content of the Bible than of the God of the Bible. Proctor believed that too many preachers hide behind a bibliolatry that substitutes a "soft salvation formula" for a real call to be disciples of Jesus. The final image is the faithful pastor, who includes in her or his ministry the aforementioned foci. Proctor argued, "This pastor is able to take ordinary words and, by the mystery of preaching in the Spirit, to lead persons into a relationship with God through the Incarnate Word, Jesus. Out of this experience is yielded the comfort and strength one needs for the journey; an awareness of the wider parameters of religious thought and feeling; a vision of the kingdom of God descending in time, space, and at City Hall; and the urge to say 'Have mercy, Lord!' and 'Thank you, Jesus!'"[24] The faithful pastor understands what the people need and serves in such a way that the balance of her ministry responds to these needs. Fundamental to this notion of the preacher-pastor's work is Spirit-led insight.

Proctor's book *Preaching about Crises in the Community* (1988) is the explicit product of his understanding of Christian ministry. In this book, he argues that the preacher is called by the crises of the times to respond to the people's needs in our communities. In his use of the word *our*, Proctor is targeting African American communities. He used the book to alert primarily black preachers to the concerns at hand. Drugs, poverty, and education led the list of crises that plagued predominantly black communities, Proctor held. These crises were not mutually exclusive. In fact, they were produced by similar causes. They created similar problems. Related to these issues was the lack of genuine community. An indicator in Proctor's time (and still in ours) is the racist attitudes that lingered from days past in America. This book was an instruction manual, meant to raise for the preacher the battles that she or he should fight. Proctor "figured out" a purpose of ministry and used this book and others to bring attention to the topics.

To be sure, the preacher's concern for the community involves more than participating in transient conflicts that arise, Proctor argued. The preacher must have the type of prophetic insight to know that the community is amiss. The preacher connects to Christ and is sensitive to the problems in society. Preachers are in position to change the moral compass of society. For Proctor, the sermon is a primary vehicle to transmit the good news that Christ proclaimed.

## The Sermon as a Conversation for Publics

Proctor saw the sermon as the preacher's ally for individual and social change. The sermon for him is a unique religious statement that wrestles with issues of immediate and ultimate concern. The sermon summons the listener(s) to think about God and humanity with relevance, for a short period. In his words, "It is a proclamation of the truth of God, through Jesus Christ by a preacher endowed with spiritual discipline."[25] The sermon employs the Christian scriptures and converses about the matters of life. The sermon's importance takes on cosmic dimensions. It can help one come to grips with life's meaning. The preacher, therefore, should approach the sermon's task with discipline and integrity. She should allow her personality to convey God's truth for God's people. In this sense, preaching is a privilege. God charges the preacher to present the Good News to people.

Proctor found his authority for preaching in the ethical teachings of the Bible. He claimed as his biblical authority the eighth-century BCE Jewish prophets, the life and teachings of Jesus, and Paul's writings on the Christ. Consistent with his black Baptist nurture and theological education, Proctor focused on the ethics in these writings. He argued for the life-changing—mind-transforming—power of Jesus the Christ. Proctor believed that preaching of this kind would result in transforming social conditions. Persons living as Christ lived and following what he taught would make the world better. His public theology applied his Christian faith to the problems of the nation. To be sure, what parishioners at the Abyssinian Baptist Church heard him preach on Sunday mornings reflected a nuanced social-political stance that he presented in other settings. Yet his concern for nurturing personhood supported his pastoral demeanor and approach to social change. He was conscious of not treading on established notions of Christian orthodoxy within his congregation. He was a pastor-preacher.

### *Proclaiming What Ought to Be: The Content of the Sermon*

Proctor proposed four main themes for preaching: that God is present and active in human affairs, that spiritual renewal and wholeness are available to human beings, that genuine community is a realizable goal, and that eternity moves through time. The themes make up the content of the preacher's sermon on any given Sunday. From these themes, the preacher has an opportunity to address the concerns of the people in the congregation. Proctor believed that persons in the pew have spiritual and social needs that lie in each of these realms of preachable content. He advised preachers to find some "arrow" from their quiver with which to point and shoot on Sunday mornings. In Proctor's words, the four faith propositions represent the core of what congregants and preachers should listen for in a sermon.[26]

First, Proctor proposed that the preacher affirm the presence and activity of God in human affairs. It is incumbent upon the preacher to keep alive or ignite a faith that gives meaning to a person's life. Preachers should discern and be sensitive to where their audiences are on a given Sunday. The faith on which the preacher builds in her his audience is that which fosters the listener's "moral response" to the world. Proctor held that leading persons into knowledge of a spiritual reality is one of the most important works a person can do.[27] The preacher's job is to make real God's immanence for the hearer. God is available and active in human affairs. For Proctor, this is an important part of a person's faith experience. Believing that God cares and is available to assist human beings provides support in ordering one's faith. The preacher's job is to make that idea real in the sermon. In true sermonic form, Proctor detailed the results of that kind of preaching. He stated that hearers of sermons that proclaim the availability of God can expect to have a coherent view of the world: "Effective preaching tries to sell a view of the world that one can live with while facing all of life's stark and bold realities. Being left with only a cold mechanistic world and with no more of a God than a 'first cause' or an 'unmoved mover' leaves large areas of our experience unaccounted for."[28] Awareness of God's presence also results in a personal moral commitment. This commitment enacts moral judgments that produce equality and the affirmation of personhood. A person, then, can find rest from the storms of life. Belief in the presence and activity of God allow persons to respond adequately to the traumas that life may produce. Persons then will be able to cope with the inconsistencies of life.

Proctor held that persons can live up to the highest values they know. The preacher also needs to make the congregation aware that spiritual renewal is possible. Preachers' tasks include assuring persons of their ability to live on a higher moral plain. Proctor argued, "One of the finest opportunities that the preacher has from the pulpit is to confront all persons with the possibilities for renewal and restoration, to begin where they are with whatever may be their degree of alienation and estrangement, and to help them find the freedom to center on Christ and experience spiritual and moral wholeness."[29] Proctor appealed to the idea that a moral good exists, and that persons continue to demonstrate this in spite of the existence of evil. He confessed that he is not naive enough to believe that evil does not exist, but he believed in the progress that humankind has made throughout the centuries. He posited that human beings have come a long way since the days of the Bible, when killing persons was "ordained" by God and women and children were property. Proctor stated that examples abound of persons who choose not to allow society's unethical practices to define their behaviors. A person who centers her or his life in Christ finds true freedom. That person receives the moral and spiritual renewal that God makes available in the life and teachings of the Christ.

A preacher's third task is to build up the hope and possibility of genuine community. This hope resides in the fundamental belief that God made all persons of one blood. The preacher must make clear that God is the creator of the human family. God has an "enduring love" for all persons. The preacher should disturb persons who take this idea for granted and awaken them to the racial, social, and gender inequalities that permeate the American experience. Proctor declared, "Preachers are obliged to point to obvious symbols of noncommunity in order to focus on the hope, the need, the possibility of change."[30] Preachers make persons aware of the facile barriers produced by the distinctions that society creates. Proctor argued that the preacher also has a job to discern the burgeoning signs of community that appear. The sermon employs persuasion to convince people of the inherent equality and interdependency of all persons.

The preacher's final objective is to address "the tension that comes with living in the world." Proctor reminds his audience that God made human beings for eternity. For Proctor, the preacher speaks to an awareness of human finitude and transcendence. The preacher has the unique responsibility of reminding persons of our destiny and fellowship with God. God created human beings above all creation, so the preacher must remind the congregation of that fact. Persons are designed to live a "dual life." Human beings exist in both *chronos* and *kairos*—time and eternity in time. Without the preacher, persons may content themselves with crass materialism. The preacher can call persons from a wasteful idolatry. The sermon makes plain the freedom that persons have to transcend the negativity of life. And it can help persons move into the orbit of God's power. Awareness of eternity allows persons to understand the transient nature of society's influence. Yet the preacher first must be freed from a reality of selfish "nowness." The preacher cannot expose persons to the truth of God's delivering power if the preacher does not receive it.[31]

The preacher's experience with God gives the preacher and the sermon credibility. Theologically, biography reified the content of Proctor's sermons. All of his sermons included stories that tied together his own experiences with the meaning he communicated. For example, he told a story about a woman in a rural home who sought his advice on getting electricity in her home. He transposed that experience into an anecdote about the need for everyone to connect to the power that God through Christ makes available. Biography, for

Proctor, affirmed and proved God's participation in human affairs. Experience sheds light on the profound truths of the gospel. Proctor encouraged preachers to make the gospel fit for today's world. His narrative was a way to accomplish that task.

### *The Sermon's Method*

Proctor believed that developing a preaching method is an important part of the preacher's ministry. He had settled upon his own sermon method as early as the 1950s. A document in the Virginia Union University archives reveals a typewritten copy of Proctor's dialectic method of sermon preparation. The document lists in detail how to construct a sermon. Proctor argued that the "competent operator"—in this case, preacher—has a method. The method, then, helps propel the sermon's message. Teaching this method in the classroom and in his writings, Proctor exposed numerous preachers to the sermon as a logical development, not necessarily an emotive one.[32] He loosely borrowed Hegel's dialectic, appropriating the terms for the method from Hegel's philosophy. Proctor stated, "A very helpful method comes to us from the German philosopher Georg Wilhelm Friedrich Hegel. He systematized a process of logical development that we use quite commonly."[33] Proctor concerned himself with the sermon's organization. Two books reveal the attention he paid to method. In *Preaching about Crises in the Community*, he dedicated the last chapter to "Putting the Sermon Together." His book *The Certain Sound of the Trumpet* is a classic textbook on the matter. He used these books as a practical way of instructing a larger audience. For him, the dialectical model allowed for constructive dialogue between tensions in life.

Proctor believed that every sermon should have a purpose. The *proposition* of a sermon states the preacher's main idea. The sermon is a faith statement that reflects an important concern in the life of the local faith community. One comes upon a proposition through biblical study or discernment of the ideas, mood, or issues the times may produce. The sermon's proposition responds to its parishioners' questions and concerns. Proctor held that preachers should be equipped to address the God questions that people bring to church on Sunday mornings. The preacher's responses to these questions take on affirmative positions. For example, Proctor used as a proposition the following statement: "We are endowed with moral choice, a margin of freedom above all conditioning factors in our lives, and we are accountable as to how that freedom is used."[34] A proposition is what the preacher shall have said once she is finished preaching.

Proctor sought relevance for the sermon. He argued that the preacher should not remain in ancient times at the neglect of the issues facing the congregation. The Bible is a primary source for the sermon's topics, and other sources provide a context for the sermon's proposition. Proctor contended that the preacher has a duty to speak to the issues of the day. A carefully crafted proposition is relevant when it takes on societal issues. Proctor stated, "There is little excuse for the preacher to have persons coming to church with burning curiosity and anxiety about events in the news . . . and have the preacher skirt around such events."[35] Proctor sought to make black clergy aware of content pertinent for the Sunday sermon. His lists of examples include matters of societal importance. The United States' military and economic leadership in the world, the spread of AIDS, and redress for historical discrimination all deserve a place in the preacher's lectionary.[36] He wanted preachers to deal with society's issues.

A sermon's antithesis (the real) made tangible the issues raised in the proposition. Proctor defined the antithesis as the condition that the sermon addresses. Located at the introduction of the sermon, the antithesis reveals the sermon's importance. It introduces listeners to the proposition's focus. Proctor noted that the sermon's antithesis can cover varied concerns. These concerns grow out of societal views, congregational concerns, and/or theological issues. His examples of antitheses vary along subject matters:

> 1. In a culture that defines success by money and power, little time is allowed for centering on God in the world (Theological Issue).
>
> 2. Problems with hunger, poverty, and illiteracy in developing nations should be handled by the people in those nations and no one else (Ethical Issue).
>
> 3. The gay community wants to sell everyone on their lifestyle. . . . They must be stopped or the nation will be damned (Social Issue).[37]

In one sermon, "Looking at the Church from the Inside, Revelation 3:4," his antithesis stated that it is easy for persons on the outside to see the shortcomings of the church. The church, therefore, has lost much of its influence on society because its shortcomings are used against it. The antithesis invites the congregation to pay attention to the sermon. Its relevance requires a hearing. Knowing that some conditions are controversial, he believed that it is important to keep the listeners focused on the content of the message. The antithesis frames the problem that the thesis addresses. One moves from what is to what ought to be.[38]

Proctor's notion of the sermon's thesis entails an expanded version of the proposition. It appeals to the Bible, history, literature, and biography to support its claims. For Proctor, "It is the preacher's opportunity to share both ethics and personal spiritual witness with the congregation."[39] The thesis is the sermon's focus. A sermon's thesis is the answer for what ails us in the antithesis. The thesis for the sermon on the church displays this fact. The antithesis states that the church's credibility is diminished based upon the shortcomings held up by outsiders. Proctor declared in the thesis that persons in the church know that there is much more to the church than its failures. Using the passage in Rev. 3:4, Proctor said that John (the writer) could see more of the good in the church than its failures. The struggle, then, is ascending to the thesis. How does one reach the ethical platform that the thesis presents?

Rhetorically, Proctor inserted a "relevant question" into the sermon's structure that anticipates the sermon's synthesis. The relevant question ties the sermon's introduction and body together. Proctor states that it keeps the sermon on course. Following the sermon outline from "Looking at the Church from the Inside," Proctor asked, "What would an insider know about the church today that an outsider may not know?" He argued that the sermon maintains its integrity when it stays on course, on topic. The relevant question draws in the listener by asking a question that allows the body of the sermon to resolve the tension between antithesis and thesis. This is the parishioner's response to the relevant question, "So what does the sermon have to do with me?" The resolution, then, is the sermon's synthesis.[40]

For Proctor, the synthesis consists of the main points of the sermon. The synthesis answers the inquiry that the relevant question presents. He used the synthesis to move the audience from the antithesis to the thesis. It lists ideas for seeing the connection between the introduction of the sermon and the relevant question. Using illustrations, mainly biographical anecdotes, in the synthesis makes concrete the ideas proclaimed in the sermon. The dialectical sermon develops in a logical fashion. The preacher intends for the thrust of the sermon to allow the congregation to think through the issues that it presents. The listener should be able to see a way to resolve the problem that the sermon raises. Consider again the sermon "Looking at the Church from the Inside." The synthesis of the sermon answers the relevant question that Proctor gleans from discerning his social context and biblical text:

> Relevant Question: "What would an insider know about the church today that an outsider may not know?"

1. The church spawned some of the most important agencies in the modern world.
2. The church's fellowship is the most inclusive in society.
3. The church's message gives the best answers on life's profound questions.[41]

Each of these answers includes its own support that argues the proposition of the sermon. Proctor believed this method to be a prime way of educating and persuading the listener.

### *At the Intersection of Pastoral, Practical, and Public Theologies*

Samuel DeWitt Proctor's approach to ameliorating the conditions of the black community resided in empowering clergy, African American clergy. During the later years of his ministry, he would draw upon the rich resources of his preaching experience and social witness. By becoming a "pastor's pastor," he conveyed these resources to the next generation of black preachers. He saw the black preacher as a person who is close enough to the pulse of the African American community to respond effectively to its needs.

Proctor remained active after his retirement from the Abyssinian Baptist Church and Rutgers University, teaching in various seminaries that included the School of Theology at Virginia Union University (now named after him), Vanderbilt Divinity School, Duke Divinity School, Harvard Divinity School, and United Theological Seminary in Dayton, Ohio. The last learning community is especially important, as it was his opportunity to mentor and influence a "talented tenth" in the black church.

Drafting the best and the brightest became a modus operandi for Proctor. As he entered retirement, he created a Doctor of Ministry program at United Theological Seminary in Dayton. He recruited several seminary-educated African American preachers to begin the journey. The first class included notable black preachers: Jeremiah Wright, Otis Moss Jr., and Suzan Johnson Cook. The courses dealt with issues of ethics in ministry and preaching for social change. Proctor desired that a group of theologically educated ministers take on the role of public theologians, contesting societal issues with a public faith. He saw a black community in crisis. The black community needed public theologians who could navigate the social-ethical boundaries of society. These preachers would need the equipment to address America on behalf of their communities. He intended to transmit the black social gospel content of his formation. The description for one of Proctor's courses, The Mission of the African American Church in the Twenty-First Century, notes, "The purpose of this course is to make an assessment of where the African American church is presently, in view of the imperatives of the Kingdom of God and the history and status of African Americans in the society; further, to project the role of the African American church as an influence upon the African American community into the 21st century."[42] The Doctor of Ministry program at the United Theological Seminary continues with tracks dedicated to Proctor's concerns.

Returning to theological education reflected Proctor's emphasis on the preacher as the person positioned best to change society. The final stage of his career was an intentional approach to theological education. He had a paradigm of public ministry upon which he based his life. Referring to his new role in ministry (i.e., as professor and lecturer), Proctor stated, "This is a wonderful way to bring the formal assignments of my career to a climax. I will use all of my time left, God willing, to preach the gospel of Jesus Christ and to advocate the pursuit of real community in America and in the world. We need educators, we need politicians, we need philosophers, but we need also those advocates, those prophets, those Elijahs who will speak truth to Ahab, and those Nathans who will remain free to say to David, 'Thou art the man.'"[43] This idea became his mission in retirement. He intentionally presented himself as a public theologian and taught that model to his students.

Proctor balanced notions of church and state with concerns for the Black Church and its community. The consummate educator, Proctor discerned that the heart of ministry is the intersection of practical, pastoral, and public theologies: "It is one of the most gratifying privileges that a preacher could ever expect; to present the claims of Christ in our personal lives and the claims of the Kingdom of God in social terms with such clarity and conviction that this creeping tribalism and racism would be seen receding before the rising tide of real community."[44] Proctor was well aware of the criticisms placed upon the Black Church and the black preacher. He refuted the charges of otherworldliness as a generalization that does not consider the depth of the African American Christian experience. He called the complaint "curious," because African American churches and preachers had responded to education and civil rights issues for well over a century.[45]

For Proctor, the pastor's role concerns more than preaching. The pastor's vocation includes ministry, as a teacher, intercessor, and counselor. He encouraged pastors to preach to their congregations about issues of diversity, liberation, and community. To be sure, Proctor was intent on teaching preachers about their significance in society. He wanted to ingrain in them an awareness of the legacy of American racism. For Proctor, the new generation of pastors needed to fight against poverty, drugs, teen pregnancy, and poor public education.[46] Proctor argued that preachers faced a world with ethical inconsistencies. He often invoked the ethical teachings of the prophets to instruct preachers. In one Hampton lecture, Proctor chided the first President Bush on the nature of his educational policies. Proctor believed that vouchers were a way to destroy the public school systems. He anticipated that churches would recruit students through the voucher system. In an uncanny parallel to recent times, he questioned the legitimacy of the war against Saddam Hussein. Proctor was concerned about America's *true* intentions for the war. These were the comments of a public theologian, providing an example for those who would preach.[47]

Like most preachers in the lecture tradition, the genre in which Proctor operated might have limited his attempts to enlighten black preachers. If C. Eric Lincoln and Lawrence Mamiya's results are near accurate today, only 20 to 25 percent of black clergy receives a professional theological education. Are the persons who need Proctor's counsel accessing it?[48] As stated earlier in this chapter, not every black preacher enrolls in seminary. Proctor, moreover, failed to appreciate the influence of the folk tradition. He could have directed some of his attention to the importance of those ministry apprenticeships. Instead, he largely disregarded the power and appeal of the emotive experience of revival preaching. Historically, folk preachers have moved crowds with their oratory. The influence of the lecture tradition did not open him up to the potential of revival preaching's allure. One could consider him an elitist on this matter.

The state of black communities in America was a matter of concern for Proctor. Justice is a goal fulfilled only in the actualization of genuine community. Preachers herald this message. Reaching that goal requires persons who participate in public dialogue about social ills, proclaiming the highest ideals of living—Christian ethics. L. Susan Bond acknowledges Proctor's preference for the preacher's vocation: "The preacher's work is always a *public* theology, done within a cultural and social context; therefore, the preacher must be informed about things such as politics, science, psychology, education, and sociology."[49] Proctor not only sought to create public theologians, he embodied his message. He fought for justice in university boardrooms, government meetings, college classrooms, and the local church pulpit. Proctor's student James Henry Harris echoes this idea: "Being a champion of justice and equality, Proctor emphasized the necessity for individuals to make decisions that are just and fair when dealing with one another."[50] Proctor saw in the preacher an advocate who can call for the type of moral conversion needed in America. He called for the preacher to herald the type of community that transcends race. The preacher would call for the community that signals the reign of God's kingdom. Proctor wrote, "When we preach about the possibility of community, it is important for us to save our people from the illusion that the distinctions created by poverty and by historic exclusions and isolation mean more than they do. Beneath such distinctions persons *are* equal."[51] Proctor embraced and embodied this message. He believed that the preacher is the herald of community.

# Notes

1. Victor Anderson, "Contours of an African American Public Theology," Journal of Theology 104 (2000): 53. See also Robert M. Franklin, Another Day's Journey: Black Churches Confronting the American Crisis (Minneapolis: Fortress Press, 1997), 122; and Steve Goldzwig, "A Rhetoric of Public Theology: The Religious Rhetor and Public Policy," Southern Speech Communication Journal 52 (1987): 130. Goldzwig's definition is appropriate for a conversation about Proctor. Goldzwig examines the content of talks given by public theologians. He argues that public theology is "theologically-based discourse intentionally targeted for mass audiences in an attempt to influence the attitudes, beliefs, and values of both religious and secular publics on public policy." Goldzwig's study says more about the way in which public theologians transmit their messages. He states that the rhetorical practices of public theologians fit three categories. Public theologians' messages speak of a partisan God who guides persons to what they should support politically (Expedient Simplicity). They fill their discourse with current problems followed by practical remedies (Existential Content). And public theologians speak to rituals that link the theologians with the audience, emphasizing action based on religious beliefs that supersede all other considerations (Action Rituals). These categories create catchalls for public theologians. Proctor has elements of these categories in many of his sermons.

2. Franklin, *Another Day's Journey*, 122.

3. Harry S. Stout, *The New England Soul: Preaching and Religious Culture in Colonial New England* (New York: Oxford University Press, 1986).

4. See E. Brooks Holifield, *God's Ambassadors: A History of Christian Clergy in America* (Grand Rapids: Eerdmans, 2007); William B. Lawrence, *Sundays in New York: Pulpit Theology at the Crest of the Protestant Mainstream, 1930–1955* (Lanham, MD: Scarecrow, 1996); and, Larry Witham, *A City upon a Hill: How Sermons Changed the Course of American History* (New York: HarperOne, 2007).

5. Black preaching is the historical and contemporary mode of preaching that wrestles with the issues in African American existence. One cannot argue cogently for black preaching as a style. Black preachers all over the world vary in style. The preacher who acknowledges and preaches from the experience of black people practices black preaching. For more on this matter, see Cleophus J. LaRue, *The Heart of Black Preaching* (Louisville: Westminster John Knox, 1999), 5. See also Henry Mitchell, *Black Preaching: The Recovery of a Powerful Art* (Nashville: Abingdon, 1990), 12; and Mervyn Warren, *Black Preaching: Truth and Soul* (Washington: University Press of America, 1977). Warren emphasizes some of the distinctions in style and emphasis in the sermon delivery of black preachers.My interpretation of black preaching is similar to the labels and characteristics that Franklin lists in *Another Day's Journey*. I choose, however, to focus on two dominant traditions of black preaching. These traditions are foundational for a conversation about the subject.

6. Charles V. Hamilton, *The Black Preacher in America* (New York: William Morrow & Co., 1972), 12.

7. Mitchell, *Black Preaching*, 39; and Hamilton, *The Black Preacher in America*, 15.

8. See C. Eric Lincoln and Lawrence Mamiya, *The Black Church in the African American Experience* (Raleigh, NC: Duke University Press, 1990), 14. The authors state, "Dr. Adams is widely celebrated as an educated preacher who can still preach in the traditional black style."

9. I believe it is necessary to note that while an overwhelming number of revivalists deliver "chanted" sermons, many revival preachers bring about the emotive congregational responses without the tonality and musicality that one experiences in the chanted sermon. The "whoop" is replaced with "shouting" or fiery appeals to the conscience of the gathered body. One may also use shouting as an emotional appeal. One can see clips of several black revivalists on the popular website YouTube.com. See Jasper William's eulogy of C. L. Franklin, http://www.youtube.com/watch?v=yBwRjFZwo5Y. See also C. A. W. Clark, http://www.youtube.com/watch?v=rHO9aqFzWtM. The revivalist preachers' appeal has not waned in black preaching.For an example of the commercialization of the folk preaching, see Alan Young, *Woke Me Up This Morning: Black Gospel Singers and the Gospel Life*, American Made Music Series (Jackson: University Press of Mississippi, 1997), 194–95. See also Evelyn Brooks Higginbotham, "Rethinking Vernacular Culture: Black Religion and Race Records in the 1920s and 1930s," in *African American Religious Thought: An Anthology*, ed. Cornel West and Eddie S. Glaude Jr., 978–95 (Louisville, KY: Westminster John Knox, 2003).

10. Albert J. Raboteau, *A Fire in the Bones: Reflections on African American Religious History* (Boston: Beacon, 1996), 141.

11. For more information on C. L. Franklin, see Nick Salvatore, *Singing in a Strange Land: C. L. Franklin, the Black Church, and the Transformation of America* (New York: Little, Brown, 2005).

12. Raboteau, *A Fire in the Bones*, 142.

13. One can scan the *Chicago Defender* and *Pittsburgh Courier* newspapers during the 1930s and 1940s to find support for this claim. I mention these names because of the nearness to Proctor. These men were either his mentors or close friends—both, in some cases.

14. J. M. Ellison, *They Who Preach* (Nashville: Broadman, 1956), 85. Ellison's idea "sounds" good in theory. A contradiction may exist in its execution. Producing the sermon as a literary piece requires attention to composition. Issues like the order of words and quality of writing are tantamount to the folk preacher's concern for sound and performance.

15. J. Pius Barbour to Samuel D. Proctor, November 1, 1951, Samuel DeWitt Proctor Papers, VUU, Richmond, VA.

16. Proctor sent at least four manuscripts to publishers. He sent his book to Judson Press, but the editor told him that his work was "too scholarly for the average reader." See Miles W. Smith to Samuel D. Proctor, August 10, 1951, Archives and Special Collections, VUU, Richmond, VA.

17. Richard Lischer, *The Preacher King: Martin Luther King, Jr. and the Word That Moved America* (New York: Oxford University Press, 1995), 68–71; see also the sermon samples and editorial pieces by Barbour in the *National Baptist Voice* during the 1940s.

18. Lionel George Crocker and Harry Emerson Fosdick, *Harry Emerson Fosdick's Art of Preaching: An Anthology*, ed. Lionel Crocker (Springfield, IL: Thomas, 1971).

19. Samuel D. Proctor, *The Certain Sound of the Trumpet: Crafting a Sermon of Authority* (Valley Forge, PA: Judson, 1994), 6–7.

20. Samuel D. Proctor, *We Have This Ministry: The Heart of the Pastor's Vocation* (Valley Forge, PA: Judson, 1996), 14.

21. Samuel D. Proctor, *"How Shall They Hear?" Effective Preaching for Vital Faith* (Valley Forge, PA: Judson, 1992), 85.

22. Samuel D. Proctor, *Preaching about Crises in the Community* (Philadelphia: Westminster, 1988), 12.

23. Ibid., 28.

24. Proctor, *The Certain Sound of the Trumpet*, 6.

25. Ibid., 9.

26. Proctor, *"How Shall They Hear?,"* 10.

27. Ibid., 20–21.
28. Ibid., 25–26.
29. Proctor, *"How Shall They Hear?,"* 35.
30. Ibid., 63, 66.
31. Ibid., 94. Proctor is adamant about the preacher and her ministry: "No one other than the preacher is charged to call us from these silly excesses and to give the preeminence and all the glory to a holy and righteous God, our supreme and *wholly other* in the world, in whose presence our souls should take delight."
32. Samuel D. Proctor, "Untitled, 1954 (?)," Archives and Special Collections, VUU, Richmond, VA.
33. Proctor, *Preaching about Crises*, 118. Proctor's system of preaching includes a thesis, antithesis, and synthesis. He stated that the antithesis is the "Real," and the thesis is the "Ideal." Persons familiar with Hegel's philosophy may accuse Proctor of holding more to the spirit of the Hegelian system than to the letter.
34. Proctor, *The Certain Sound of the Trumpet*, 42.
35. Ibid., 46.
36. Ibid., 47.
37. Ibid., 57–59. See also Proctor, *Preaching about Crises*, 119.
38. Proctor, *The Certain Sound of the Trumpet*, 66–67.
39. Ibid., 74.
40. Ibid., 66–67, 95.
41. Ibid., 67.
42. Timothy Binkley from the United Theological Seminary Library in Dayton, Ohio, supplied the course description from the United Theological Seminary catalog (1992–1994).
43. Samuel D. Proctor, *My Moral Odyssey* (Valley Forge, PA: Judson, 1989), 176.
44. Proctor, *The Certain Sound of the Trumpet*, 15.
45. Proctor, *"How Shall They Hear?,"* 98.
46. Samuel D. Proctor and Gardner C. Taylor, *We Have This Ministry: The Pastor's Vocation* (Valley Forge, PA: Judson, 1996).
47. Samuel D. Proctor, *Fruits of the Spirit*, lecture presented at the Hampton University Minister's Conference, Hampton, VA, 1990 (Hampton, VA: Hampton University, 1990), audiotape.
48. C. Eric Lincoln and Lawrence Mamiya, *The Black Church in the African American Experience* (1990; Durham, NC: Duke University Press, 1998), 399. At the time of the study (c. 1990), Lincoln and Mamiya posited that "only" one out of every four or five ministers had graduated from a professional school. The study reflects some of the most recent information on the topic of professional education for black clergy.
49. L. Susan Bond, *Contemporary African American Preaching* (St. Louis: Chalice, 2003), 41.
50. James Henry Harris, *The Word Made Plain: The Power and Promise of Preaching* (Minneapolis: Fortress Press, 2004), 33.
51. Proctor, *"How Shall They Hear?,"* 67.

# 6

# Creating a Genuine Community

## *A Black Christian Vision for Transforming American Public Space*

The notion and construction of a "genuine community" was Samuel DeWitt Proctor's remedy to the racial crisis in the United States. The nation's glaring social disparities were the product of centuries of racist practices, he believed. He envisioned a world in which justice and fairness prevailed. And he believed that the United States could achieve community. He saw it in his own life. Moments of kind, collegial relationships across racial lines were a glimpse of genuine community to Proctor. He knew that real community was possible, and he committed to working for it.

Proctor, like other black religious intellectuals of the liberal tradition, resolved that America's citizens needed to become a community. These black Christian thinkers understood "beloved" or "genuine" community to be a moral-spiritual human existence that embraces and celebrates personhood through racial and ethnic inclusiveness, economic equity, and social justice for the world's residents. Proctor differed, however, from liberal black religious intellectuals in this tradition by emphasizing faith as the impetus of genuine community's creation. This faith lay primarily in God's dealings in human history and in persons' potential to make community possible. In this way, Proctor pushed for a public faith that expressed his hope in social progress and in the inherent good of humanity. His biography proved to him that progress was possible, even inevitable. He was among a cadre of significant black religious thinkers who also held forth a definition of community as a remedy for the cultural crisis of twentieth-century America.[1]

As with many thinkers, Proctor nuanced his concept of creating community as he matured. At the beginning of his public ministry, from about the 1950s to the 1970s, Proctor touted education as the catalyst for creating community in America. That idea remained constant for him. Government officials, the president and legislators, who could enact policies to eliminate racism, became the agents for change in this model. They were in positions of power to affect the state of affairs in America. After years of public service, however, Proctor saw how powerless these same persons could be without the moral support of the American public. This insight led him to revise his thoughts on the creation of community. The latter portion of Proctor's career, from the 1980s to 1997, marked a shift in focus. He placed more responsibility on the vocation of the minister. The minister, he argued, could herald the message of moral and spiritual regeneration and nurture the development of community. Preachers, especially black preachers, Proctor insisted, had the unique opportunity to fight racism by moral-spiritual suasion. Built into the gospel was the message of community that could change the ethical tilt of the United States. For Proctor, the rationale was simple. The nation's principles were consistent with the ethics and teachings of Jesus. Proctor, informed by the black Christian tradition and the liberal theological view of humanity, affirmed the inherent dignity and worth assigned by God to every person. The nation's founding documents did the same, in theory. He saw, therefore, the pursuit of genuine community as the logical end in the social progress of humanity. Reaching genuine community meant that the United States would wage war against racism, poverty, and the conditions that create them.

## Defining Genuine Community

Genuine community is the idea that guided Proctor's beliefs about change in American society. It is the conclusion of his theological principles of humanity and the objective of his public faith. His definition of community consists of three interrelated components. The first of these components is the affirmation of the personhood of all humanity. Every person is a part of the family of God. The second concept is the removal of arbitrary impediments for persons to attain full status in society. A third component is the moral obligation of the "haves" to the disadvantaged members of society). Proctor understood that these interrelated parts would not come without effort. A moral framework needed to be in place before genuine community could exist. Proctor believed that genuine community requires the choice of persons to yield to an interdependent existence that affirms the accountability of each person to all humanity.

Four decades of Proctor's thoughts and writings went into understanding the meaning of community. A sermon he presented at the 1954 American Baptist Churches convention in Minneapolis displays the sprouts of this concept. The sermon, entitled "The Other Sheep," interpreted his missionary journey to Asia on behalf of the denomination. He concluded that human beings are fundamentally alike. The next step for humanity was to break down the categories that separate persons from living in community. He argued, "The next advance in ideas must furnish us with a concept of man which will educate us for citizenship in a world community, one that will include some suggestion of the possibility of a fraternity of men in spite of our infinite varieties."[2] He was already thinking in terms of a world community in 1954. His missionary journey opened his eyes to the global nature of racism. The trip gave him license to speak confidently about the state of race relations in the United States. The sermon represents his optimism for the possibility of community and his understanding of what must take place to make it a reality. Community can happen. But persons must be reeducated in terms of their working anthropology. His goal was to "furnish" persons with a concept of humanity that would allow world community to happen one person or group at a time.

Proctor's description of community went beyond superficial meanings. He understood that persons labeled community too loosely. For example, any connection of people who inhabit a certain space for a certain period might fit a definition of community. He also acknowledged that one could consider a gathering of persons for a sporting event or concert to be a community. One could call a neighborhood a community. The basic values of persons in these neighborhoods could be similar, thereby granting them some semblance of community. Yet their existence as community is temporary, transient. When a game or concert ends, that community dissolves. Geographical space connects and binds residents of a neighborhood. But does anything else bind them? Proctor believed that genuine community calls for a higher standard of social participation. Genuine community requires persons to make a moral choice about their entry into it. He stated, "Genuine community is limited by choice, not by other arbitrary constraints. It is volitional, not circumstantial. We have freedom, men choose rapprochement rather than estrangement."[3] Persons commit to being in genuine community. They recognize that it is their choice to join it. Community cannot be authentic if it is forced, supported only by a tenuous moral contract. Proctor's notion of community demands a moral basis, a theological foundation. He posited that genuine community reflects the community's depth of kinship, an inclusive and "ever-widening" embrace of humanity, and its volitional participation of persons of different backgrounds and perspectives. Community comes by choice, not compulsion.[4]

Choice, a basic aspect of humanity's "margin of freedom," is integral in community. Persons choose to accept the Christian moral principles that champion the inherent dignity of all humanity. Denying this basic principle is to deny the fundamental ground of Jesus' ethics. The source of a person's motivation decides the nature of her or his moral choice. Does money, fear, or love determine the way the person relates to other human beings? For Proctor, the love of Christ is the foundation for genuine community. The ethical teachings of Christ have spiritual power to convert and change the moral tilt of American life. Persons have the opportunity to move beyond narrow nationalistic and/or ethnocentric understandings of humanity to a Christ-centered inclusive appreciation of and accountability for it. Walter E. Fluker describes this idea in his study on community in the thought of Howard Thurman and Martin Luther King Jr.: "Concretely expressed, then, the beloved community is 'the mutually cooperative and voluntary venture' of persons in which they realize the solidarity of the human family by assuming responsibility for one another as children of God."[5]

## Creating a Family of Justice and Love

Justice and love were important ideas within Proctor's view of community. A concept of justice that seeks the good of all persons is necessary for creating community. Proctor wrestled with questions of African American poverty, unemployment, and education. He attempted to address them in the Great Society–era programs as an agent of the government. Yet he discerned that apathy and "moral inertia" were influential factors that deterred action that rectified the aforementioned social conditions. He argued that many Christians fail to discern the need for justice in American society. The type of self-sacrifice that community requires also needs love to make it happen. Love for one's neighbor is a part of the Christian mandate. He appealed to the Christian sensibilities of society by arguing that the human family is one, thereby calling for Christian empathy and charity to ameliorate the social conditions that impede human flourishing.

### *The Parenthood of God*

Genuine community's theological commitment affirms God's parenthood of humanity. Proctor often invoked this theological premise to support his arguments. All persons are God's children and deserve such recognition. Each neighbor looks at the other, appreciating the inherent dignity and worth of the other. Using Acts 17:19-28 as his guide, Proctor contended, "The hope and the possibility of genuine community rest firmly upon the basic understanding that all persons are indeed created equal. God did make of one blood all persons to dwell on the face of the earth."[6] Proctor believed that this notion of God's parenthood is foundational for genuine community. This is his major claim for community: everybody is God's somebody! Proctor stated, "We are one human family, with one Creator, and God cares about the total human family with infinite love. Love of God requires love of all of God's children."[7] One cannot know true community if one does not start with this idea at its core. Authentic community defies the boundaries of race, religion, nationality, and class. Personhood is the transcendent aspect of humanity's nature that allows it to occupy these distinctions but not be limited by them. For Proctor, details like race are geographical and genetic accidents in the sense that one cannot choose where and to whom one is born.

Proctor's theology models the biological family when considering God's parenthood. One begins to learn about genuine community in the biological family; family is the microcosm of community for Proctor. It is the individual's foray into understanding real community. He celebrated family as the community in which life begins and values are defined. Family aids in developing the person. Family represents the relationship in which persons share space, resources, and ideas. A good family exhibits the type of sacrificial love that seeks the good of every other member in the unit. Family also models community in that it is intergenerational. The parents establish the principles for kinship and set the values and standards by which each member of the community/family relates to society. Children explore moral boundaries and test the experiences of life through the lens of family. Children also learn what to value from what they see their parents do. Parents encourage or discourage entry into the life of the mind, and teach their children that the interest of one is the interest of all. Family is the incubator for how a person grows morally and spiritually. Proctor felt that such an important community influences the life choices and chances for a person. Family is the foundational social paradigm for genuine community.[8]

### *Justice*

Proctor called upon Christians to recognize that some persons are victims of social neglect and unfair treatment. He was concerned that Christians were not empathizing with poor and marginalized persons. He expressed a belief that Christians have sided with those who are apathetic about poverty. He stated, "Christians are slow to see the Spirit of Christ in such situations. In fact, today many Christians are altogether too closely identified with the political mentality that is most indifferent toward the poor."[9] Proctor held that Christians needed to make justice a public issue. In a sermon titled "Relevant Religion," he implied that Christians had made justice a private matter. He maintained that they are obligated to make justice a policy issue. In his words, "It is not enough for Christians to be buried in their own piety and in their own sense of justice. We've got to participate and make our institutions just and fair."[10] Christians, with ethics at the core of their faith, could lead humanity toward the just society that God requires. Justice, though, is a by-product of the faith that Christians display in God. Justice represents a belief in God's desire for human affairs.

### *Selfless Love*

Accepting the idea of human personhood requires action that expresses self-sacrificial love. Proctor called upon persons to open their hearts to others because of their unique kinship through God. Assuming this moral-spiritual posture allows persons to do good for others—to love others selflessly. Proctor wrote, "This unmeasured love flows from our awareness of God's love for all of us. True love is always the willingness to take the initiative in seeking good in the life of another."[11] Proctor stated that love must transform the heart. The love of God is the catalyst for this transformation. Seeing people through the love of God helps persons empathize and enter into relationship with others. Selfless love also demands, Proctor noted, a sacrifice of material excess so that others might experience contentment.

Proctor used as his examples the Peace Corps teachers he directed in Africa. He described their self-sacrifice as vicariousness. The volunteers lived with the indigenous population of people by giving up the comforts they knew in the United States. The young persons who volunteered also entered the lives of others in Africa without foolish notions about the people they served. He maintained that this relationship helped those volunteers see the humanity of the people that they served. The Africans also learned about Americans. Proctor maintained that selfless love would seek the good of persons suffering in other lands. Nationality and ethnicity could not limit the expression of selfless love. What Proctor observed, however, as a barrier to the full realization of selfless love was that this love, in practice, did not extend into policy/legislation. Selfless love lacked structural support on government levels. He claimed that one of the challenges for preachers is fighting to make love a part of the political consensus.[12] Genuine community calls for the moral sense of obligation that can only come with conviction of one's heart. Proctor demanded that a response follow. He affirmed, "Compassion must become actualized. Genuine community calls us to go beyond sentiment and pity to intervene effectively."[13]

### *Eliminating Social Impediments*

Proctor identified the moral-spiritual duty of human beings in the struggle against the disparities brought about by racism. It was here that he targeted poverty and problems in public education as impediments to social uplift. Proctor argued that prejudice and "economic deprivation" go hand in hand. He did not accept the notion of social determinism, but he did believe that social impediments are unjust in nature. He noted that some persons are born with advantages. For example, at birth, some persons inherit good parents who raise their children with a good set of morals, nurture their self-esteem, and sometimes support them with sizable financial backing. Other persons are not born into similar circumstances. The child without a stable home environment, parental concern for education, and health (mental and physical) has numerous impediments to overcome. The latter circumstance, for Proctor, was a dismal portrait of reality for many urban black youth. The responsibility of helping persons with impediments and disadvantages, Proctor argued, falls upon persons who were born with undeserved benefits.[14] Removing constructed and superficial impediments and affirming personhood can correct the random results that come with birth (parent's income, social status, etc.). Some people deserve extra help: "It's based on the assumption that no one has any right to the arbitrary assignment of preferential treatment. Everyone stands at the same level with an equal opportunity to earn the good things of life. But some persons, having impediments placed in their path, deserve some extra help in order to have equal opportunity."[15] For Proctor, equal opportunity was crucial to genuine community. He witnessed during his life the denial of equal rights in African American communities. The presence of racism created many social obstacles for African Americans. To move in the direction of equality of opportunity, the "least" in the community need the assistance of persons who are socially content or well off.

Constantly reminding his audiences of the global moral and economic status of the United States, Proctor celebrated the notion of justice inherent in the American system of government. In this way, Proctor believed in the structural integrity of American democracy. He saw the failures in the execution of democratic principles, but not in their ideals. A just society necessitates moral action to correct its injustices; Americans did not always act. Proctor stated, "Justice requires fairness. The just person and the just society are committed to rectify those inequalities that result from an unfair distribution of advantages and disadvantages."[16]

The moral obligation of the "advantaged" members of community requires a redistribution of wealth, Proctor held. He employed, on occasions, the writings of the philosopher John Rawls to bolster his case. Proctor suggested that persons should consider an original position for each member of the human family. From there, he held that human beings must figure out what we owe the least in our society. We must wish for others what we would want for ourselves. He understood that people do not always relate well to persons from different racial and/or ethnic backgrounds. He recognized that persons with money and power have a hard time identifying with persons in poverty. He identified this as a problem. He believed that persons would have a hard time showing sympathy if they could not understand the struggles of persons with dismal circumstances. He wrote, "It is not easy for us to understand what it takes for deprived people to command that discipline to launch out with faith, to pursue goals that they have never seen realized, and to achieve objectives that have always been nothing but theoretical."[17]

That "advantaged" members of society control the major institutions concerned Proctor. Persons in poverty would need to play by the rules of a system that kept them in poverty. The rich and the powerful, Proctor noted, maintain the structures that oppress people. The "winners" do not understand the ones who struggle. The uphill climb for marginalized members of society reflects, in many instances, the ill regard shown to them by persons who base their judgments of certain racial/ethnic groups and people in poverty upon largely inadequate information or contempt.[18] Securing help can be a difficult task.

Proctor held that some persons are not able to navigate the free enterprise system of America. Many persons struggle to succeed because they are not able to negotiate the terms of the competitive systems of a capitalist society. Proctor realized that only a few persons advocate on behalf of these societal "losers." Few persons are concerned about balancing the economic and social scales that beset disadvantaged members of society. But a focused effort to affirm personhood in community produces the ethical acts of good will that attenuate the unjust conditions of society.

## On Racism, Big Money, and the Religious Right

Proctor knew that attaining genuine community in the United States—in the world—was an elusive task. His life had shown him that the possibilities existed, but the moral will of the nation did not always follow. He experienced the racial problems of the United States and spoke freely about the nation's long struggle with black-white relations. Proctor was a veteran of the civil rights movement and a survivor of the segregated South. He lived through turbulent periods of race relations in America. He identified, as a result, several factors that blocked the formation of real community in the United States. He was realistic about the social crises in the United States. The historical consequences of a racialized America, the greedy materialism of its culture, and the rise of a conservative Christianity represented the most daunting barriers to Proctor's idyllic community.

### *Racial Estrangement*

Proctor argued that numerous persons are accustomed to narrow and divisive, primarily racial, categories for understanding life. The categories provide persons with easy designations to exclude persons or groups from full participation in society. He asserted that America has had a lot of practice in exclusion. Divisive categories are an easy way to negate personhood and label differences as "other." With such categories, people erected walls between groups by emphasizing the notion of difference. Proctor stated, "It relieved one group of any responsibility for the other. It suggested complete difference, and it suggested this difference so strongly that it appeared to be inherent, natural, ordained, immutable and desirable."[19] Proctor determined that racism was a historical phenomenon—an antecedent of poverty and poor systems of education for African Americans and some other ethnic groups. Proctor held that one could not pinpoint the date on which the process of racism in the United States advanced.

For Proctor, racism is the precursor to many of today's social and economic problems among minority populations. Residual effects of racism influence many aspects of society. He argued, "Today the remaining residuals of injustice are not quite so poignant, but they are there. There is inertia in upscaling minorities in industry, government, the media, the fine arts, and education. So the black/white income gap is widening."[20] Proctor was also clear about the direct causes of the problems. The racism that constructed racial slavery and segregation was at the core of the crises that plagued the black community. To be sure, noncommunity in America has seen the historical expressions of racism create the conditions that deny many African Americans the equality that they deserve.

Slavery and segregation were two explicit barriers produced by history, Proctor maintained. Placing this idea within a global framework, he posited that many groups have experienced such historical racial and ethnic conflicts. He argued that many of the impediments to community are the results of problems from the past. Examples of these historical conflicts include the Jewish-Palestinian conflict, Protestants and Catholics of Northern Ireland, South African apartheid, and slavery in the United States. He also mentioned colonization. Colonialism left many nations unequipped to work through the problems in their lands. He wrote, "The community that we hope for is frustrated by the awful disparities in opportunity and quality of life between the former colonies and the former colonizers. And it is not fair."[21] He traced the tensions in America's urban areas to the injustices and inequalities produced by racist structures and systems. Referring to the conflict between whites and blacks in the United States, he perceived that the breakdown of the black family was a critical problem that had its roots in slavery.[22]

Proctor argued that the slaveholder's tampering with African and African American families produced many of the problems in the black community. The destruction of the black family and the denial of education for most African Americans in the antebellum era were initial effects of slavery, and those effects had long-term consequences. He claimed, "This meant that at the emancipation, except in a few notable cases, the 4 million blacks emancipated were penniless, separated from parents and other family, landless, and illiterate."[23] Numerous problems persist because of the United States' immaturity on matters of race. Proctor believed that many whites had not come to realize the historic damage done by racial slavery and racism. Alluding to affirmative action, Proctor argued that white persons had problems with many government-proposed policy solutions to offset or eliminate racial injustices. He stated that the solutions were "deemed intolerable" by many persons in the white community.[24] A fitting comment summarizes his view on the matter: "Our society flounders terribly, for example, on the whole business of welfare, open admissions, a better chance for blacks, Chicanos, and native Americans. Bright people put their racial and tribal interests out front and say the silliest things; they talk as though slavery never happened and the slaughter of Indians was a watermelon feast or fish fry."[25] For Proctor, racist notions and practices hold the nation back from its destiny of national purpose. He argued on several occasions that one could acknowledge one's particular ethnic and racial heritage while tying it to larger identities of nation and humanity.

## *"Big Money"*

American society's obsession with material things also prevents genuine community from existing. Proctor held that Americans' obsession with money has blinded the United States to the larger realities in the world. Proctor recalled that while he was in Africa, many Africans were reminding him of how the United States treated its impoverished minorities. He maintained that the United States had not set the moral standard on such matters, and other countries knew it. He understood that the nation could be a moral power in helping persons in urban areas of the United States and developing nations. But he also recognized that money could easily dominate the nation's agenda in the opposite direction. He was skeptical of the way in which the United States "idolized big money."[26] He concluded that many persons in the United States are more loyal to status and comfort than they are to the struggling persons in their cities. Implicit in Proctor's critique is an indictment of the influence of American capitalism. He was skeptical of a society that could afford to pay athletes millions of dollars but not invest enough money in moving persons out of poverty.

Money's major influence on the political system also troubled Proctor. He despised the fact that a person running for the American presidency had to be a millionaire to be viable in the race. The wealthiest segment of society controls the political institutions, and Proctor discerned this in what he believed were policies of noncommunity. He knew that big money supported the status quo. And the status quo represented the racist agendas that have always been in place. He wrote, "The domination of party politics by the privileged holds the country captive to the old paradigm of the superiority of the rich."[27] Elected officials could not really know the problems of the people they served if their lives were so distant from their constituents. There could be no solution to "rescue" the government with such money behind its officials.

### *Conservative Christians and Churches*

The most troubling obstacle to genuine community in the 1980s and 1990s, Proctor thought, was the Religious Right. His description of the Right indicates his suspicion: "The saddest resistance to a new human paradigm comes from the very place where it should be most enthusiastically supported, the Protestant church. A special brand of churches—usually smaller, quasi-churches on the fringes of major denominations—cluster around right-wing leaders who support nationalism, heavy defense expenditures, and Christian schools that deliberately subvert racial integration."[28] Proctor was concerned about the Right's opposition to social uplift for African Americans. The Religious Right presented one of the greatest challenges to community because of its allegiance to a political agenda that was racist and militaristic. The Right, Proctor argued, dismissed the needs of racial minorities and impoverished persons while dressing its views in a "Christian" piety. He condemned the Right's motives and tactics as the unchristian attempt of a few religious groups to wed government to its program. (Proctor rarely named persons in the Religious Right. But he did have concerns about Jerry Falwell and Pat Robertson.)

The Right capitalized on the opening of a weak moral moment in the history of the United States, Proctor claimed. He identified the rise of the new Religious Right with a moral vacuum that had been created following the Kennedy and Johnson era in the 1960s. Maybe due to Proctor's ties to the Kennedy and Johnson administrations, he saw their work as a sort of ethical apex in the history of American government. The Great Society was a career investment for Proctor. The war on poverty that Proctor waged as a part of the Office of Economic Opportunity helped to shape his understanding of appropriate government responses to the plight of the black community. He attributed the downfall of those endeavors to a distracted American public. The U.S. campaigns in the Indo-Chinese conflict and Vietnam War helped erode the moral backing of American citizens for domestic programs. It would not be long after the Johnson administration that the Right asserted itself onto the political landscape. Proctor claimed that the Religious Right overturned the gains and programs implemented by the aforementioned Democratic presidents. He would attribute a significant portion of the blame to the focus on the Vietnam conflict.[29] Proctor addressed what he saw as the Right's idolatrous "supernationalism," callous disregard for the poor, racist response to school integration, childish preoccupation with defense spending, disregard of the risks of nuclear war, and subservient attitude to the rich were traits that galvanized a large segment of Americans. As Proctor saw it, the budding relationship between the Religious Right and the government would place African Americans on the margins. Religion—Christianity—supported the right-wing political leaders and affirmed segregation.[30]

Proctor argued that the Right made racism seem "justifiable." He maintained that the Religious Right caught black people off guard. The relationship between a type of white "Christianity" and the federal government lacked definition for African Americans:

> Black people never really saw any clear distinction in the nature of their enemy, church people or secular forces, because they were the very same persons. For over two centuries they observed that the persons who held them in physical bondage, the ones who denied them a fair chance at education, health care, jobs, housing, and recreation, and the ones who resisted every move for justice and equal opportunity were persons who also frequented the churches, befriended pastors, studied the Bible, sent mission funds to Africa and Asia, and talked much about prayer, heaven and salvation.[31]

He also implied that African Americans could not trust a sizable number of flag-waving Americans during segregation. He suggested that those Americans who displayed such signs of patriotism were the main ones threatening the rights, and in some cases lives, of blacks.[32] He provided as his primary example the fact that the 1954 decision by the Supreme Court to integrate schools led conservative white Christians to start "Christian" academies. Proctor came back to this point in several addresses. He believed that the Right had done much to set back the aspirations of African Americans. It troubled Proctor that blacks could enter the state universities and colleges before they could enter the private schools that were founded on "Christian" principles. What may have been even more dejecting for Proctor was the representation of Christianity that the Right put in the public sphere. The Christianity that the Right espoused did not match the Christianity that Proctor embraced as a child of the Black Church.

Proctor indicted the Right's unchristian social witness. He held that the religion of the Right was contradictory to that of Jesus. He identified the flaws in its language and social mission as a contrast to the mission of Christ. He labeled the language of the Right as "simplistic passwords" that do not reflect the true intention of its religion. A pious "shibboleth" like prayer in school does not celebrate the religious plurality of the students. What the Right wants taking place in the school is only a certain type of prayer from a certain religious community. Proctor posited that the Right would not like it if a Quaker minister or a Jewish rabbi came to school and prayed with the children. For Proctor, the real goal of the Right was clear. He wrote, "It is obvious that this is a misguided attempt to erase the separation between church and state and favor a partisan religious group with special privileges." Yet the Right allied itself with conservative media ("electronic fundamentalists"). Proctor called the Right's message an "oblong blur of pious generalities."[33] Unfortunately, Proctor added, its message betrayed the gospel of Jesus. Proctor asserted that the Right did not mimic Jesus' concern for the poor, sick, disenfranchised, and disinherited.

## On Democracy, Education, and the Preacher

Proctor resolved that the barriers to community were curable. Ambassadors to community existed in American religious and educational settings. Optimistic about the prospects of creating genuine community, he saw this potential in the ideals of the American governmental, educational, and religious institutions. He wanted the ideas, entities, and persons that could further the coming of community to have a fair hearing. The world had known noncommunity, but it had not realized the alternative. At the heart of his optimism was a belief in the possibility of transforming persons morally. This would imbue structures and institutions with ethics that mirror a Judeo-Christian tone. Contrary to the Religious Right, Proctor situated this ethic in a pro-civil-rights liberal black Christianity and social gospel theology. Barriers existed through racist attitudes and the policies that turned those attitudes into laws. The love ethic of Jesus, Proctor argued, provides the moral suasion needed to convert the hearts and minds of the persons who constructed the barriers. Reorienting the motivations and actions of prejudicial persons and organizations could begin the process of change that the country needed. Community could not come without the help of a dedicated American citizenry that invested in implementing the ethics of Jesus as national policy. A variety of concerned persons would need to carry out this task through participating in the institutional processes that effect change in the society.

### *American Democracy*

Proctor believed that America was the best place for genuine community to take place. He argued that its political theory affirms principles that echo biblical views of personhood. There is no political system equal to American democratic principles, he held. His appeal to democratic ideals was more than rhetorical fodder. In a published sermon, he remarked, "We ought to be extremely grateful as a people, having the most perfect system of government, based on the distilled fragrance of the best ideas men have ever conceived."[34] Without a state religion, with more than one political party, without a lineage of royalty, but with a multiethnic population, America could forge a path toward community. But the foundation of the country's ability to reach genuine community is its ideas. Proctor wrote, "We have the ideas in America on which world community can be built: the innate worth of persons, government by the consent of the governed, personal freedom, due process of law, and rights that the state neither confers nor can deny."[35] The primary belief in the worth of all persons could provide a space for community to flourish.

This faith in personhood and its potential gave Proctor hope. He had hope that the factors of noncommunity would relinquish their hold on the society. Proctor wanted to see transformative social ideas actualized. He was critical of investing lip service in the nation's symbols (the flag, the military, etc.) without true "liberty and justice for all." He commented that the nation's symbols do not make it great; the people standing for the nation's principles lift it to excellence. "A nation is no better than her people," he asserted.[36] But the nation can bring about community when the voice of the people and the action of the government usher in its advent.

A democratic system of government allows the society to support community. Proctor said that American government is supposed to have "built-in correctives for the uneven beginnings of life."[37] He had a list of crises (many produced by the effects of racism) in which government intervention was necessary. Proctor was adamant that the government could implement programs that could help reorient urban youths victimized by a slum mentality. He was concerned about the crime and poverty statistics that emanated from urban residential areas with African American residents. But he recognized that change could not happen without a merger of interests from public and private sectors. He called for a "surge of decency and fairness emanating from the public will."[38] Proctor argued that if this surge did not take place, the statistics would remain into the twenty-first century. A champion of civil rights initiatives like affirmative action, Proctor encouraged persons to engage the political process for the sake of community.

Crucial to Proctor's hope for genuine community is an appeal for persons to be accountable for the opportunities they make and/or receive. Government can provide only so much assistance. He did not think America had yet put in place the mechanisms that would balance the scales of justice. He felt this was the case for persons in poverty and members of certain racial and/or ethnic minorities. He had a conciliatory approach to the limits and responsibilities of government. He wrote, "Community will be hard to achieve if an underclass of poor, uneducated African Americans and whites fails to recognize that self-reliance, accountability, and personal pride are the trademarks of a free and just society. Nothing will change significantly if the society has to provide sustenance for large numbers of people who have no hope of becoming self-supporting."[39] Proctor was for programs—government or other sponsored—that helped make sure children had a fair start in the world. At the same time, he wanted to limit dependency on aid and encourage work that built character. He evoked the benefits of the Works Progress Administration and the Public Works Administration of the Roosevelt years. Proctor contended that these programs exhibit a way in which a successful labor program could work in the contemporary setting. The public works program required the effort and ingenuity of the nation's leaders to guarantee respectable employment for able-bodied persons.[40] The same, Proctor believed, could happen in the current United States. But this would require that America aid persons challenged by the historic effects of racial estrangement. America had to live up to its political charter. Specifically, Proctor desired an America that honored racial and ethnic pluralism as an idea whose time had come.

Proctor emphasized racial pluralism in his vision of genuine community. He insisted that America has the making of a genuine community with its ethnic and cultural diversity. He was concerned, however, that the citizens of the United States lacked the deeper ties that community requires. The national community we have, Proctor argued, is more symbol than substance. An America that ignores the voices of its marginalized persons is not yet eligible for genuine community. He called upon the nation to recognize that the fates of blacks and whites are tied together. He stated, "Our destinies, social, cultural, economic and political, are inexorably bound together unless we pursue an irrational, illegal and immoral course that would lead to an intransigent estrangement."[41] He claimed that there is a common national destiny. Racial pluralism was high on the list of its priorities. It is a goal every American must work to achieve. The alternative to working toward a common national purpose consists of a destructive dualism that fosters an environment of American racism. Rejecting community on matters of racial pluralism is the denial of the best we know in American ideals.[42] Rejecting a racially pluralistic community denies the common origin of all persons.

### *Education and Human Development*

For Proctor, education was "the primary agent of change" for the pursuit of genuine community.[43] To be sure, Proctor relied upon education and religion—Christianity—to "humanize" society. His dedication to these aspects of society as transformational entities was due, in large part, to his vocational and professional responsibilities as an educator and Christian minister. The role of educator was a part of who he was. He never relinquished that position. He saw the benefits of education, watching urban and rural youth matriculate at Virginia Union University and North Carolina A&T State College (now University). He knew that education was a way to access the "mainstream" of American economic prosperity. Education in America could be an investment in black personhood. As Proctor saw it, it might have been the most effective agent for receiving full participation in American life.[44] He claimed that a new approach to education has the power to celebrate the racial and ethnic pluralism that would make community a more achievable reality. Integrating narratives from the pluralistic racial and ethnic communities into the educational curriculum was a key part of this process.

Proctor wanted education to be a liberating force for African Americans. He wanted children to enter "the life of the mind" at an early age as a part of their growth. In his biography of his moral development, he dedicated a whole chapter to the ways in which he engaged his environment as a student of

life. For Proctor, education needed to be an opportunity to grow morally and spiritually. Education, he maintained, has the capacity to "humanize" society. By humanize, Proctor meant the process by which human beings develop their abilities as human beings and are sensitized to the sufferings of others. Humanization is contingent upon humanity's search for a new relationship with nature and nature's God. To an extent, education allows for a theological encounter. In education, one learns what it means to be human (based on the faculties that God provides to persons).[45] Education could also serve as a corrective to the racial problems in the nation: "Building community is a problem in America. If American education can show us how to overcome the racial polarization in our land, how to correct the abuses of the past, how to compensate adequately for a glaring moral failure in the slave system, how to protect the domestic tranquility, to promote the general welfare, to form a more perfect union—education deserves at least a generation of special effort."[46]
Ideally, Proctor noted, education is committed to the uplift of persons in society. Implicit in education is its ability to prepare persons to live in a pluralistic nation and intervene in the lives of the socially and economically impoverished. "We want to learn to live among people with widely differing starting points and watch them move forward at their optimum pace,"[47] he acknowledged. Early experiences in quality, integrated learning environments could provide that type of opportunity. Education could remove some of the barriers to community, shoring up deficiencies caused by various circumstances. In a 1977 commencement address at North Carolina A&T, he responded to an argument that education in a capitalist society was a cause of African American docility and contentment with their circumstances. He countered by saying, "Black folk who are educated have developed a sensitivity to their conditions, they have become aware and ambitious, and they have fallen in love with freedom and the betterment of their conditions."[48] Proctor called education the "definitive test" of the nation's ability to live up to its democratic principles of freedom and diversity.

These ideas led Proctor to envision a strategy for building relationships that would connect urban black youth to quality education. His solution required several areas of improvement to the current educational system.[49] He argued that teachers should learn the history and background of all students. He concluded that many teachers, mainly white teachers, had no knowledge of the circumstances of their African American students from urban areas. To learn more about these students, the teachers needed to do some research on their students' lives. This idea was consistent with his notion of vicarious participation in the lives of others. Presupposing diversity in the classroom,

Proctor questioned whether teachers could be effective without understanding their students' backgrounds. Real education is the product of relationships. A teacher cannot adequately assess a student's learning ability based upon appearances. Proctor was afraid that this took place too often. He recalled the fact that his grade school principal and teachers had promoted him several grades because he had a "large head." The teachers believed he looked smart, and the principal and many of the teachers were familiar with his family. They knew that his parents (and grandmother) would do whatever it took to help him be successful in the higher grades. He lamented the fact that several students had remained in the lower grades because the teachers and principal had no history with them. The educators did not know the students' family stock, or the students did not look smart enough. Proctor contended that teachers should search for learning ability in all students.

This was not his only point of contention, however. During the middle years of his career, Proctor called for a broadening of the American educational curriculum, especially in the university setting. American students, he held, must begin to learn more about "non-Western" cultures. Proctor called America's lack of knowledge about these cultures an embarrassment. He charged that the exclusion of such cultures reflected American arrogance. He declared that America led itself to believe that "The rest of the world somehow lay in the shadow of stupidity and barbarism with a slight interruption by Socrates, Aristotle, and Cicero."[50] Proctor pointed to what he called Moslem (Muslim) culture in Africa, Egyptian achievements, and the Japanese culture(s) as models for Americans to study in this new curriculum. A new curriculum would change the focus of the social sciences. Proctor also challenged social scientists to do more than analyze and describe. He called for academics to determine where the society is headed based upon the problems of the time. What problems would the next generation of Americans inherit? Proctor also encouraged academics in the humanities to prepare students to live in a global community.[51] This required that students learn the humanities anew. "We need a more balanced diet for the young, nurturing the notion that modern man belongs to a total human community that stretches far beyond the Mediterranean and the Atlantic cultures."[52] In the 1954 sermon "The Other Sheep," Proctor called for an educational awakening that would prepare persons for a "world community." He preached, "The next advance in ideas must furnish us with a concept of man which will educate us for citizenship in a world community, one that will include some suggestion of the possibility of a fraternity of men in spite of our infinite varieties."[53]

Proctor also called upon the university community. That so many academics used their intellectual resources to promote racism troubled Proctor. Academics, he feared, were stuck in racial modes of thinking—stereotyping. He called the gathering of social data based upon race in studies such as the Bell Curve one of the worst ways to study cause and effect. Yet he noted that several universities continued to publish these data without including in their results the possibility of other factors. He called the Bell Curve a "cacophony of racist propaganda."[54] He challenged the university community to move beyond racial categories and promote a world that judges persons on their merits: "It is time for us to say that we should get rid of racism in the world once and for all and let people be judged on personal merits."[55]

At the end of his career, Proctor realized that creating the type of educational experiences that many inner-city youth needed would require years of reform and government support. Proctor understood the dynamics of several urban school systems. He acknowledged that many public schools are "coping with crime, guns, gangs, and drugs."[56] He compared the schools to forts. He argued that the intent of the voucher system was the destruction of the public school system. As an alternative, he called for programs that would prepare better teachers, keep the schools open with productive activities until 5:30 p.m. throughout the year, and equip schools with personnel for disciplinary problems. He called for a National Youth Academy that would create a boarding school type of experience for low-income black youth. But he recognized the need for faith to support the persons who administer and are served by the educational system:

> So even though it would seem that education is a large part of the answer, it is not all. The truly educated person, in my view, is never content until a satisfactory, operational answer is found to the questions of purpose and destiny. In our early years, school is largely in control of the life of the mind and the world of ideas. But eventually we must turn our focus outward and upward to look for our own larger frame of reference. Religion brings our quest for purpose and direction to closure and our soul to ease by revealing our place in the scheme of things.[57]

### *Preacher and Church*

The preacher cannot sit still on the issue of community, Proctor declared. Preachers' failure to act was a crime of noncommunity. Proctor's ideal of community depended upon preachers to make it visible through sermons and ministry activities. There was urgency in Proctor's appeal. In 1976, he told participants at a Duke University–sponsored conference that it was the wrong time for university and Christian communities to keep silent when racism and economic disparities existed.[58] He also sounded the trumpet in a 1991 publication (his Lyman Beecher Lecture) to preachers in which he stated that it was necessary for them to speak about community. He declared, "When we become silent on community we are in complicity with *noncommunity*."[59] Proctor envisioned the preacher and the church participating in the work of community building by raising awareness of and modeling the relationships and processes that could ensure genuine community's place in society.

Preaching community was a priority for Proctor's view of the preacher's ministry. He argued that community is a fundamental message of the gospel. Preaching the gospel means preaching community. Presenting a God who made inclusive love available to all humankind was the ethics and teaching of Christ. The preacher's sermon challenges the audience to embrace a higher standard for living and know that God loves all of humanity. Transmitting that fact is the preacher's vocation. "As remote and far-fetched as the idea of community may seem, those who preach cannot escape the imperative to make clear God's prevailing and enduring love for the whole human family."[60] This is the moral imperative for Proctor. The preacher's role is to preach the gospel and let the teachings and example of Christ transform the minds and hearts of the listeners.

Community is one of the most important messages for the preacher to proclaim. Community coexists with the kingdom of God. It is an important attribute of God's kingdom. Community and kingdom reveal that depth of human-divine relations that knows no superficial differences (e.g., class, race, nationality, political): "The kingdom of God that Jesus and John the Baptist preached did indeed reach across all of the distinctions of race and culture. . . . The kingdom was a new allegiance with no reference to a bloodline or an ethnic origin. And the kingdom never seems so much like a structured, geographic organization or program as it is a controlling, constraining force in the hearts of persons under the rule of God's love."[61]

On a political and moral level, the preacher attempts to construct the processes that will make community real. Someone must give the clarion call for moral progress. Proctor proclaimed, "Preachers have to give support to ideas and plans that move us toward community in modern urban America."[62] Proctor realized that public theology is the preacher's work every Sunday. The preacher as public theologian needs a word for the people that will inch community closer. The preacher, Proctor believed, is an agent of change who encourages moral reform. He wanted the preacher to participate in the political conversation.

Proctor conceded that change needed to happen morally and legislatively. This did not necessarily mean that the preacher needed to become a politician. But Proctor knew that times could call for the preacher to be more active in politics. Preachers have the power, Proctor argued, to make selfless love a part of "society's agenda." The preacher, therefore, ought to fight for persons by being a voice in the public square. The preacher can put community in the nation's moral purview.[63] God works through the preacher to effect change. Preachers were crucial to Proctor's thoughts on community. Installed in the preacher's vocation is the gospel message that affirms the dignity and worth of all persons.

The (black) preacher, Proctor insisted, has the unique opportunity to save (black) people from the disillusionment of the racial and economic segregation of America. Proctor did not believe that segregation ended with the civil rights movement. Preachers, he asserted, are still needed to attack racist and class distinctions. Proctor challenged preachers to "save our people" from the consequences of racial isolation and oppression. He wanted preachers to spread the word about the equality of all persons. That message could contend with racism. Preaching about community has that potential to change society.[64]

Proctor was aware that the preacher carries out her vocation within the framework of a community that must also be politically active. He called upon Christian churches to help sway public-policy conversations. At the same time, he realized that members of "Christian" coalitions could abuse the privileges and responsibilities of participating in the political process. The church, Proctor stated, must stand up for itself against the religious views of the Right. He called upon the church to articulate the true concerns of Jesus: "It is our purpose to winnow and refine our values so that true community begins to emerge, one that binds people not by ties of blood, money, race, or class, but which has the nexus of justice, compassion, and human dignity as our agglutinating force, a force made strong by the contribution of Jews, Catholics, Protestants, and others, nurtured and sustained by their own respective faiths."[65]

In an earlier sermon, Proctor posited that the Christian message has something to offer everyone. Christ makes a legitimate claim on the lives of all persons. Persons are fundamentally alike in needs and destiny. Christian churches bear witness to the essence of this gospel. God made of one blood all of humanity. Proctor's notion of community would not exist without this core principle: "This is the Christian contribution to the secular pluralistic culture, our estimation of the worth of persons. In our preaching we must advocate this basic approach to the building of community in a free, pluralistic nation.

It is a prerequisite for a genuine community."[66] For Proctor, the principle of a human family was essentially Christian. He held that Christianity provides the highest ideals of American democratic principles, and America has the potential to embrace all humanity because of this Christian influence.

## Community: A Liberal Black Protestant Creation

Proctor was not alone in his desire for genuine community. Persons will attribute the concept of "Beloved Community" to the Johannine tradition in the Bible and Josiah Royce and his influence on the social gospel theology of Walter Rauschenbusch, but manifestations of the beloved community exist in the black Christian experience. Lawrence Jones argued that African American Christians since before the Civil War desired an integrated community that affirms the equality and humanity of every person in it.[67] In the twentieth century, a generation of black Protestant theologians (who matriculated at liberal theological institutions) made community the norm for their theological-ethical ideal. Specifically, persons such as Proctor's mentor, John Malcus Ellison, Howard Thurman, and Martin Luther King Jr. shared the work of heralding a notion of community grounded in a Christian ethic of racial and ethnic integration based upon the equality of all persons promised in the political and social ideals of the United States.

In 1943, John Malcus Ellison wrote an article entitled "The Problem of Community in America," in which he spelled out the aspects of society that resist community. He begins the article by appealing to democratic ideals and principles. He states that there existed in that time elements of disunity and conflict that "belie" the principles of democracy. He does not state explicitly a definition for community. But his definition for the spiritual aim of democracy is similar to Proctor's understanding of genuine community. Ellison merges his idea of community with his ideals for democracy: "From the human and spiritual side it means the recognition of human worth, respect for persons, and the use of the principle of love as a leaven for determining the quality of human relations. As a way of life it aims at the creative development of human personality."[68] Love functions as a "principle" for gauging the grade of the relationships in this community. But freedom that is granted by human rights within a democracy sustains these relationships.

Thematically, Ellison distinguishes his understanding of community by focusing on the rights of the human being. Life, liberty, and the pursuit of happiness find their expression in social freedom. They provide for all of humanity to participate in economic and political endeavors equally. These are important "affirmations" for the freedoms of persons within society. Ellison connects these rights and affirmations with human growth: "All of these affirmations are aimed not only at the creative growth of the individual but at the cooperative development of society."[69] Community, for Ellison, then, is the space in which humanity can flourish within those freedoms and affirmations.

But barriers do exist in American society, in Ellison's perspective. Ellison identified several areas of American society that were inconsistent with democracy. For Ellison, capitalism, a racist and disenfranchising political system, and American Christianity all fought off community. They operated in a way that reduced the freedoms of certain racial and ethnic populations in America. Reform in all three areas would mean for Ellison the redistribution of wealth, fair and free political access and participation, and the affirmation of black personhood as human and equal. He saw, however, that these ideas were not on the list of priorities in American Christianity. He states, "Too often those who are strong, economically secure, and possessors of an inherited faith and religion are never stirred by the challenge to make religious faith vital and aglow by attacking social, political, and economic injustice."[70]

Howard Thurman developed a similar idea of community in his essay "Desegregation, Integration, and the Beloved Community." For Thurman, the beloved community requires a depth of human relationship that does not know the superficial barriers of race and class. Love is that profound depth. Walter Fluker argues that Thurman believed community to be "inherent in the process of life" as an expression of the will of God.[71] This is why segregation is problematic. Thurman noted that segregation was "ingrained in the structure of our society." He contended that economic, political, social, and religious measures propped up segregation and maintained it as a system. Thurman also believed that community could be realized in integration—not desegregation. He suggested that banishing segregation laws would help America know the depth of ties necessary to know what God intended for humanity. He wrote, "That which makes any community become the beloved community is the quality of the human relations experienced by the people who live within it. . . . It cannot be brought into being by fiat or by order; it is an achievement of the human spirit as men seek to fulfill their high destiny as children of God."[72] Thurman understood that every person has a responsibility to make community a reality. Persons embracing others and affirming personality across racial and class boundaries are necessary for community to exist.

Martin Luther King Jr. also concluded that community is the telos of the moral order. King wanted America to commit to the laws of its society. He was concerned about the democratic image it projected throughout the world. Racial prejudice, he stated in a 1963 speech, remained the country's "greatest moral dilemma." He too celebrated the worth and dignity of all humanity. In that same speech, he argued, "There must be a recognition of the sacredness of human personality. Deeply rooted in our political and religious heritage is the conviction that every man is an heir to a legacy of dignity and worth. Our Hebraic-Christian tradition refers to this inherent dignity of man in the Biblical term *the image of God*."[73] The Declaration of Independence echoes this fact, King stated. The dignity of all humanity, moreover, was the foundation for a world or beloved community for King. The beloved community, for King, was a voluntary cooperative experience of persons who understood their solidarity as a human family. The family achieved this goal by taking on responsibility for each other by affirming the worth of every person in the group. National purpose would be achieved when Americans reached that point.

Walter Fluker's work on Thurman and Martin Luther King Jr. reveals a connection between the four thinkers in this section. They all identified similar barriers to community. King and Thurman, however, saw love as the power that can overcome the barriers. Fluker concludes that Thurman expressed a belief in the power of love through self-awareness. A creative encounter with God brings about love's fight with the internal demons that prevent self-actualization. King saw love as the catalyst for social justice. Jesus' model of redemption through love is King's basis for the power of love's social witness. Proctor could agree with either emphasis. But his route placed less emphasis on love. He identified faith as the modus operandi for creating community.

Faith became the primary component upon which Proctor built his notion of genuine community. Faith for genuine community is a trust in God and human fulfillment, foreseeing and anticipating the kingdom of God on earth. The title of his memoir (*The Substance of Things Hoped For: A Memoir of African American Faith*) is a testament to this premise. In the opening chapter, "The Crucible of Faith," he argues that African and African American slaves countered the dehumanization of chattel slavery with their faith. Biblical passages cemented their faith in a God that was able to deliver them. Stories from the Old Testament (e.g., the deliverance of Joseph, Daniel, and the Hebrew men in the furnace) were proof that God could deliver black people from slavery. Proctor wrote, "And by repeating the narratives over and over again, slaves began to fashion a faith hypothesis that would see them through every conceivable scheme of dehumanization." He went on to write, "The spiritual resilience derived from their faith allowed most enslaved African Americans to come through their degrading experience whole, without losing their humanity. When the hour was upon them, they set out to create something entirely novel in the history of the world: In America, they dreamed of being free, side by side with their former masters. . . . With nothing but faith, they *imagined* the future. They fixed their trust in God and began the journey up the road to equality."[74] But faith produced more than dream and imagination. It had to reconcile dreams with the facts on the ground.

In a 1973 sermon, "Making the Most of Our Faith," Proctor identified the heavy lifting that faith must do to create community. Faith cannot be a substitute for the facts. The facts suggest reality, but they do not define it. Integral to faith is an ability to hope for the good, regardless of the facts. Faith, he believed, picks up where the facts end. He stated, "Faith is never a soft-headed escape into fantasy land. It is a tough-minded approach to the real world. It is the substance of things earnestly hoped for."[75] Faith can address the challenges that life presents by wading into an active hope. The facts, Proctor implied, can paralyze a person's psyche and hinder moral development. He said, "We can't make it with economists and sociologists repeating the facts to us. The facts are drowning us with despair." But faith can overcome these obstacles with the possibilities that hope presents. He offered a way to reconcile faith with facts. He proclaimed, "We need somebody with a heart full of faith to be the architect of a greater nation than we now have." Faith engineers the plans for a better world. For Proctor, faith gives persons the vision of a better day, a better world, and a God who cares.

Genuine community requires a new vision of humanity, Proctor realized. Christianity provides the model for this vision. Jesus exhibited the faith in humanity that humanity should show in itself. Proctor saw this as a liberating type of self-awareness. He saw this type of faith in the words and practices of enslaved African Americans—including his grandmother—and following generations of black Americans. That is how they survived and overcame the heinous crimes committed against them. Refusing to accept misguided definitions of their humanity, they believed they were children of God. They enacted a faith in God that appreciated a different vision of their destiny. Knowing the inherent worth of their personhood, numerous African Americans made a positive influence on American life. The world, Proctor held, needed this vision of the equality and worth of black personhood to produce community. Christianity, moreover, has broadcast that vision for some time. Proctor concluded that the world has looked forward to this community.

This section stands as a survey of the similar strands of thought concerning community within a sample of the "liberal" black Baptist tradition. It exhibits the fact that certain prominent black Protestants determined that community is essential for true human relationship and the imminent "kingdom of God." Though there are many similarities within their ideas of community, Proctor distinguishes his thematic tone from Ellison, Thurman, and King. He presents a public theology that privileges a concept of faith that suggests the ability to engage a marginalizing society with a vision of the "ought to be" that God intends.

It is clear that Proctor's understanding of community displays his confidence in American democracy. On occasions, he blurred the distinctions between community and American democracy. He even began several speeches and sermons by appealing to the common ground between Christianity and American democracy. Yet that trust in American democracy revealed his lack of a real plan to redistribute the "advantages" of society to persons with deficits.

Proctor's call for a National Youth Academy could do little to offset the economic disparities in society. The call for a national educational academy relied heavily on the goodwill of persons who were among the advantaged. Thus, the burden of responsibility for social uplift fell upon the advantaged members of society. Proctor had faith in what would be a sustained showing of goodwill from people. That is admirable. He did not answer, in most cases, what would be the responsibility of persons with life deficits. Can they do for themselves only after they have been helped? Proctor treads a thin line on such questions. He seems to rely upon the ability of the middle and upper classes to make things better. He depends upon the possibility of moral-spiritual conversion to convict persons to give up their advantaged positions in society to aid others. He also does not concern himself with communities that have chosen poverty as a way of life. This is obvious by his limited exposition on that issue of choice and its moral-spiritual path. But it is clear that Proctor was a practical-public theologian who only dabbled in theoretical theology, economics, and ethics.

As a public theologian, Proctor would not keep silent about the greatest issue of his time, American racism. He understood theology to be a public activity, and he encouraged Christians to participate in processes that would make community a reality. By doing this, persons with a social gospel perspective had the opportunity to influence secular publics to become community. He proclaimed, "Those of us who believe the gospel and love our country need to find a way to share the good news on terms compatible with our pluralism and our separation of church and state."[76]

Proctor situated himself within a tradition of black Protestant thinkers who promoted community as the logical end for our religious and political ideals, and he developed his understanding of community over the course of a career. He concluded over time that the American embrace of genuine community could fight racism and its consequent problems. He stated, "Now we are challenged to transform a political state into a pluralistic, moral and spiritual *community*, which can accommodate sectarianism."[77] He believed that community could not exist without love and justice at its foundation. He also argued against the barriers of community and argued that education and "liberal" Christianity could overcome the barriers. A politically involved preacher who embraced the teachings of Jesus has much work to do, in Proctor's view. The payoff, though, is worth the travail:

> If we can pull it off here in this country, America, it will be a triumph greater than the marches of Alexander of Macedon into the East, greater than the achievements of Athens under Pericles, and greater than the empire built by Augustus Caesar.[78]

The American society, Proctor maintained, was ripe for community to blossom.

## Notes

1. For a brief introduction to the "Beloved Community" in Thurman's and King's thought, see Walter E. Fluker, They Looked for a City: A Comparative Analysis of the Ideal of Community in the Thought of Howard Thurman and Martin Luther King, Jr. (Lanham, MD: University Press of America, 1989); Katie G. Cannon, Black Womanist Ethics, American Academy of Religion Series (Atlanta: Scholars, 1988); Kenneth L. Smith and Ira G. Zepp Jr., Search for the Beloved Community (Valley Forge, PA: Judson, 1974); Noel Leo Erskine, King among Theologians (Cleveland: Pilgrim, 1994); Charles Marsh, The Beloved Community: How Faith Shapes Social Justice, from the Civil Rights Movement to Today (New York: Basic Books, 2005). Charles Marsh's book is an important contribution on the way in which notions of community shaped the black civil rights struggle.

2. See Samuel D. Proctor, "The Other Sheep, 1954" (photocopy), p. 2, Samuel DeWitt Proctor Papers, VUU, Richmond, VA.

3. Samuel D. Proctor, "Education for the Humanization of Society," *Educational Record* 57, no. 4 (1977): 243.

4. Samuel D. Proctor, *My Moral Odyssey* (Valley Forge, PA: Judson, 1991), 149; and Proctor, "Education for the Humanization of Society," 243.

5. Fluker, *They Looked for a City*, 111.

6. Samuel D. Proctor, *"How Shall They Hear?" Effective Preaching for Vital Faith* (Valley Forge, PA: Judson, 1992), 59. See also Proctor, *My Moral Odyssey*, 149; and Samuel D. Proctor, "Everybody Is God's Somebody," in *Sermons from the Black Pulpit*, ed. Samuel D. Proctor and William D. Watley (Valley Forge, PA: Judson, 1984), 31.

7. Samuel D. Proctor, *The Certain Sound of the Trumpet: Crafting a Sermon of Authority* (Valley Forge, PA: Judson, 1994), 42.

8. Proctor, *My Moral Odyssey*, 151–52.

9. Samuel D. Proctor, *Preaching about Crises in the Community* (Philadelphia: John Knox, 1989), 100.

10. Samuel D. Proctor, "Relevant Religion," in *Outstanding Black Sermons*, ed. Milton E. Owens Jr. (Valley Forge, PA: Judson, 1982), 3:58.

11. Proctor, *"How Shall They Hear?,"* 69.

12. Ibid., 71.

13. Proctor, *Preaching about Crises*, 103.

14. Samuel D. Proctor, "Equity from a Racial/Ethnic Perspective," Research and Development Series, April 26, 1983, ERIC, ED 215166, p. 21.

15. Proctor, "Relevant Religion," 56.

16. Samuel D. Proctor, "A Mind Is a Terrible Thing to Waste," *Phi Delta Kappan* 60, no. 3 (1978): 203S.

17. Samuel D. Proctor, "The Wrong Time to Be Silent," in *Christianity amid Rising Men and Nations*, ed. Creighton Lacy (New York: Association Press, 1965), 176.

18. Proctor, "Education for the Humanization of Society," 243.

19. Proctor, "The Other Sheep," 1.

20. Proctor, *My Moral Odyssey*, 170.

21. Proctor, *"How Shall They Hear?,"* 74–75.

22. See Proctor, *My Moral Odyssey*, 152–53.

23. Proctor, "Equity from a Racial/Ethnic Perspective," 4.

24. Proctor, *"How Shall They Hear?,"* 58.

25. Samuel D. Proctor, "On Overcoming Moral Fatigue," in *The Struggle for Meaning*, ed. William Powell Tuck (Valley Forge, PA: Judson, 1977), 68.

26. Proctor, *My Moral Odyssey*, 171.

27. Samuel D. Proctor, *The Substance of Things Hoped For* (New York: G. P. Putnam's Sons, 1995), 232.

28. Ibid., 233.

29. Samuel D. Proctor, "Post–Vietnam War America: Its Sense of Purpose and Set of Priorities," lecture presented at the Union Theological Seminary–Presbyterian School of Christian Education, Richmond, VA, 1973, audiotape.

30. Samuel D. Proctor, "The Black Community and the New Religious Right," *Foundations* 25 (1982): 180.

31. Ibid., 183.

32. Samuel D. Proctor, "What the Law Cannot Do," lecture presented at the Hampton University Ministers' Conference, Hampton, VA, 1990 (Hampton, VA: Hampton University, 1990), audiotape.

33. Proctor, "The Black Community and the New Religious Right," 184–85. Proctor wrote, "At present we have the New Right in alliance with the electronic fundamentalists. And the message is one oblong blur of pious generalities and a blind neglect of the Jesus who walked the roads of Judea, who healed the sick, who was a friend of sinners, who warned the rich of their idolatry, and whose love transcended all national, racial, and class boundaries."

34. Samuel D. Proctor, "A Nation under God," in *Outstanding Black Sermons*, ed. Walter B. Hoard (Valley Forge, PA: Judson, 1979), 2:90.

35. Proctor, *My Moral Odyssey*, 173.

36. Proctor, "A Nation under God," 90–91.

37. Proctor, *Preaching about Crises*, 102.

38. Proctor, *The Substance of Things Hoped For*, 219.

39. Ibid., 234.

40. Ibid., 236.

41. Proctor, *Preaching about Crises*, 94.

42. Samuel D. Proctor, "Racial Insularity and Racial Integration, 1968," photocopy, State Historical Society of Wisconsin, Madison, 1, 4–6.

43. See Proctor, "Equity from a Racial/Ethnic Perspective," 6. Proctor wrote, "Nevertheless, our commitment to pluralism, our democratic ideal of equality, our enviable history of creating upward mobility, and the ethical demands of the Judeo-Christian ethos which forms the basis of our culture all require that this issue be resolved at every level, and that the pursuit of a genuine community, with education as its primary agent of change, should continue."

44. Proctor, "A Mind Is a Terrible Thing to Waste," 202S.

45. Proctor, "Education for the Humanization of Society," 241.

46. Ibid.

47. Proctor, "Education for the Humanization of Society," 243–44.

48. Samuel D. Proctor, "Commencement Address at North Carolina A&T University, 1977," photocopy, The F. D. Bluford Library Archives, North Carolina Agricultural and Technical State University, Greensboro, NC, p. 7. See also Proctor, *My Moral Odyssey*, 161;and, Proctor, "Racial Insularity and Racial Integration," 6.

49. Proctor, "Equity from a Racial/Ethnic Perspective," 12, 18.

50. Proctor, "Education for the Humanization of Society," 245.

51. Ibid., 244, 254.

52. Samuel D. Proctor, "Education for Genuine Community," in *A Man for Tomorrow's World*, ed. Robert R. Leeper (Washington: Association for Supervision and Curriculum Development, 1970), 7.

53. Proctor, "The Other Sheep," 2.

54. Proctor, *The Substance of Things Hoped For*, 184.

55. Proctor, "The Wrong Time to Be Silent," 178.

56. Proctor, *The Substance of Things Hoped For*, 213–14, 221.

57. Ibid., 215.

58. Proctor, "The Wrong Time to Be Silent," 173.

59. Proctor, *"How Shall They Hear?,"* 60.

60. Ibid., 63.

61. Ibid., 64.

62. Proctor, *Preaching about Crises*, 103.

63. Proctor, *"How Shall They Hear?,"* 71.

64. See ibid., 67; and, Proctor, *Preaching about Crises*, 96.

65. Proctor, "The Black Community and the New Religious Right," 187.

66. Proctor, *Preaching about Crises*, 95, 98–99.

67. See Lawrence N. Jones, "Black Christians in Antebellum America: In Quest of the Beloved Community," *Journal of Religious Thought* 38 (1981): 12–19. It is tempting to connect the "Beloved Community" in King's thought to Josiah Royce through Rauschenbusch. A more fitting connection is the black Christian tradition described by Peter Paris in *The Social Teachings of the Black Churches* (Minneapolis: Augsburg Fortress, 1998), 10–12.

68. John M. Ellison, "The Problem of Community in America," *Journal of Religious Thought* 1 (1943): 8.

69. Ibid., 6–7.

70. Ibid., 17.

71. Fluker, *They Looked for a City*, 55.

72. Howard Thurman, "Desegregation, Integration, and the Beloved Community," unpublished manuscript, n.d., 16.

73. Martin Luther King Jr., "The Ethical Demands of Integration," in *Testament of Hope: the Essential Writings and Speeches of Martin Luther King Jr.*, ed. James Melvin Washington (San Francisco: Harper Collins, 1991), 118–19.

74. Proctor, *The Substance of Things Hoped For*, 5.

75. Samuel D. Proctor, *Making the Most of Our Faith,* audiotape of sermon presented at the Massanetta Springs Bible Conference, Harrisonburg, VA, 1973 (Harrisonburg, VA: Massanetta Springs Camp and Conference Center, 1973), audio recording.

76. Proctor, *Preaching about Crises*, 95.

77. Ibid., 94.

78. Proctor, "A Mind Is a Terrible Thing to Waste," 201S–202S.

# Conclusion

Samuel DeWitt Proctor has been a neglected person in research on American Christianity. This book makes the case for his inclusion into the "canon" of American church history. He was a public theologian who channeled his faith claims into strategic activities meant to transform American society. He forged his theological position in the nurture of an African American community, a black Baptist experience and institution, and a liberal theological seminary and graduate education. Proctor is a product of a social Christianity, a black social gospel, which he employed to fight the largest social problem of his lifetime: racism. He argued from that social gospel though the landscape of black public faith changed. His was a public theology in that it brought to a national conversation distinctly Christian commitments in order to influence public policy on the matter of racial equality. The implications of this study suggest that his faith in God was as much a part of the fight against racism as his belief in American democracy. His public faith saw as its foundation the inherent dignity given by God to every human being. The end of that faith was the preacher's ability to herald a genuine community of persons who celebrate and affirm this belief.

## Black Middle-Class Religion in the Twentieth Century

Several conclusions result from an investigation of Samuel DeWitt Proctor's life and thought. First, as this book has shown, it was influenced by the black Christian tradition. He was a product of the tradition, and similar to its public expressions, he did not divorce culture and theology. The biblical anthropology that affirms the parenthood of God and the kinship of all humanity is evident in Proctor's faith. To be sure, Proctor, like many African American Christians, derived much of his theology of humanity from the Bible. His theological anthropology was also informed by his knowledge of African American history and the struggle for human rights. And the fundamental display of his public faith was the way in which he addressed racism in the United States. This falls in line with Dwight Hopkins's argument that building a constructive statement on theological anthropology requires a critical look at the theory and history of race in the United States.

Proctor's defense of black humanity is thoroughly black, Christian, and middle class. This judgment is more than a mere curtsy to notions of race and its interaction with religion and class. I argue that his public faith maintains a hierarchical position heavily influenced by his understanding of his economic and social position in society. By this statement, I mean that Proctor was raised with a middle-class (Protestant) ethic that emphasized moral, political, and formal education. His education and occupations, moreover, placed him among a privileged group in black life. I also attribute this to his upbringing. It is probable that the Proctor family's income and professional standing would not have made it middle class in theory. I believe, however, that one can make a case that a middle-class ethic and ethos pervaded the home. This ethic was Puritanical in nature, focusing on education, morals, and evangelical Christianity.

While I am aware of the restrictive nature of such labels as *middle class* and *underclass* and the pejorative meanings they may signify, they represent indicators—however flawed—of income and social mobility. While class is a social construct, I employ the term and its descriptors because of its frequent usage in scholarly literature. They are flawed inasmuch as they fail to describe the totality of a person's or family's value system, work ethic, and the religious or social beliefs that inform them. Consider, however, the following comments about a black middle class.

In E. Franklin Frazier's book *The Black Bourgeoisie*, he argues that the education of the black middle class is a by-product of the influence of Puritan missionaries in post-Reconstruction schools. Frazier identified piety, thrift, and respectability as the characteristics that remained a part of the black middle-class ethos. The Puritan missionaries made sure they educated former slaves and newly freed persons in their form of Protestantism.[1] Statements from Proctor seem to suggest that his rearing and nurture represent the values and the ethics of a middle-class black family. Consider Samuel Proctor's primary professions, minister and educator, and one can make a solid case for his status in the middle class by way of the respect afforded these careers.

What does all of this have to do with religion and Proctor's Christian theology of humanity? One cannot divide Proctor's theoretical understanding of the God-human encounter from Proctor's social location and practice of Christianity. Black, Christian, and middle class are who he was as a person. Consider his words on the matter when he described his family, church family, and community: "They had all reached a consensus about the good life and how it was to be lived. This consensus was a blend of the Ten Commandments, the teachings of Jesus, and the values of middle-class strivers."[2] He inherited and embraced these values.

Bart Landry's study of the black middle class is relevant to this assessment of Proctor as a member of a black middle class. In Landry's book *The New Black Middle Class*, he argues that class status is the result of "impersonal market dynamics" that display a person's earned or inherited economic position. As mentioned earlier in this section, we may not really be able to measure the influence of the Protestant missionaries who brought the residue of New England Puritanism and budding evangelicalism to the southern portion of the United States in the postbellum period. Landry writes, "In the south, early elite contact with whites came in the academies established by northern white missionaries to educate blacks following emancipation. There they received not only a basic education but training in the culture and values of white New England society, training they attempted to follow later in life."[3] While Proctor's family did not make up the economic black elite of Landry's description, it was among the most privileged in terms of opportunity. Proctor's grandmother was a graduate of the Hampton Institute, an American Missionary Association college, and became a teacher. Presbyterians established the Norfolk Mission College from which his parents graduated. To be sure, an established middle-class ethos resided in the Proctor family home. The family valued education, piety, and thrift.

### *The Black Middle Class: Saviors of the Race*

In a 1971 article, "Survival Techniques and the Black Middle Class," Proctor concluded that black people in the United States needed a strategy that would allow for the black middle class to "selflessly identify their interests with those of the black lower classes."[4] Although he believed that class was an American construction that insulated communities from one another, he addressed the class issue in his article. He argued that the black middle class needed to move beyond self-interest. At the same time, he defended the black middle class for its stance on certain forms of protest and activism. He maintained that certain activities and rhetoric went against the survival tendencies of the black middle class. This article took on an elitist posture in its obvious bias and apologetic tone. It is worth exploring to see the main argument that Proctor makes: the black middle class can save the lower-class members of the black race.

Culturally, Proctor believed there was little difference between middle-class blacks and African Americans in urban ghettos and the rural South. Many middle-class blacks were products of those environments, he claimed. This equipped the African American middle class with knowledge of the situation that plagued blacks. He believed that the black middle class was aware of the social problems of poverty and the adverse effects it had on many African

Americans. He believed that socially constructed myths produced the chasm between upper- and lower-class African Americans. Concerning this, he stated, "But the American class structure, the media, and the messiahs operate as insulating agents."[5] A "wall" between African Americans was only a thin obstacle they could overcome, however. In this regard, he took on E. Franklin Frazier's depiction of the black bourgeoisie. He did not believe that the middle class was as self-absorbed as Frazier depicted.

Proctor conceded that the black middle class wanted to hold on to its gains. In doing this, he acknowledged that some truth existed in the perception of the black middle class. Some members of the middle class left the ghetto and left it unchanged. He observed, "It is the extent to which the black middle class has been co-opted by the system that the young militant finds hard to take." Admittedly, Proctor understood the fine line between success and American individualism. He called upon the black middle class to play a role in changing society, not accepting the worst of it. A polarized black race would delay change; an active, involved middle class would usher it in. Proctor saw race as a point of solidarity among African Americans. He held that it defined a black person in America more than the issue of class. He stated, "Black people, therefore, have a common cause that requires attending to, and this course does not allow for the rigid class separation that is the luxury of American whites."[6] He was concerned about separatists and "Afrocentrists" who demanded a separate community within the United States or a return to Africa.

The divide within the African American race weighed heavily on Proctor's mind. Although he saw himself as a bridge between several persons and ideological positions, his association with a black "avant-garde" helped determine the perceptions of his social stance. He was understandably conflicted by the division. He describes an example of this in his memoir. In the 1960s, he attended a fraternity function at the Commodore Hotel in New York. A group of "black men dressed in African attire" from the National Association of Black Educators followed him into the meeting room. As he described it, his meeting consisted of persons who "represented signs of success and change, a new image, new movement toward inclusiveness and fairness."[7] Consider his summary of the encounter (between the Afrocentrists and the fraternity members): "I felt frustrated, feeling that both sides had legitimate platforms yet, at least that night, at the Commodore, with one group dressed in tuxedos and the other in African garb, both appeared excessive. We did need agitation to make schools alert to the needs of black students for affirmation and identity. And the fraternity members were the big link between black problems and the resources needed to solve them. They were in touch with the power structure and they were sincere in their advocacy."[8]

The uplift of the African American race relied upon the initiative of the black middle class, in Proctor's perspective. The main point of his argument was that middle-class blacks were in a better position to promote and sustain leadership in American society. Tacitly, he embraced the idea that the black middle class had a more calculated—better—approach to activism. Within this class of African Americans lay the talent and intellect to achieve "long-term gain." Proctor wrote, "The middle class has effective representation at the council tables, but the poor are scattered, leaderless, and defenseless."[9]
Proctor's dream of a National Youth Academy may represent best the expression of his faith in the middle-class African American. Proctor wanted to transform defunct military bases into educational academies all across the United States. Youth in the seventh through the twelfth grades would enroll based on income and receive an education from experts in various fields. These young persons would learn basic survival skills from volunteers. The volunteers would be accomplished individuals who had acquired such skills through professional and academic achievement. (Proctor copied this idea from the Peace Corps.) These leaders in their fields would give their time to combat the poor education and economic status of the academy's students.

Proctor could not help but see the issue of race in a class perspective. Education, economics, and morality were all within the purview of the Black Church's concerns. His theological equipment was in service to a black middle-class hermeneutic. To be sure, he was educated in such a way that he was sensitive to American capitalism and the problems it created for poor and marginalized persons and communities. Inasmuch as there was a disparity in aspects of life among African Americans, it was obvious to a keen observer like Proctor. Few blacks received the same opportunities that he did, and not all of the ones who did accomplished as much as Proctor accomplished.

Ethically, Proctor's understanding of racial uplift and African American morality was similar to that of Martin Luther King Jr., as is evident in Robert Michael Franklin's book *Liberating Visions*.[10] Franklin describes this idea of human fulfillment in the thought of four prominent African American intellectuals, Booker T. Washington, W. E. B. Du Bois, Malcolm X, and Martin Luther King Jr. In the section on King, Franklin argues that King had four main concerns for living a moral life: civic idealism, economic reformation, integrative education, and African American prophetic Christianity. Civic idealism represented a concern for the "moral hygiene of society." Franklin states that King saw the importance of civic obligation and cooperative living.

Economic reformation displays the Protestant work ethic and the importance of hard work and thrift. Economic justice for the society was also a requirement. Integrative education emphasized education as a tool for moral awareness and social uplift. African American prophetic Christianity spoke to the transformative countercultural ethic that sought to bring forth racial and religious plurality. King's middle-class background (family, education, etc.) and sensibilities may have forged the ideas that Franklin examined in his work. To be sure, Proctor grew up with a similar middle-class ethic. And his value system reflected his middle-class status; he even recognized that in his background. Therefore, the same categories are credible descriptors for a "Proctorian" ethic of racial uplift.

This class-conscious religion raises several questions when considering Proctor's public faith. Did he place too much hope in integration? Theologically, I believe he underestimated his own middle-class biases and did not see the way it parted African Americans by class. He remained troubled by the notion of unifying the "two black Americas." He expected the two to bridge the divide, but that meant middle-class blacks lifting lower-class blacks. He recommended, moreover, that lower-class blacks get the education and jobs they needed to integrate into the larger society. His vision seemingly depended upon the goodwill of those socially and economically established African Americans. Proctor, therefore, seemingly participates in a form of discrimination. His view of the black middle class may negate the substance of his argument for the worth of all personhood. It would be fair to ask him, "What does the black underclass have to offer the black middle class—the whole nation?" He unintentionally devalued the contribution of a black underclass by tying the worth of one's social contribution to one's education and economic quality of life. He argued that black folk would not make it without talented—middle-class—people who will give their time for the good of the society.

Proctor's self-identification with the social gospel theology raises other questions about his public faith. His optimism and belief in the inevitable progress of the world deserves attention. His statements on the matter of progress reflect his belief in a God who is slowly but surely bringing about the fullness of the kingdom of God in cooperation with humanity. Proctor embraced education as a way to ameliorate the society and achieve this goal. In this belief, he may have underestimated the power of willful sin in social forces such as capitalism and racism. Could the best moral education dampen persons' greed? Would more than a few persons give up their advantages to live in solidarity with or in proximity to persons who are socially disadvantaged?

While touting the power of Christ to transform the hearts of racist persons and other ethical felons, Proctor misidentified the more problematic foe. The main source of the battle for equal rights was not a spurious anthropology, as Proctor proposed, as much as it was American political and economic pragmatism. Racism as a social construct provided the cover for the capitalistic endeavors of generations of American citizens. At the same time, however, his optimism is refreshing.

A social Christianity seemed to be the priority in Proctor's theology. Christianity, for him, is an ethical religion. He understood personal salvation in social terms. Jesus enlightened one's social awareness and provoked responsibility toward members of the human family. Proctor, however, does not demarcate the spiritual and the ethical. For him, the spiritual is the ethical. He was a proponent of pastoral care and a concern for the soul. But his writings and sermons display his intentional concern for an ethical Christianity that orders human relationships in society. He explained Christianity's transcendent quality in social terms, thereby limiting a transcendent quality.

Critics of the social gospel will also point to its tendency to hold up American democracy as an ideal system for Christianity to accomplish its social mission. Proctor, like many social gospel theologians, emphasized a realized eschatology, not the future heavenly kingdom of many evangelical Protestants. The kingdom, therefore, mirrors an ideal social order. For Proctor, the immanence of the kingdom looked more like Lyndon Johnson's Great Society than a heavenly city in John's Apocalypse. Proctor supported social programs that were meant to establish the equality and justice of God's coming kingdom. Proctor was a member of the Kennedy and Johnson administrations, so it follows that the merger of his theological commitments with the Democratic politics of 1960s America was a source of his optimism for the coming kingdom and change in the United States. Although Proctor acknowledged that the legislation of the civil rights era could not bring about the totality of changes necessary to eradicate racism, he believed that the legislation (i.e., the equal-rights and voting rights legislation) of that era reflected the possibilities of American democracy. For Proctor, American democracy—at its best—displayed the ethical traces of a Judeo-Christian foundation. But American democracy also produced the Nixon, Reagan, and Bush administrations that Proctor opposed.

## Final Considerations

Much more research is needed to understand Proctor's contributions to conversations in American Christianity. His belief in America's democratic system of government, his understanding of church-state relations, and a more detailed look at his formal theological education deserve more attention. His education and subsequent career suggest related questions. How did African Americans of his generation translate their liberal theological education? How much of a disconnect existed between the "liberation theology" of African American theologians from the liberal era and persons such as James Cone and J. Deotis Roberts who came behind them? Analysis beyond this work will show the merits and flaws of the black social gospel tradition.

A black social gospel tradition needs more attention.[11] Painted in broad strokes, it is responsible for black social organizations and protest groups. The face of the modern civil rights movement, Martin Luther King Jr., studied Rauschenbusch *and* Benjamin Mays and Howard Thurman. But theologians and ethicists have not attended to the content of a black social gospel tradition as much as to its results. Proctor held on to his social gospel roots and saw no adequate replacement for them. He died in 1997. By that time, James Cone's work was over a quarter of a century old. Womanist thought was in its adolescence. Jesse Jackson had become a political and diplomatic force. And E. V. Hill was a mainstay on black and white revival circuits, a presidential candidate in the National Baptist Convention, and a frequent guest on the Trinity Broadcasting Network. There was something to the black social gospel tradition. That something requires more research on its leaders, influence, and theological content.

Proctor was a profound thinker and preacher whose public faith influenced many persons. The true measure of his legacy may be the ways in which his students and associates have embraced his person and ideas. His legacy lives on in his students' ministries. Jesse Jackson, Jeremiah Wright, and others have felt his influence and made significant contributions to society and public conversations. A group of clergy started the Samuel DeWitt Proctor Conference, Inc., to honor his theological influence. The conference seeks to promote awareness of social issues and mobilize church publics in the face of injustice. Its board has consisted of notable black religious leaders. The conference has also engaged in activist ministries that range from restoring post-Katrina New Orleans to educating its constituents on the mass incarceration of black men. Marian Wright Edelman and the Children's Defense Fund honored Proctor by naming the Fund's Institute for Child Advocacy Ministry after him. These organizations embrace the ideas that Proctor proclaimed. That is more than a notion. His public faith left an impression that awaits more critical attention in and from the academy.

## Notes

1. See E. Franklin Frazier, *Black Bourgeoisie* (Glencoe, IL: Free Press, 1957), 71.

2. Samuel D. Proctor, *My Moral Odyssey* (Valley Forge, PA: Judson, 1989), 20.

3. Bart Landry, *The New Black Middle Class* (Berkeley: University of California Press, 1987), 33.

4. Samuel D. Proctor, "Survival Techniques and the Black Middle Class," in *Black Life and Life Culture in the United States*, ed. Rhoda L. Goldstein (New York: Cromwell, 1971), 280–94.

5. Ibid., 289–90.

6. Ibid.

7. Samuel D. Proctor, *The Substance of Things Hoped For: A Memoir of African-American Faith* (New York: G. P. Putnam's Sons, 1995), 120.

8. Ibid.

9. Proctor, "Survival Techniques and the Black Middle Class," 289.

10. Robert Michael Franklin, *Liberating Visions: Human Fulfillment and Social Justice in African-American Thought* (Minneapolis: Fortress Press, 1990), 114–17.

11. I make this claim knowing that excellent work on the black social gospel tradition sits on the shelves of academic libraries. Such works tend to examine activities, however, and lack detailed assessments of the theology that informs those actions.

# Appendix: Photo Gallery

*From left to right: Marvin McMickle, Samuel DeWitt Proctor, Calvin O. Butts III, William S. Epps. Dr. Marvin McMickle is president of the Colgate Rochester Crozer Divinity School. Dr. Calvin Butts is pastor of the Abyssinian Baptist Church and president of the State University of New York College at Old Westbury. Dr. William Epps is the current pastor of the Second Baptist Church in Los Angeles.*

**Samuel DeWitt Proctor, Th.D.**

**Nineteenth Pastor of**
**Abyssinian Baptist Church**
**during the years**
**1972 – 1989**

*This is the cover of the program for Proctor's retirement celebration. He served the Abyssinian Baptist Church from 1972–1989.*

*Dr. Samuel DeWitt Proctor (ca. 1970s).*

*Come Sunday! Samuel DeWitt Proctor participates in worship at the Abyssinian Baptist Church.*

# Bibliography


The Abyssinian Baptist Church, New York (Harlem), New York, maintains a collection of Proctor's audiotapes of sermons (approximately thirty-five audiocassettes). Kevin McGruder, church archivist, has aided me in my research of this collection.

The Morton-Smith Library, Union Theological Seminary Presbyterian School of Christian Education, Richmond, Virginia, maintains a collection of Proctor's audiotapes of sermons (approximately twenty audiocassettes).

The Massanetta Springs Camp and Conference Center maintains a collection of compact discs and audiocassettes from the numerous presentations that Proctor made at the Bible conference (approximately twenty-five lectures or sermons).

The L. Douglas Wilder Library, Virginia Union University, Richmond, Virginia, maintains a collection of audio- and videotapes of sermons. In addition, the library is the repository for Proctor's correspondence during his teaching and administrative tenure at the school.

Bank Street Memorial Baptist Church. *Bank Street Memorial Baptist Church, 1840–1985*. Norfolk, VA: Bank Street Memorial Baptist Church, 1985.

Brinson, Albert Paul. "Ministering to the Black Middle Class." Thesis, United Theological Seminary, 1990.

Cady, Linell E. "A Model for a Public Theology." *Harvard Theological Review* 80, no. 2 (1987): 193–212.

Callahan, Allen Dwight. *The Talking Book: African Americans and the Bible.* New Haven, CT: Yale University Press, 2006.

Cannon, Katie Geneva. *Teaching Preaching: Isaac Rufus Clark and Black Sacred Rhetoric.* New York: Continuum International, 2002.

Clarke, John Henrick. *Harlem, U.S.A.* Berlin: Seven Seas, 1964.

———, ed. *Harlem: A Community in Transition.* New York: Citadel, 1964.

Cone, James H. *A Black Theology of Liberation.* 2nd ed. Maryknoll, NY: Orbis, 1986.

Cooper-Lewter, Nicholas C., and Henry H. Mitchell. *Soul Theology: The Heart of American Black Culture.* 1st ed. San Francisco: Harper & Row, 1986.

Crawford, Evans E., and Thomas H. Troeger. *The Hum: Call and Response in African American Preaching.* Nashville: Abingdon, 1995.

Dabney, Virginius. *Richmond: The Story of a City.* Charlottesville: University of Virginia Press, 1990.

Deats, Paul, and Carol Robb. *The Boston Personalist Tradition in Philosophy, Social Ethics, and Theology.* Macon, GA: Mercer University Press, 1986.

Dorrien, Gary J. *Soul in Society: The Making and Renewal of Social Christianity.* Minneapolis: Fortress Press, 1995.

Ellison, John Malcus. *The Art of Friendship.* Richmond:, 1943.

———. *Tensions and Destiny.* Richmond: John Knox, 1953.

———. *They Who Preach.* Nashville: Broadman , 1956.

———. *They Sang through the Crisis; Dealing with Life's Most Critical Issues.* Chicago: Judson, 1961.

Evans, James H. Jr. *We Have Been Believers: An African-American Systematic Theology.* Minneapolis: Fortress Press, 1992.

Faulkner, Isaac Devereaux. "A Study of the High-School Achievement of a Group of 225 Negro Boys and Girls Admitted at the End of the First Term of the Eighth Grade as Compared with the High-School Achievement of a Group of Pupils Admitted at the End of the Second Term of the Eighth Grade during 1933–1936, Inclusive, in the Booker T. Washington High School, Norfolk, Va." Thesis, Hampton University, 1937.

Fluker, Walter Earl, ed. *The Stones that the Builders Rejected: The Development of Ethical Leadership from the Black Church Tradition.* Harrisburg, PA: Trinity Press International, 1998.

Fosdick, Harry Emerson. *The Modern Use of the Bible.* New York: Association Press, 1924.

———. *The Man from Nazareth as His Contemporaries Saw Him.* 1st ed. New York: Harper, 1949.

———. *The Living of These Days, an Autobiography.* 1st ed. New York: Harper, 1956.Foss, William O. *The United States Navy in Hampton Roads.* Norfolk: Donning, 1984.

Frazier, E. Franklin. *The Negro Church in America.* New York: Schocken, 1964.

Hapgood, David, and Meridan Bennett. *Agents of Change: A Close Look at the Peace Corps.* 1st ed. Boston: Little, Brown, 1968.

Harris, James H. *Pastoral Theology: A Black-Church Perspective.* Minneapolis: Fortress Press, 1991.

Hoopes, Roy. *The Peace Corps Experience.* 1st ed. New York: C. N. Potter, 1968. Distributed by Crown.

Hopkins, Dwight N. *Being Human: Race, Selves, Culture.* Minneapolis: Fortress Press, 2005.

Irving, Richard F. "Toward Equal Opportunity: The Story of the Providence Urban League in the 1940's." Thesis, Brown University, 1974.

King, Martin L. Jr. *The Trumpet of Conscience.* New York: Harper & Row, 1967.

———. *Where Do We Go from Here: Chaos or Community?* Boston: Beacon, 1967.

Kinney, John William. "Adam Clayton Powell, Sr. and Adam Clayton Powell, Jr.: A Historical Exposition and Theological Analysis." Ph.D. diss., Columbia University, 1979.

Lacey, Adolphus Clarence. "Congregation as Community Developer: A Socio-Historical Reading of the Social Ministry of the Abyssinian Baptist Church." Ph. D. diss., Northwestern University, 2002.

Levine, Lawrence W. *Black Culture and Black Consciousness: Afro-American Folk Thought from Slavery to Freedom.* New York: Oxford University Press, 1977.

Lewis, Earl. *In Their Own Interests: Race, Class, and Power in Twentieth-Century Norfolk, Virginia.* Berkeley: University of California Press, 1991.

Lincoln, C. Eric. *The Black Church since Frazier.* New York: Schocken, 1974.

———. *Race, Religion, and the Continuing American Dilemma.* New York: Hill and Wang, 1984.

Lincoln, C. Eric, and Lawrence Mamiya. *The Black Church in the African American Experience.* Durham, NC: Duke University Press, 1990.

Lischer, Richard. *The Preacher King: Martin Luther King, Jr. and the Word That Moved America.* New York: Oxford University Press, 1995.

Martin, Sandy D. "The American Baptist Home Mission Society and Black Higher Education in the South, 1865–1920," *Foundations* 24 (1981): 310–327.

Mays, Benjamin, and Joseph William Nicholson. *The Negro's Church.* New York: Institute of Social and Religious Research, 1933.

McClendon, James W. Jr. *Biography as Theology: How Life Stories Can Remake Today's Theology.* Eugene, OR: Wipf and Stock, 2002.

Moses, Wilson. "Civil Religion and Crisis of Civil Rights." *Drew Gateway* 57, no. 2 (1986): 24–42.

Niebuhr, H. Richard. *The Responsible Self.* New York: Harper & Row, 1963.

Niebuhr, Reinhold. *Moral Man and Immoral Society.* New York: Charles Scribner's Sons, 1932.

———. *The Nature and Destiny of Man.* New York: Charles Scribner's Sons, 1949.

Paris, Peter J. *Black Religious Leaders: Conflict in Unity.* Louisville: Westminster/John Knox, 1991.

Parramore, Thomas C., Peter C. Stewart, and Tommy L. Bogger. *Norfolk: The First Four Centuries.* Charlottesville: University of Virginia Press, 1994.

Pinn, Anthony B. *The Black Church in the Post–Civil Rights Era.* Maryknoll, NY: Orbis, 2002.

Pipes, William H. *Say Amen, Brother! Old-Time Negro Preaching, a Study in American Frustration.* Detroit: Wayne State University Press, 1992.

Richardson, Frederick. "American Baptists' Southern Mission," *Foundations* 18, no. 2 (1975): 136–45.

Roberts, J. Deotis. *A Black Political Theology.* Louisville: Westminster, 1974.

Roberts, Samuel K. *In the Path of Virtue: The African American Moral Tradition.* Cleveland: Pilgrim, 1999.

———. *African American Christian Ethics.* Cleveland: Pilgrim, 2001.

Rose, Ruth A. *Norfolk, Virginia.* Charleston, SC: Arcadia, 2000.

Rosenberg, Bruce A. *The Art of the American Folk Preacher.* New York: Oxford University Press, 1970.

Ruegsegger, Gary. *The History of Norfolk Public Schools, 1681–2000.* Norfolk, VA: Norfolk Public Schools, 2000.

Smith, R. Drew, ed. *New Day Begun: African American Churches and Civic Culture in Post-Civil Rights America.* The Public Influences of African American Churches, vol. 1. Durham, NC: Duke University Press, 2003.

Taylor, Gardner C. "A Mighty Oak Fallen." *African American Pulpit* 4, no. 1 (2001): 76–79.

Thurman, Howard. *Jesus and the Disinherited.* New York: Abingdon-Cokesbury, 1949; Boston: Beacon, 1996.

Warren, Mervyn Alonzo. *Black Preaching: Truth and Soul.* Washington, DC: University Press of America, 1977.

White, Forrest R. *Pride and Prejudice: School Desegregation and Urban Renewal in Norfolk, 1950–1959.* Westport, CT: Praeger, 1992.

Wimbush, Vincent L., and Rosamond C. Rodman, eds. *African Americans and the Bible: Sacred Texts and Social Textures.* New York: Continuum, 2000.

Woodward, C. Vann. *The Strange Career of Jim Crow.* New York: University of Oxford Press, 1966.

## Primary Sources

Proctor, Samuel DeWitt. "New Testament Interpretation within the Northern Baptist Convention." Th.D. diss., Boston University School of Theology, 1950.

———. "The Social Philosophy of John C. Bennett." *Journal of Religious Thought* 11, no. 2 (1955): 93–104.

———. "Inaugural Address, March 18, 1961," TMs (photocopy). Library Archives, Ferdinand D. Bluford Library, North Carolina Agricultural and Technical State University, Greensboro.

———. "The Wrong Time to Be Silent." In *Christianity amid Rising Men and Nations*, ed. Creighton Lacy, 171–81. New York: Association Press, 1965.

———. *The Young Negro in America: 1960–1980.* New York: Association Press, 1966.

———. "Racial Insularity and Racial Integration," Speech given at the State Historical Society of Wisconsin, Madison, Wisconsin, November 30, 1968.

———. "The Black Contribution to the American Experience." *National Elementary Principal* 49, no. 1 (1969): 19–22.

———. "The Church in Society." *Encounter* 30 (1969): 126–33.

———. "The College and the Urban Community: Racial Insularity and National Purpose." *Liberal Education* 55, no. 1 (1969): 78–85.

———. "Education for Genuine Community." In *A Man for Tomorrow's World: Addresses by Samuel D. Proctor, Theodore Roszak, and Alexander Frazier and Two ASCD Position Papers from the 25th Annual Conference, San Francisco, California, March 14–18, 1970*, ed. Robert R. Leeper, 3–11. Washington: Association for Supervision and Curriculum Development, NEA, 1970.

———. "Reversing the Spiral toward Futility." *Personnel Guidance Journal* 48, no. 9 (1970): 707–12.

———. "Survival Techniques and the Black Middle Class." In *Black Life and Culture in the United States*, ed. Rhoda L. Goldstein, 280–94. New York: Thomas Y. Crowell, 1971.

———. Commencement Address, Speech given at North Carolina A&T State University, Greensboro, NC, May 8, 1977. (Library Archives, Ferdinand D. Bluford Library, North Carolina Agricultural and Technical State University, Greensboro.)

———. "Education and the Humanization of Society." *Educational Record* 57, no. 4 (1977): 241–46, 277.

———. *The Epistle to the Abyssinians and other Sermons of Inspirations.* New York: printed by author, 1977.

———. "On Overcoming Moral Fatigue." In *The Struggle for Meaning*, ed. William Powell Tuck, 63–69. Valley Forge, PA: Judson, 1977.

———. "Aborted Hopes and Promises." *Christian Century* 95, no. 2 (1978): 47–48.

———. "A Mind Is a Terrible Thing to Waste." *Phi Delta Kappan* 60, no. 3 (1978): 201–3.

———. "A Nation under God." In *Outstanding Black Sermons*, vol. 2, ed. Walter B. Hoard, 89–94. Valley Forge, PA: Judson, 1979.

———. "The Black Community and the New Religious Right." *Foundations* 25 (1982): 180–87.

———. "How to Believe if the Worst Should Come." *Journal of Religious Thought* 40 (1983): 34–44.

———. "The Theological Validation of Black Worship." *Journal of the Interdenominational Theological Center* 14 (Fall 1986–Spring 1987): 211–23.

———. "Meeting the Challenge." *Selections* 14, no. 3 (1987): 43–55.

———. *Preaching about Crises in the Community*. Preaching About . . . Series. Philadelphia: Westminster, 1988.

———. *Samuel Proctor: My Moral Odyssey*. Valley Forge, PA: Judson, 1989.

———. "The Black Church and Crises in the Black Community." *Chicago Theological Seminary Register* 80 (1990): 5–10.

———. "The Four Daughters of Philip, the Deacon." In *Women: To Preach or Not to Preach*, ed. Ella Pearson Mitchell, 99–103. Valley Forge, PA: Judson, 1991.

———. Interview by Tommy Bogger. Transcript, History of Norfolk Project, City of Norfolk, VA, June 5, 1991.

———. *How Shall They Hear? Effective Preaching for Vital Faith.* Valley Forge, PA: Judson, 1992.

———. "The Metes and Bounds of Black Theology." *Journal of Theology* 96 (1992): 33–41.

———. *The Certain Sound of the Trumpet: Crafting a Sermon of Authority*. Valley Forge, PA: Judson, 1994.

———. *The Substance of Things Hoped For: A Memoir of African-American Faith.* New York: G. P. Putnam's Sons, 1995.

———. "Introspection, Outreach and Inclusion: Achieving Pluralism at MIT." In *Reflections of the Dream, 1975–1994: Twenty Years Celebrating the Life of Dr. Martin Luther King, Jr. at the Massachusetts Institute of Technology*, ed. Clarence G. Williams, 205–14. Cambridge, MA: MIT Press, 1996.

———. "King: What Progress since the Dream?" In *Reflections of the Dream, 1975–1994: Twenty Years Celebrating the Life of Dr. Martin Luther King, Jr. at the Massachusetts Institute of Technology*, ed. Clarence G. Williams, 89–112. Cambridge, MA: MIT Press, 1996.

———. *We Have This Ministry: The Heart of the Pastor's Vocation.* Valley Forge, PA: Judson, 1996.

Proctor, Samuel D., and William D. Watley. *Sermons from the Black Pulpit.* Valley Forge, PA: Judson, 1984.

## *Providence Chronicle* Articles

Proctor, Samuel D. "Resources for Monday Morning." The Letter and the Spirit. *Providence Chronicle*, March 8, 1947, p. 7.

———. "Christianity and World Unity." The Letter and the Spirit. *Providence Chronicle*, March 15, 1947, p. 7.

———. "Abundant Living." The Letter and the Spirit. *Providence Chronicle*, March 22, 1947, p. 7.

———. "On Being Neutral." The Letter and the Spirit. *Providence Chronicle*, March 29, 1947, p. 7.

———. "The Life of The Inner Man." The Letter and the Spirit. *Providence Chronicle*, April 5, 1947, p. 7.

———. "From Inspiration to Power." The Letter and the Spirit. *Providence Chronicle*, April 12, 1947, p. 7.

———. "The Magnetic Christ." The Letter and the Spirit. *Providence Chronicle*, April 19, 1947, p. 7.

———. "Religion and the Juvenile Mind." The Letter and the Spirit. *Providence Chronicle*, April 26, 1947, p. 7.

———. "The Beatitudes." The Letter and the Spirit. *Providence Chronicle*, May 3, 1947, p. 7.

———. "The Science of the Soul." The Letter and the Spirit. *Providence Chronicle*, May 10, 1947, p. 7.

———. "Faith and Moods." The Letter and the Spirit. *Providence Chronicle*, May 17, 1947, p. 7.

———. "How Important Am I?" The Letter and the Spirit. *Providence Chronicle*, May 24, 1947, p. 7.

———. "Honoring the Dead." The Letter and the Spirit. *Providence Chronicle*, May 31, 1947, p. 7.

———. "What Do You Worship?" The Letter and the Spirit. *Providence Chronicle*, June 7, 1947, p. 7.

———. "Divine Guidance." The Letter and the Spirit. *Providence Chronicle*, June 14, 1947, p. 7.

———. "The Fellowship of Belief." The Letter and the Spirit. *Providence Chronicle*, June 21, 1947, p. 7.

———. "The Higher Citizenship." The Letter and the Spirit. *Providence Chronicle*, June 28, 1947, p. 7.

———. "The Least of These." The Letter and the Spirit. *Providence Chronicle*, July 5, 1947, p. 7.

———. "Sons of God." The Letter and the Spirit. *Providence Chronicle*, July 12, 1947, p. 7.

———. "Finding God." The Letter and the Spirit. *Providence Chronicle*, July 19, 1947, p. 7.

———. "David." The Letter and the Spirit. *Providence Chronicle*, July 26, 1947, p. 7.

———. "The Second Birth." The Letter and the Spirit. *Providence Chronicle*, August 2, 1947, p. 7.

———. "Evangelism and Social Concern." The Letter and the Spirit. *Providence Chronicle*, August 9, 1947, p. 7.

———. "The Holy Spirit." The Letter and the Spirit. *Providence Chronicle*, August 16, 1947, p. 7.

———. "Are There Any Atheists?" The Letter and the Spirit. *Providence Chronicle*, August 23, 1947, p. 7.

———. "The Good Life." The Letter and the Spirit. *Providence Chronicle*, August 30, 1947, p. 7.

———. "The Silent Partner." The Letter and the Spirit. *Providence Chronicle*, September 13, 1947, p. 7.

———. "To Each His Own." The Letter and the Spirit. *Providence Chronicle*, September 20, 1947, p. 7.

———. "The Gateway to God." The Letter and the Spirit. *Providence Chronicle*, September 27, 1947, p. 7.

———. "The Christian and His Government." The Letter and the Spirit. *Providence Chronicle*, October 4, 1947, p. 7.

———. "Hero of the Series." The Letter and the Spirit. *Providence Chronicle*, October 11, 1947, p. 7.

———. "Galatians 5:4." The Letter and the Spirit. *Providence Chronicle*, October 18, 1947, p. 7.

———. "A Forewarning." The Letter and the Spirit. *Providence Chronicle*, October 25, 1947, p. 7.

———. Untitled. The Letter and the Spirit. *Providence Chronicle*, November 1, 1947, p. 7.

———. Untitled. The Letter and the Spirit. *Providence Chronicle*, November 8, 1947, p. 7.

———. "Our Holy Alliance." The Letter and the Spirit. *Providence Chronicle*, November 15, 1947, p. 7.

———. "The Threat to Religion." The Letter and the Spirit. *Providence Chronicle*, November 22, 1947, p. 7.

———. "Was Jesus Really Unfair?" The Letter and the Spirit. *Providence Chronicle*, November 29, 1947, p. 4.

———. "Abiding in the Light." The Letter and the Spirit. *Providence Chronicle*, December 6, 1947, p. 7.

———. "An Eye for Opportunity." The Letter and the Spirit. *Providence Chronicle*, December 13, 1947, p. 7.

———. "We Need Christmas This Year." The Letter and the Spirit. *Providence Chronicle*, December 20, 1947, p. 2.

———. "Manger Religion." The Letter and the Spirit. *Providence Chronicle*, December 27, 1947, p. 7.

———. "Pressing On." The Letter and the Spirit. *Providence Chronicle*, January 3, 1948, p. 7.

———. "Take Your Choice." The Letter and the Spirit. *Providence Chronicle*, January 10, 1948, p. 7.

———. "The Forerunner of Jesus." The Letter and the Spirit. *Providence Chronicle*, January 17, 1948, p. 7.

———. "Jerusalem: The Holy City." The Letter and the Spirit. *Providence Chronicle*, January 24, 1948, p. 7.

———. "Part of the Problem." The Letter and the Spirit. *Providence Chronicle*, January 31, 1948, p. 7.

———. "Taking Religion Seriously." The Letter and the Spirit. *Providence Chronicle*, February 7, 1948, p. 7.

———. "Mahatma Gandhi." The Letter and the Spirit. *Providence Chronicle*, February 14, 1948, p. 7.

———. "Shall the Meek Inherit the Earth?" The Letter and the Spirit. *Providence Chronicle*, February 21, 1948, p. 7.

———. "A Positive Faith." The Letter and the Spirit. *Providence Chronicle*, February 28, 1948, p. 7.

———. “Stewardship.” The Letter and the Spirit. *Providence Chronicle*, March 6, 1948, p. 7.

———. “Simon Peter: A Character Study.” The Letter and the Spirit. *Providence Chronicle*, March 13, 1948, p. 7.

———. “Did He Have to Do It?” The Letter and the Spirit. *Providence Chronicle*, March 20, 1948, p. 7.

———. “The Resurrection in Your Life.” The Letter and the Spirit. *Providence Chronicle*, March 27, 1948, p. 7.

———. “The Real Test.” The Letter and the Spirit. *Providence Chronicle*, April 3, 1948, p. 5.

———. “Organized Good.” The Letter and the Spirit. *Providence Chronicle*, April 10, 1948, p. 5.

———. “The Christian Answer.” The Letter and the Spirit. *Providence Chronicle*, April 17, 1948, p. 3.

———. “In His Care.” The Letter and the Spirit. *Providence Chronicle*, April 24, 1948, p. 3.

———. “Praying for the Material.” The Letter and the Spirit. *Providence Chronicle*, May 1, 1948, p. 3.

———. “Whose Child Was It?” The Letter and the Spirit. *Providence Chronicle*, May 8, 1948, p. 3.

———. “Church Building.” The Letter and the Spirit. *Providence Chronicle*, May 15, 1948, p. 3.

———. “Will We Ever Learn?” The Letter and the Spirit. *Providence Chronicle*, May 22, 1948, p. 3.

———. “How Evil Are We?” The Letter and the Spirit. *Providence Chronicle*, May 29, 1948, p. 3.

———. “Making the Most of Youth.” The Letter and the Spirit. *Providence Chronicle*, June 5, 1948, p. 3.

———. “What to Do with Discouragement?” The Letter and the Spirit. *Providence Chronicle*, June 19, 1948, p. 3.

———. “Is Any Nation Independent?” The Letter and the Spirit. *Providence Chronicle*, June 26, 1948, p. 3.

———. “It Can Happen.” The Letter and the Spirit. *Providence Chronicle*, July 3, 1948, p. 3.

———. “Open Letter to Church Members.” The Letter and the Spirit. *Providence Chronicle*, July 10, 1948, p. 3.

———. “A Different Kind of Delight.” The Letter and the Spirit. *Providence Chronicle*, July 17, 1948, p. 3.

———. "The Answer to Your Suspicion." The Letter and the Spirit. *Providence Chronicle*, July 24, 1948, p. 3.

———. "The Things Religion Takes for Granted." The Letter and the Spirit. *Providence Chronicle*, July 31, 1948, p. 3.

———. "How Urgent Is the Gospel?" The Letter and the Spirit. *Providence Chronicle*, August 7, 1948, p. 3.

———. "Candidates for Membership." The Letter and the Spirit. *Providence Chronicle*, August 14, 1948, p. 3.

———. "Consequences of Sin." The Letter and the Spirit. *Providence Chronicle*, August 21, 1948, p. 3.

———. "Christian Liberation." The Letter and the Spirit. *Providence Chronicle*, August 28, 1948, p. 3.

———. "Foundation for Living." The Letter and the Spirit. *Providence Chronicle*, September 4, 1948, p. 3.

———. "The Unknown God." The Letter and the Spirit. *Providence Chronicle*, September 11, 1948, p. 3.

———. "Moral Dwarfs." The Letter and the Spirit. *Providence Chronicle*, September 18, 1948, p. 3.

———. "Man's Lead for the Future." The Letter and the Spirit. *Providence Chronicle*, September 25, 1948, p. 3.

———. "The Ministry of Reconciliation." The Letter and the Spirit. *Providence Chronicle*, October 2, 1948, p. 5.

———. "The Aim of Jesus' Teachings." The Letter and the Spirit. *Providence Chronicle*, October 9, 1948, p. 5.

———. "Our Spiritual Legacy." The Letter and the Spirit. *Providence Chronicle*, October 16, 1948, p. 5.

———. "Jesus' Humility." The Letter and the Spirit. *Providence Chronicle*, October 23, 1948, p. 7.

———. "Where Religion Begins." The Letter and the Spirit. *Providence Chronicle*, October 30, 1948, p. 11.

———. "Early Church Revivals." The Letter and the Spirit. *Providence Chronicle*, November 20, 1948, p. 7.

———. "Divine Contempt." The Letter and the Spirit. *Providence Chronicle*, November 27, 1948, p. 7.

———. "The Edge of the Abyss." The Letter and the Spirit. *Providence Chronicle*, December 4, 1948, p. 7.

———. "Church Cooperation." The Letter and the Spirit. *Providence Chronicle*, December 11, 1948, p. 7.

———. "Getting the Most out of Christmas." The Letter and the Spirit. *Providence Chronicle*, December 18, 1948, p. 7.

———. "Carrying Christmas through the Year." The Letter and the Spirit. *Providence Chronicle*, December 25, 1948, p. 7.

———. "Starting Together." The Letter and the Spirit. *Providence Chronicle*, January 1, 1949, p. 7.

———. "The Beginning of the Ministry." The Letter and the Spirit. *Providence Chronicle*, January 8, 1949, p. 7.

———. "Taking Jesus Seriously." The Letter and the Spirit. *Providence Chronicle*, January 15, 1949, p. 7.

———. "Base of Operations." The Letter and the Spirit. *Providence Chronicle*, January 22, 1949, p. 7.

———. "Capernaum." The Letter and the Spirit. *Providence Chronicle*, January 29, 1949, p. 7.

———. "The Jesus Program." The Letter and the Spirit. *Providence Chronicle*, February 5, 1949, p. 7.

———. "The Family of God." The Letter and the Spirit. *Providence Chronicle*, February 19, 1949, p. 7.

———. Untitled. The Letter and the Spirit. *Providence Chronicle*, March 5, 1949, p. 7.

———. "Demons Today and Yesterday." The Letter and the Spirit. *Providence Chronicle*, March 12, 1949, p. 7.

———. "Among the Home Folk." The Letter and the Spirit. *Providence Chronicle*, March 26, 1949, p. 7.

———. "The Source of Evil." The Letter and the Spirit. *Providence Chronicle*, April 2, 1949, p. 7.

———. "Fulfilling the Law." The Letter and the Spirit. *Providence Chronicle*, April 9, 1949, p. 7.

———. "Dead Jesus or Living Christ." The Letter and the Spirit. *Providence Chronicle*, April 16, 1949, p. 7.

———. "Strength in Unity." The Letter and the Spirit. *Providence Chronicle*, April 30, 1949, p. 7.

———. "Our Mothers." The Letter and the Spirit. *Providence Chronicle*, May 7, 1949, p. 7.

# Index of Names and Subjects

# Index of Biblical References